C000217403

THE ISLAMIC TRII

VOLUME 4

AN ABRIDGED KORAN

THE RECONSTRUCTED HISTORICAL KORAN

BILL WARNER, PHD

THE ISLAMIC TRILOGY SERIES

VOLUME 1

MOHAMMED AND THE UNBELIEVERS

VOLUME 2

THE POLITICAL TRADITIONS OF MOHAMMED

VOLUME 3

A SIMPLE KORAN

VOLUME 4

AN ABRIDGED KORAN

THE ISLAMIC TRILOGY

VOLUME 4

AN ABRIDGED KORAN

THE RECONSTRUCTED HISTORICAL KORAN

BILL WARNER, PHD

CENTER FOR THE STUDY
OF POLITICAL ISLAM

CSPI PUBLISHING

THE ISLAMIC TRILOGY

VOLUME 4

AN ABRIDGED KORAN

THE RECONSTRUCTED HISTORICAL KORAN

BILL WARNER, PHD

ISBN 0-9785528-4-9
ISBN13 978-0-9785528-4-8
PERFECT BINDING

V 10.09.2016

PUBLISHED BY CSPI

WWW.CSPIPUBLISHING.COM

TABLE OF CONTENTS

PREFACE

The Center for the Study of Political Islam, CSPI, teaching method is the easiest and quickest way to learn about Islam.

Authoritative

There are only two ultimate authorities about Islam—Allah and Mohammed. All of the curriculum in the CSPI method is from the Koran and the Sunna (the words and deeds of Mohammed). The knowledge you get in CSPI is powerful, authoritative and irrefutable. You learn the facts about the ideology of Islam from its ultimate sources.

Story-telling

Facts are hard to remember, stories are easy to remember. The most important story in Islam is the life of Mohammed. Once you know the story of Mohammed, all of Islam is easy to understand.

Systemic Knowledge

The easiest way to study Islam is to first see the whole picture. The perfect example of this is the Koran. The Koran alone cannot be understood, but when the life of Mohammed is added, the Koran is straight forward.

There is no way to understand Islam one idea at the time, because there is no context. Context, like story-telling, makes the facts and ideas simple to understand. The best analogy is that when the jig saw puzzle is assembled, the image on the puzzle is easy to see. But looking at the various pieces, it is difficult to see the picture.

Levels of Learning

The ideas of Islam are very foreign to our civilization. It takes repetition to grasp the new ideas. The CSPI method uses four levels of training to teach the doctrine in depth. The first level is designed for a beginner. Each level repeats the basics for in depth learning.

When you finish the first level you will have seen the entire scope of Islam, The in depth knowledge will come from the next levels.

Political Islam, Not Religious Islam

Islam has a political doctrine and a religious doctrine. Its political doctrine is of concern for everyone, while religious Islam is of concern only for Muslims.

Books Designed for Learning

Each CSPI book fits into a teaching system. Most of the paragraphs have an index number which means that you can confirm for yourself how factual the books are by verifying from the original source texts.

LEVEL 1

INTRODUCTION TO THE TRILOGY AND SHARIA

The Life of Mohammed, The Hadith, Lectures on the Foundations of Islam, The Two Hour Koran, Sharia Law for Non-Muslims, Self Study on Political Islam, Level 1

LEVEL 2

APPLIED DOCTRINE, SPECIAL TOPICS

The Doctrine of Women, The Doctrine of Christians and Jews, The Doctrine of Slavery, Self-Study on Political Islam, Level 2, Psychology of the Muslim, Factual Persuasion

LEVEL 3

INTERMEDIATE TRILOGY AND SHARIA

Mohammed and the Unbelievers, Political Traditions of Mohammed, Simple Koran, Self-Study of Political Islam, Level 3, Sources of the Koran, selected topics from *Reliance of the Traveller*

LEVEL 4

ORIGINAL SOURCE TEXTS

The Life of Muhammed, Guillaume; any *Koran, Sahih Bukhari,* selected topics, *Mohammed and Charlemagne Revisited,* Scott.

With the completion of Level 4 you are prepared to read both popular and academic texts.

INTRODUCTION

The Koran must be the world's most famous book that very few have read and even fewer have understood. But we know that this was not true during Mohammed's day. We know from both the Hadith (the traditions of Mohammed) and the Sira (Mohammed's biography) that the Arabs of Mohammed's day not only understood the Koran, but held debates about its meaning.

Why could an illiterate Arab of Mohammed's day understand the Koran and we cannot? Simple. The Koran of Mohammed's day had a context, the life of Mohammed.

The Koran you buy at the bookstore has no context to the verses. There is no time in the Koran, since the chapters are laid out in order of their length, not in time sequence. Imagine that you took a novel and cut off the spine and rebound the book starting with the longest chapter and ending with the shortest chapter. The novel would have been randomized and the plot would be destroyed. That is what has been done with the Koran at the bookstore.

An Abridged Koran solves all of these problems by taking the standard Koran and reconstructing the historical Koran by integrating Mohammed's life. Then anyone can pick it up and understand it, just like the Arabs of Mohammed's day.

After reading this Koran, you will be able to pick up a "real" Koran and understand it. Think of this *Abridged Koran* as the map or key to the Koran.

KAFIR

The first step in learning about Islam is to know the right words. The language of Islam is dualistic. There is a division of humanity into believer and *kafir* (unbeliever). Humanity is divided into those who believe Mohammed is the prophet of Allah and those who do not.

Kafir is the actual word the Koran uses for non-Muslims. It is usually translated as unbeliever, but that translation is wrong. The word unbeliever is neutral. As you will see, the attitude of the Koran towards unbelievers is very negative. The Koran defines the Kafir.

In Islam, Christians and Jews are infidels and "People of the Book"; Hindus are polytheists and pagans. The terms infidel, People of the Book, pagan and polytheist are religious words. Only the word "Kafir" shows the common political treatment of the Christian, Jew, Hindu, Buddhist, animist, atheist and humanist. What is done to a pagan can be done to a Jew or any other Kafir. Likewise, what is done to a Jew can be done to any other Kafir.

The word Kafir will be used in this book instead of "unbeliever", "non-Muslim" or "disbeliever". Unbeliever or non-Muslim are neutral terms, but Kafir is extremely bigoted and biased.

The Kafir is hated—

> 40:35 *They [Kafirs] who dispute the signs [Koran verses] of Allah without authority having reached them are greatly hated by Allah and the believers. So Allah seals up every arrogant, disdainful heart.*

A Kafir can be enslaved [Bukhari is a sacred text, see page xi.]—

> Bukhari 5,58,148 *When some of the remaining Jews of Medina agreed to obey a verdict from Saed, Mohammed sent for him. He approached the Mosque riding a donkey and Mohammed said, "Stand up for your leader." Mohammed then said, "Saed, give these people your verdict." Saed replied, "Their soldiers should be beheaded and their women and children should become slaves." Mohammed, pleased with the verdict, said, "You have made a ruling that Allah or a king would approve of."*

A Kafir can be raped—

> 1759 *On the occasion of Khaybar, Mohammed put forth new orders about forcing sex with captive women. If the woman was pregnant she was not to be used for sex until after the birth of the child. Nor were any women to be used for sex who were unclean with regard to Muslim laws about menstruation.*

A Kafir can be beheaded—

> 47:4 *When you encounter the Kafirs on the battlefield, cut off their heads until you have thoroughly defeated them and then take the prisoners and tie them up firmly.*

A Kafir can be confused—

> 6:25 *Some among them listen to you [Mohammed], but We have cast veils over their [Kafirs'] hearts and a heaviness to their ears so that they cannot understand our signs [the Koran].*

A Kafir can be plotted against—

> 86:15 *They plot and scheme against you [Mohammed], and I plot and scheme against them. Therefore, deal calmly with the Kafirs and leave them alone for a while.*

A Kafir can be terrorized—

8:12 *Then your Lord spoke to His angels and said, "I will be with you. Give strength to the believers. I will send terror into the Kafirs' hearts, cut off their heads and even the tips of their fingers!"*

A Kafir can be made war on and humiliated—

9:29 *Make war on those who have received the Scriptures [Jews and Christians] but do not believe in Allah or in the Last Day. They do not forbid what Allah and His Messenger have forbidden. The Christians and Jews do not follow the religion of truth until they submit and pay the poll tax [jizya], and they are humiliated.*

A Muslim is not the friend of a Kafir—

3:28 *Believers should not take Kafirs as friends in preference to other believers. Those who do this will have none of Allah's protection and will only have themselves as guards. Allah warns you to fear Him for all will return to Him.*

THE THREE VIEWS OF ISLAM

There are three points of view in dealing with Islam. The point of view depends upon how you feel about Mohammed. If you believe Mohammed is the prophet of Allah, then you are a believer. If you don't, you are a *Kafir*. The third viewpoint is that of a Kafir who is an apologist for Islam.

Apologists do not believe that Mohammed was a prophet, but they never say anything that would displease a Muslim. Apologists never offend Islam and condemn any analysis that is critical of Islam as being biased.

Let us give an example of the three points of view.

In Medina, Mohammed sat all day long beside his 12-year-old wife while they watched as the heads of 800 Jews were removed by sword.[1] Their heads were cut off because they had said that Mohammed was not the prophet of Allah.

- Muslims view these deaths as necessary because denying Mohammed's prophet-hood was an offense against Islam and beheading is the accepted method of punishment, sanctioned by Allah.
- Kafirs look at this event as proof of the jihadic violence of Islam and as an evil act.
- Apologists say that this was a historic event, that all cultures have violence in their past, and that no judgment should be passed. According to the different points of view, killing the 800 Jews was either evil, a perfect godly act or only another historical event, take your pick.

1   *The Life of Muhammad*, A. Guillaume, Oxford University Press, 1982, pg. 464.

Apologists ignore the Islamic belief that the Sunna, Mohammed's words and deeds in the past, is the perfect model for today and tomorrow and forever. They ignore the fact that this past event of the beheading of 800 Jewish men continues to be acceptable in the present and the future, thus the fate of Kafirs today.

This book is written from the Kafir point of view and is therefore, Kafir-centric. Everything in this book views Islam from how it affects Kafirs, non-Muslims. This also means that the religion is of little importance. Only a Muslim cares about the religion of Islam, but all Kafirs are affected by Islam's political views.

Both the apologists and the Muslims believe in an authoritarian philosophy of knowledge. The Muslim accepts without question every aspect of the Sunna and the Koran. The apologist bows to the authority and opinion of the Muslims and never contradicts them.

The Kafir approach to knowledge is analytic or critical. Critical thinking seeks truth through the friction of debate in order to tease out the resolution of an idea. Authoritarians forbid critical thought for the simple reason that it cannot co-exist with authoritative thinking. Muslims forbid critical thinking by threatening and inducing fear. Apologists forbid critical thinking on the basis that offending any minority is a social evil. The offending speech is considered bigoted. The proof of bigotry is that the minority is offended. Even if the statement is true, it can still be called bigotry.

"Truth" has no meaning in authoritative knowledge. There are only thoughts that are allowed and thoughts that are forbidden. "Truth" is determined by appeal to authority, but only to the correct authority. Authoritative knowledge forbids debate. Those who want to debate are demeaned and insulted or simply locked out of the venue. Both political correctness and Islam agree that only "allowed" opinions may be expressed and "forbidden" opinions are declared to be bigotry—a moral evil.

Critical thinking, however, exists by debate. There are no forbidden ideas in critical or analytic thinking.

Notice that these different points of view that cannot be reconciled. There is no possible resolution between the view of the Kafir and the Muslim. The apologist tries to bring about a bridge building compromise, but it is not logically possible.

THE ISLAMIC BIBLE—THE TRILOGY

Islam is defined by the words of Allah in the Koran, and the words and actions of Mohammed, the *Sunna*.

The Sunna of Mohammed is found in two texts—the Sira (Mohammed's life) and the Hadith. His words and actions are considered to be the divine pattern for humanity acceptable to Allah and the best source for these are the biographies, or Sira, by Ishaq and Al Tabari.

A hadith, or tradition, is a brief story about what Mohammed did or said. A collection of hadiths is called a Hadith. There are many collections of hadiths, but the most authoritative are those by Bukhari and Muslim.

So the Trilogy is the Koran, the Sira and the Hadith. Most people think that the Koran is the "bible" of Islam, but it is only about 14% of the total textual doctrine. Statistically, Islam is 14% Allah and 86% Mohammed. The Trilogy, not the Koran, is the foundation of Islamic doctrine.

WHAT IS THE KORAN?

According to Islam, the Koran is the exact words of the only god of the universe. It is complete, perfect, eternal and universal. It is also unintelligible.

What Mohammed recited as the revelations of Allah was memorized and written down on paper, palm leaves, and even the shoulder blades of animals.

Shortly after Mohammed's death, Zaid (Mohammed's secretary) compiled all the known Koranic material. There was a problem, however, since there was disagreement and variation between different collections of Koranic material. About 20 years after Mohammed's death, Uthman, the caliph, empowered Zaid to gather all of the known versions of the Koran and produce the Koran we know today. The Koran is considered to be the exact, precise recording of the words of Mohammed reporting what he heard from the angel Gabriel. Since Mohammed's transmission of the revelation is taken to be perfect, the Koran is considered by all Muslims to be the perfect, exact words of Allah, without a single error.

Uthman then took and burned all of the sources. No comment is ever made about this burning, but it is telling. Why would Uthman burn all of the original source material?

The Koran that Uthman produced was not the Koran of Mohammed. In the historical Koran each chapter followed the other as Mohammed's life unfolded. This is the Koran that has the original time sequence and includes events Mohammed was involved in at the time.

The historical Koran was easy to understand. An illiterate Arabian could understand it because each verse was in the context of what was happening at the time. If that original historical form is reproduced, then the resulting Koran can be understood by anyone who reads it.

The public image of the Koran is that everybody has heard about it, but no one knows anyone who understands it. As a result of the lack of knowledge, there are myths about it: The Koran is very profound; it is full of wisdom; it is so deep that you must be highly trained or a Muslim to comprehend it; it is in the same category as the Bible. Even though people don't know what it is, they have firm conclusions.

THE DIFFICULTY OF KNOWING THE KORAN

The form of the Koran found in the bookstore is designed to not be understood.

The problems

1. When Zaid compiled all the copies of the Koran, he arranged them from the longest chapter to the shortest chapter. The sequence of events is scrambled. As a result, no one can understand the original story.
2. Each chapter has a bewildering array of topics. One topic abruptly ends and an unrelated one begins.
3. It is very repetitive. The story of Moses is told 39 times. This is an important clue about the true nature of the Koran, but it is tiresome to read the same story again and again. Not only are the stories repetitive, but also there are 290 different verses about Hell. The constant repetition is tiresome.
4. There is no context to many verses. Subjects just lurch up in front of you from out of nowhere. This is very confusing.
5. There are many strange names and foreign terms.
6. It is contradictory. One verse will teach tolerance and the next will call for the death of Kafirs. The contradictions confuse the reader.
7. The Koran contains a great deal of violence towards Kafirs. It threatens and insults Kafirs and calls them foul names. This makes a Kafir want to avoid reading it.

The sum total is that the Koran is confusing, contradictory, makes no sense, and is strange, violent, threatening and unpleasant. It's difficult to understand and daunting to attempt.

The most common comment is that a better translation is needed. That is absolutely not the case. No translation will fix a single one of the problems that make the Koran unreadable. Besides, anyone who wants to go onto the web can read the Koran in many translations. The only difference between them is how they handle the violence.

All of this is unfortunate, because when the Koran is made readable, it becomes a truly epic story with an incredible plot. It is also the most frightening book you will ever read because once it is clear, you can see the future.

There is a way to solve each and every difficulty that has been discussed while retaining every verse.

Problem 1: There is no time in the Koran

The Koran cannot be understood without time being reintroduced. Zaid had the Koran arranged in order of chapter length and destroyed the historical Koran. Thus, the classical Koran that is found in the book-store is obscure. Taking out the time-line has randomized it. Uthman did two things that totally changed the Koran. By burning all of the source material, he made the Koran "superior" to the New Testament and Old Testament, since they have known variations in their historical texts. And since Uthman destroyed all of the variations, the Koran could be claimed to be exactly like the one Allah gave to Mohammed.

But more importantly, by rearranging the Koran, he removed the story. The story of the Koran is that Islam triumphed over all Mohammed's enemies. It is a political story of triumph and conquest. By removing the political ending, Uthman cloaked the politics in rhetoric and made it seem more religious. Confusion passes for profoundness.

So, the first step is to put the elements of the document in the proper historical order. That turns out to be an almost trivial process. The correct order of the chapters is well known to scholars[2]. Anybody with access to the web can download a version of the Koran and use a word processor to produce a Koran in the right time order. It is a cut-and-paste job, no more, no less. Once you have the Koran on your word processor and the proper sequence of each chapter, it takes about an hour to produce a Koran with the proper chronological sequence.

Problem 2: Topics

When you read a chapter in the Koran it jumps from one topic to the next. The first clue is that the Arabic word, sura, which is translated as "chapter" is not a chapter in the normal sense. A better term would be folder, because it is just like a file folder with many different letters in it. The problem is that one runs on into the next. Most versions of the Koran introduce their own topic breaks.

---

2   *Discovering the Quran*, Neal Robinson, SCM Press Ltd, 1996, pgs. 78-79.

One powerful method of organizing the suras into chapters is the Koranic Argument. This method is discussed in the final chapter, "Conclusions" page 197.

Problem 3: Repetition

The Koran is filled with stories that allow easy categorization. The story of Moses is easily recognized as a topic. Then there are the repetitive Arabic stories of Thamud and others. But there remains a lot of verbiage that is not a story. How should it be arranged into topics?

Once the Koran is placed into the right chronological order, the next step is to group together all of the similar repetitive material. One of the most tiresome things about the Koran is the endless repetition.

The reason for the repetition is simple. The Koran is an exact recording of Mohammed's campaign of persuasion. Imagine that you are a reporter and follow a political candidate around as he speaks. You will find that he constantly repeats the same points, but with slight variations. This is what happened with the Koran. Mohammed covered the same points over and over again. Hence, the repetitive Koran. The Koran is an exact history of Mohammed's career as a prophet of Allah.

Once the Koran is categorized, similar topics can be grouped together. This greatly simplifies the comprehension and ease of reading. When similar topics are grouped, it becomes easy to skip over them and not feel like you are missing anything. It also allows the reader to see the small changes in the stories. The Koran did not always repeat the story in the same way.

When the stories are grouped, another thing really stands out. Allah was no storyteller. A story has a beginning, middle and an end. Not one story in the Koran can stand on its own. There are always missing pieces. Even the Joseph story, technically the best told story in the Koran, is incomplete.

Problem 4: Context

There is a missing piece to the Koranic puzzle. The missing piece is Mohammed. Only Mohammed can make the Koran coherent. Take as an example:

> Koran 59:5 *Allah gave you permission to cut down some palm trees and leave others intact so as to shame the wicked [the Jews]. After Allah gave the spoils to His Messenger, you made no move with horses or camels to capture them [the Jews], but Allah gives His messengers power over what He chooses. Allah is all-powerful.*

As you read along, this verse, without any context, just jumps out at you. Why does Allah suddenly talk about palm trees? The answer is that Mohammed attacked the Jews near Medina and he wanted to destroy their economy by cutting down their date palm plantations.

So, if we weave Mohammed's life into the Koran, then the Koran has a context and all of the mystery is gone. By including Mohammed, we have reproduced the original version. The Koran unfolded as needed by Mohammed. The Koran frequently gives a solution to an ongoing problem in his life. When Mohammed's life is integrated into it, the Koran becomes an epic story that ends with the triumph of Islam.

Problem 5: Arabic

Islam frequently claims that the Koran cannot be translated. Much of the Koran is written in a poetic style that is similar to the ancient classical texts such as the Greek *Odyssey*. The *Odyssey* is an epic tale that is written in poetry, which makes it easy to memorize. The Koran is also written, in great part, in a poetic form that is easy to memorize.

Take an English proverb: "Birds of a feather, flock together." We have the information that a flock of birds only contains one type of bird, but it is written in poetic form. Can the poetry of "Birds of a feather, flock together" be translated into Arabic? No. But the meaning of "a flock of birds contains only one type of bird," can be easily translated into Arabic.

The poetry of the Koran does not translate, but the meaning can be translated. Read many different translations of the Koran and you will find the meaning is consistent across the translations.

So, can the Koran be translated? In one sense, no. Can the meaning be translated into any other language? Yes. If the meaning of a particular section of the Koran cannot be translated, then that implies that the concept is not applicable to that language. Or said another way, that part of the Koran would not be universal. But the Koran is very insistent upon the fact that it is universal. It follows that the universal meaning can be translated into all languages. In particular, anything that is said about the Kafir can be understood by the Kafir. If there are religious verses that only those trained in classical Arabic can read, it does not concern the Kafir. Kafirs do not care about the religion of Islam.

Problem 6: Strange names and terms

Nothing can be done about the names, as such. But it is simple to define the names and terms and put them in brackets as an in-line comment.

Problems 7, 8, 9: Contradictions, violence and Kafir

There is no way to temper these verses, except to say that they provide the deepest insight into the true inner nature of the Koran. The violence against the Kafir is central to the Koran, since it is frequent. The contradictions are part of Koranic doctrine called abrogation. The Koran directly addresses the contradictions within it and provides a way to resolve the issues. There will be much more said about this in the next chapter. The contradictions are part of Islamic dualism. None of these problems can be removed.

SUMMARY

The Koran can be made understandable by using:
- Chronology—putting the verses in the original historical order
- Categorizing—the method of grouping verses around the same subject.
- Context—using Mohammed's life to explain the circumstances and environment of the text.

Any Muslim will tell you that this book is not a Koran. That may or may not be, but this book is a key or map to the "real" Koran. After you read this Koran, you will be able to pick up a "real" Koran and it will be easily understood.

READING THE KORAN

The Koran is a difficult book when it is viewed as a religious text. But when it is viewed as an historical and political text as well as a religious text, it is a straightforward story. To understand the language, you need some background. Islam holds that the Koran is the perfect record of what the angel Gabriel (also called a spirit) told Mohammed. When the words I, We, Us, and Me are used, they refer to Allah. I and We can occur in the same verse.

The term "Say:" is used frequently and means that Gabriel is telling Mohammed to say this to the people.

Another common term is "signs." Signs can be manifestations of nature, *e.g.* rain after a drought, or signs can be verses of the Koran. Each verse is considered a miracle by Islam.

With this background, read one of the epic stories of history. When you finish it, you will be able to pick up any translation of the Koran and read it with understanding.

HOW THE VERSES ARE GROUPED

The classical arrangement of the Koran is by chapters (suras) and verses. The verses are not so useful in understanding since a verse is usually a sentence, not an complete idea. So the first step for easy understanding is to group the verses into paragraphs that contain a coherent thought (*pericope*). As an example:

> 93:4 *Certainly the future will be better than the past.*
> 93:5 *In the end your Lord will be generous to you, and you will be satisfied.*
> 93:6 *Did He not find you living like an orphan and give you a home?*
> 93:7 *Did He not find you lost and give you guidance?*
> 93:8 *Did He not find you poor, and did He not give you enough?*

These verses have been grouped into a paragraph:

> 93:4 *Certainly the future will be better than the past, and in the end your Lord will be generous to you, and you will be satisfied. Did He not find you living like an orphan and give you a home? Did He not find you lost and give you guidance? Did He not find you poor, and did He not give you enough?*

REFERENCE NUMBERS

The information in this book can be traced back to the source by use of the reference numbers:

I234 is a reference to Ibn Ishaq's *Sirat Rasul Allah*, translated by A. Guillaume as *The Life of Muhammad*. This is a reference to margin note 234.

T123 is a reference to *The History of al-Tabari* by the State University of New York. The number refers to the margin note 123.

M234 is a reference to *The Life of Mohammed* by Sir William Muir, AMS Press, New York, NY, 1975. The number is page 234.

B2,3,45 is a reference to Bukhari's Hadith. The three example numbers are volume 2, book 3, and number 45, a standard reference system.

M2,345 is a reference to Muslim's Hadith. The example would be book 2, number 345.

12:45 is Koran chapter (sura) 12, verse 45.

It is the present state of knowledge of the West about Islam that there is no standardized spelling of proper Arabic nouns. Examples: Muslim/Moslem, Mohammed/Muhammad, Koran/Quran.

IN THE BEGINNING

CHAPTER 1

33:21 You have an excellent example in Allah's Messenger
for those of you who put your hope in Allah and the
Last Day and who praise Allah continually.

Be sure to read the Introduction.

Fourteen hundred years ago in Arabia, there was an orphan who be-came the first king of Arabia. Mohammed's name would become the most common name in the world. He was to create an empire that would dwarf the Roman Empire, and he was to become the ideal pattern for all men and make the god of the Arabs the god of all. The smallest aspect of his behavior would be recorded in great detail and would set the pattern of life for billions of people over 1400 years.

Mohammed's father was called Abdullah, meaning slave of Allah. Allah was a high god of the many gods worshiped in the town of Mecca. His father died while his mother was pregnant. When he was five years old, his mother died and his grandfather took over his upbringing. Then Mo-hammed was orphaned for the third time when his grandfather died and his raising was assumed by his uncle, Abu Talib. All were of the Quraysh tribe. These brief facts are the history known about his early childhood.

MOHAMMED'S TRIBE—THE QURAYSH

When Mohammed was born, there was no nation of Arabia, no Ara-bian king, no political unity. The society was tribal in nature and had the usual tribal aspects. A person was not an individual as much as he was a part of a tribe. Blood relations were everything, and when someone met someone outside the tribe, the first question was what is your tribe and your lineage? Your name gave a portion of your lineage. Without your tribe you were fair game and very weak. Squabbling and fighting amongst clans were common and were ruled by blood laws.

The Quraysh came to Mecca five generations before Mohammed under the leadership of Qusayy. Under Qusayy the rituals of worship at the Ka-bah [a stone temple] were established. The Quraysh became the priestly tribe of Mecca. They were the nobility of the town and held the ceremonial offices.

In addition to being religious leaders, the Quraysh were traders and business men. Religion and business came together in the form of the different religious pilgrimages and the accompanying business transactions.

Mohammed's clan was the Hashim clan of the Quraysh tribe. The Hashimite clan is active in politics today.

MECCA AS A RELIGIOUS CENTER

In Mecca there was a stone building in the shape of a cube called the Kabah. The Kabah was a religious site that contained many images of several tribal gods. We know of at least six other square stone houses called Kabahs that were in other towns in Arabia. However, Islam holds that the Kabah in Mecca was built by Abraham, the patriarch of the Jews.

The Kabah was the focus of religious rituals and a community center. Rituals established by Qusayy included prostrations, ritual prayers, and circling the Kabah while praying and drinking from the well called Zam Zam. Other rituals included throwing stones at pillars which symbolized the devil. Islam's rituals come from the aboriginal Arabic religions.

Stones played an important part of the religions of Arabia. The Kabah was made of stone and had an important stone, the Black Stone, built into the corner of the Kabah. It was probably a meteorite and was a composite of several stones. It is small in size, roughly seven inches in diameter. This stone was touched only with the right hand and kissed by pilgrims. All of these native rituals were incorporated into Islam.

The god, Allah, seems to have been a male god of the moon and was probably the god of the Quraysh. Each tribe had its gods. There was not much organization of gods, unlike the Greeks or Romans. Mohammed's father was named after Allah, but his other brothers were named after other Arabic gods.

EARLY LIFE

CHAPTER 2

3:131 Obey Allah and His messenger so that you may receive mercy.

CHILDHOOD

I115[1] When Mohammed was eight years old, his grandfather died. He was then taken in by Abu Talib, his uncle. His uncle took him on a trading trip to Syria, which was a very different place from Mecca. Syria was a sophisticated country that was Christian and very much a part of the cosmopolitan culture of the Mediterranean. It was Syrian Christians who gave the Arabs their alphabet. When Mohammed was a child there had never been a book written in Arabic. Only poems and business correspondence were written in Arabic.

MARRIAGE

I120 Mohammed was grown when he was hired by the wealthy widow and a distant cousin Khadija to act as her agent in trading with Syria. Mohammed had a reputation of good character and good business sense. Trading from Mecca to Syria was risky business because it took skill to manage a caravan and then to make the best deal in Syria. He managed Khadija's affairs well, and she returned a good profit on the trading.

I120 Khadija was a widow and well known among the Quraysh tribe. Sometime after hiring Mohammed as her business agent, she proposed marriage to him. They married and had six children. Their two sons died in childhood, and the four daughters lived to adulthood.

MONOTHEISM IN ARABIA

I144 The Arabs referred to monotheism as Hanifiya and to those who were monotheists as Hanifs. By far the strongest strain of monotheism was represented by the Jews. After the destruction of Jerusalem by the Romans due to the Zealot's rebellion, Jews dispersed throughout the Middle East, so there was a strong presence of Jews in Arabia. There were a few Christians who were local Arabs, in fact, Mohammed's wife had a cousin

---

1. This reference is to Ishaq's *Sirat Rasul Allah*

who was a Christian. But the type of Christianity in the area of Mecca was unorthodox with a Trinity of God, Jesus and Mary.

I144 Jews and Christians were called the People of the Book. Since there was no book yet published in Arabic, this distinction was a strong one. The sources of the Arabic religions were found in oral tradition and custom. The Meccans were aware of the Jewish Abrahamic myths, and though Mecca was a long way from Syria where Abraham dwelt, the Meccans claimed that Abraham and Ishmael had built the Kabah in ancient times.

I144 Even though there was a pull towards monotheism, it mixed with ancient Arabic tribal religions in a society that had a tolerance for different religious beliefs. In one clan, families would differ in the deities they included in their worship. These included deities that were brought into the home through marriage outside of the clan and a belief of spirits, or jinns, that could influence lives in good or bad ways.

I144-149 One monotheist, Zayd, abandoned all religion and created his own monotheistic religion, making his own prayers and rituals. They were a fusion of Judaism theology and tribal rituals, including use of the Kabah for a prayer focus and prostrations. He said that Abraham prayed facing in a sacred direction and condemned and publicly attacked his tribal members for their religion. The one god was to be feared, heaven was a garden, and infidels would burn in Hell. He condemned any form of worship of a god except the one god, and people submitted to the un-named one god. Much of his poetry used the same language as the Koran did. He referenced his worship to the Jewish patriarchs as they were pure in their worship. Mohammed recognized him as a precursor.

THE KORAN OF MECCA

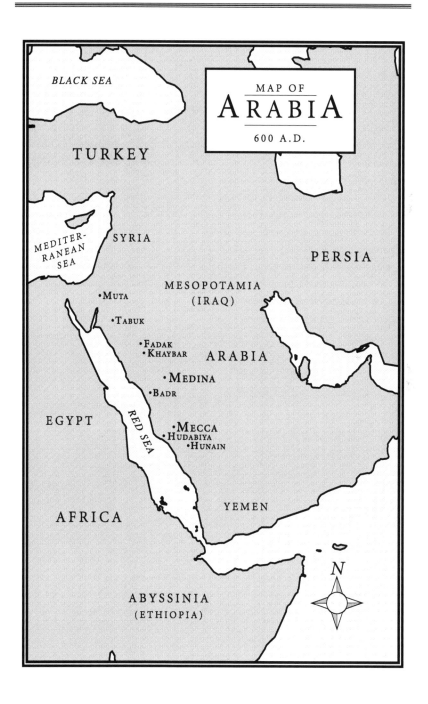

MAP OF
ARABIA
600 A.D.

BLACK SEA

TURKEY

MEDITER-
RANEAN
SEA

SYRIA

PERSIA

MESOPOTAMIA
(IRAQ)

•MUTA

•TABUK

•FADAK
•KHAYBAR

ARABIA

• MEDINA

•BADR

EGYPT

RED SEA

•MECCA
•HUDABIYA
•HUNAIN

AFRICA

YEMEN

N

ABYSSINIA
(ETHIOPIA)

BEGINNING TEACHINGS

CHAPTER 3

4:13 These are the limits set up by Allah. Those who obey Allah
and His Messenger will be led into the Gardens watered by
flowing rivers to live forever. This is the ultimate reward!

I150 Mohammed would take month long retreats to be alone and do the Quraysh religious practices. After the retreat he would go and circumambulate (circle and pray) the Kabah.

I152 At the age of forty Mohammed began to have visions and hear voices. His visions were first shown to him as bright as daybreak during his sleep in the month of Ramadan. Mohammed said that the angel, Gabriel, came to him with a brocade with writing on it and commanded him to read. "What shall I read?" The angel pressed him and said, "Read." Mohammed said again, "What shall I read?" The angel pressed him again tightly and again commanded, "Read!" Again the reply, "What shall I read?"

The angel said:

> *96:1 Recite: In the name of your Lord, Who created man from clots of blood.*
> *96:3 Recite: Your Lord is the most generous, Who taught the use of the pen*
> *and taught man what he did not know.*

T1150 Mohammed awoke from his sleep. Now Mohammed hated ecstatic poets and the insane. His thoughts were that he was now either a poet or insane, that which he hated. He thought to kill himself by jumping off a cliff. And off he went to do just that. Half way up the hill, he heard, "Mohammed, You are the apostle of Allah and I am Gabriel." He gazed at the angel and no matter which way he turned his head the vision followed his eyes. Mohammed stood there for a long time.

Then Mohammed began to receive what he called revelations such as:

> *97:1 Surely, We have revealed it [the Koran] on the night of power. And who*
> *will explain to you what the night of power is? The night of power is better*
> *than a thousand months. On that night the angels and the spirit descended*
> *with their Lord's permission, to do their every duty and all is peace until*
> *the break of day.*

55:1 *Merciful Allah has taught the Koran, has created man, and has taught him to speak. The sun and the moon follow their exact courses, and the plants and the trees bow down in adoration. He has uplifted the sky and set the balance of justice so that you may not exceed the right measure. Measure fairly, and do not cheat the balance.*

55:10 *He has prepared the earth for his creatures. On it there are fruits and palms with sheathed clusters and husked grains and fragrant plants. Which of your Lord's blessings would you deny?*

55:14 *He has created man from clay like a potter, and He created the jinn[1] from smokeless fire. Which of your Lord's blessings would you deny?*

55:17 *He is the Lord of the east. He is the Lord of the west. Which of your Lord's blessings would you deny?*

55:19 *He has freed the two seas [fresh water and salt water] so that they meet, but separated them with a barrier that they cannot breach. Which of your Lord's blessings would you deny?*

55:22 *From the seas come pearls and coral. Which of your Lord's blessings would you deny?*

55:24 *His ships sail the seas, towering like mountains. Which of your Lord's blessings would you deny?*

55:26 *Everything on the earth will perish, but the majestic and glorious face of your Lord will endure forever. Which of your Lord's blessings would you deny?*

55:29 *Everything in the heavens and the earth look to Him. Every day He exercises absolute power. Which of your Lord's blessings would you deny?*

55:31 *Soon We will settle the affairs of men and jinn [invisible beings made of fire]. Which of your Lord's blessings would you deny?*

THE FIRST CONVERT

I156 Mohammed's wife, Khadija, was the first convert. From the first she had encouraged him, believed him. She knew him to be of good character and did not think him to be deceived or crazy.

Soon he stopped hearing voices or seeing visions and became depressed and felt abandoned. Then his visions started again and said:

93:1 *By the brightness of the noonday sun and by the night at its darkest, your Lord has not forgotten you, and He does not hate you.*

93:4 *Certainly the future will be better than the past, and in the end your Lord will be generous to you, and you will be satisfied. Did He not find you living like an orphan and give you a home? Did He not find you lost and give you guidance? Did He not find you poor, and did He not give you enough?*

1.   Islam has an entire world of spirits called jinns (genies). They can influence humans for good or bad.

93:9 *Therefore, do not oppress the orphan, and do not scold the beggar. Instead, announce the bounty of your Lord.*

Then Mohammed began to tell others who were close to him of words in his visions.

1:1 *In the Name of Allah, the Compassionate, the Merciful.*
1:2 *Praise be to Allah, Lord of the worlds. The Compassionate, the Merciful. King of the Judgment Day.*
1:5 *Only You do we worship, and to You alone do we ask for help. Keep us on the straight and narrow path. The path of those that You favor; not the path of those who anger You [the Jews] nor the path of those who go astray [the Christians].*

107:1 *What do you think of him who treats Our religion as a lie, who trusts that others will raise the orphan, and does not urge others to feed the poor? Woe to those who pray, but whose prayers are careless and to those who make a show of devotion, but refuse to help the needy.*

70:22 *Not the devout, who pray constantly and whose wealth has a fixed portion set aside for beggars and the destitute, and those who believe in the Judgment Day, and those who fear their Lord's punishment—because no one is safe from their Lord's punishment—and who control their sexual desires (except with their wives or slave-girls, with them there is no blame; but whoever indulges their lust beyond this are transgressors), and who keep their trusts and promises, and who tell the truth, and who are attentive to their prayers. These will live with honors in Gardens.*

92:5 *He who gives alms and fears Allah and accepts the good, to him We will make the path to happiness easy. But he who is greedy and does not think he needs Allah's help and calls the good a lie, to him We will make the path to misery easy. And what good will his wealth do him when he dies?*
92:12 *Certainly it is up to Us to guide man and certainly the future and the past belong to Us. Therefore I warn you of the blazing Fire. Only the most wretched will be thrown into it, those who call the truth a lie and turn their backs.*
92:17 *Those who fear Allah will escape it and so will those who give away their wealth so that they may be purified; and who give freely without hope of reward, except seeking the pleasure of his Lord, the most high, certainly in the end they will be content.*

95:1 *I swear by the fig and the olive, by Mount Sinai, and by this inviolate land [Mecca]! We have created man in a noble image then reduced him to the lowest of the low, except those who believe and do the right things, because their reward will never fail.*

95:7 Then, who can convince you that the judgment is a lie? Is Allah not the best of judges?

PRAYER

1157 Mohammed began to do his prayers with his new understanding. At first he did two prostrations with each prayer. Later he understood that he should use four prostrations per prayer and use two prostrations when he was traveling.

1158 Then when he was on a mountain he saw a vision in which Gabriel showed him how to do ritual ablutions as a purification ritual before prayer. He went home and showed his wife, Khadija, how he now understood the prayer rituals to be done and she copied him.

T1162 Mohammed, his wife and nephew, Ali, started praying at the Kabah with their new rituals of ablutions and prayer with prostrations. A visitor asked about this new ritual and was told that it was a new religion and that Mohammed said that he would receive the treasures of Rome and Persia.

> *73:1 You [Mohammed] wrapped up in your robe, awake half the night, more or less, to pray and recite the Koran in a measured rhythm, because We will send down to you a weighty message. Certainly nightfall is a time when impressions are stronger and speech is more certain. Obviously, the day is filled with constant work.*
>
> *73:8 Remember the name of your Lord, and devote yourself to Him with complete devotion. Lord of the east and the west; there is no god except Allah. Take Him for your protector.*

THE FIRST MALES TO ACCEPT ISLAM

1159 A famine overtook the Quraysh and Mohammed's uncle Abu Talib had a large family. Abu Talib was a well respected tribal leader, but had fallen on hard times. Mohammed went to another uncle, Al Abbas, and they both went to Abu Talib and offered to help raise two of his children. Ali went into Mohammed's house to be raised by him and Khadija. When Ali turned ten he joined with Mohammed in his new religion, Islam.

1160 Mohammed and Ali used to go to the edge of town to practice their new ritual prayers. One day Abu Talib came upon them and asked what were they doing? Mohammed replied, "Uncle, this is the religion of Allah, His angels, His prophets and the religion of Abraham. Allah has sent me as an apostle to all mankind. You, my uncle, deserve that I should teach you the truth and call you to Islam." His uncle said that he could not give up the religion of his ancestors, but that he would support Mohammed.

The native Arabic religions were tribal in that every tribe had its deities, but the ceremonies and traditions were passed down by oral tradition, not in writing.

Mohammed lived in Mecca, which had been a religious center for many generations. It had a stone building that was roughly shaped like a cube and was called a Kabah. There were at least five other Kabahs in other towns in Arabia. The Kabah was a religious center for many of the native religions. Some sources say that there were as many as 360 deities worshiped in Mecca, a city that was profoundly polytheistic and tolerant. There were religious festivals that involved pilgrimages to Mecca, so at different times of the year, many tribes would gather to trade and do religious ceremonies.

One of the many gods in Mecca was Allah, a moon god. The native religions did not have any formal structure to the many deities, but Allah was a high god. Allah was the primary god of the Quraysh tribe of Mohammed, and Mohammed's father was named Abdullah, slave of Allah.

The idea of having an Arabian prophet was new. The sources of the native religions were unknown, but the new religion of Islam had a self-declared prophet. The Jews had prophets, and now the Arabs had a prophet in Mohammed.

> 87:1 *Praise the name of your Lord, the Most High, who has created and proportioned all things, who has determined man's destinies and guided them, who brought forth the pasture, and reduced it to dusty stubble.*
> 87:6 *We will teach you to recite [the Koran] so that you do not forget, unless Allah wishes. He knows everything manifest and secret, and We will make it easy for you [Mohammed] to attain a state of ease. Therefore give warning because the warning is profitable. He who fears Allah will receive the warning, and only the most unfortunate ones will avoid it. They will be flung into Hellfire, in which there is no death or life.*

Since Mohammed was a prophet, it was natural that the Koran should pick the thread of the history of the Jews and their prophets, such as Abraham and Moses.

Abraham

> 51:24 *Have you heard the story of Abraham's honored guests? They went to him and said, "Peace!" And he replied, "Peace, strangers." And he went among his household and brought out a fatted calf, and he set it before them and said, "Do you want to eat?" They did not, and he became afraid of them. They said to him, "Do not be afraid," and gave him the news that he was going to father a wise son. Abraham's wife came forward with a cry, striking her face, and said, "But I am old and barren!"*

51:30 *They said, "Your Lord says it is true, and he is wise and knowing."*
51:31 *Abraham said, "What errand are you on, messengers?" They replied, "We are sent to a wicked people, to shower them with stones of clay, sent by your Lord for their excesses."*
51:35 *We went to evacuate the believers in the city, but We only found one Muslim family, and We left signs warning those who fear the painful punishment. Moses was another sign. We sent him to Pharaoh with manifest authority. But Pharaoh was confident of his might and turned his back and said, "You are a magician, or insane." So We seized him and his army and cast them into the sea, and he had only himself to blame.*

Moses

79: 15 *Have you heard the story of Moses? How his Lord called to him in the sacred valley of Tuwa, saying, "Go to Pharaoh. He has rebelled, and say, 'Do you want to be purified?' Then I will guide you to your Lord so that you may fear Him."*
79:20 *And Moses showed Pharaoh a great miracle. But Pharaoh denied it and disobeyed. Furthermore, he turned his back and rebelled against Allah. He gathered an army and made a proclamation, saying, "I am your lord, the most high." So Allah punished him and made an example of him in this life and the hereafter. Surely this is a lesson for those who fear Allah.*

Mohammed preached the doctrine of the Day of Judgment.

88:1 *Have you heard the news of the overwhelming event?*
88:2 *Some faces will be downcast that day, troubled and weary, burnt at the scorching Fire, forced to drink from a fiercely boiling fountain, with only bitter thorns for food, which neither nourishes nor satisfies hunger.*

88:8 *Other faces that day will be joyous, and in a lofty Garden, very pleased with their past efforts. No vain talk will be heard there. There will be gushing fountains. There will be raised couches, and goblets placed nearby, and cushions arranged, and carpets spread out.*

88:17 *Will they consider the camels and how they were made? Or consider how the sky was upraised, and how the mountains are rooted, and how the earth is spread?*
88:21 *Warn them, because you [Mohammed] are merely a warner. You have no authority over them, but whoever turns back and disbelieves, Allah will punish them terribly.*
88:25 *Truly they will return to Us. Then it will be time for Us to settle their accounts.*

After the day of doom would come Paradise and Hell.

56:1 *When the inevitable day of terror arrives, no one will treat its sudden arrival as a lie. That day many will be crushed! That day some will be exalted!*

56:4 *When the earth is shaken to its core, and the mountains crumble to powder and become scattered dust, and the people are divided into three groups, the people of the right hand—Oh, how happy the people of the right hand will be!*

56:9 *The people of the left hand—Oh, how wretched they will be!*

56:10 *The people who were foremost on earth [the first to follow Mohammed], they will be foremost in the hereafter. A large number of those who lived before are the people who will be brought close to Allah, in Gardens of delight. A few of those who lived later [after Islam was well established] will be on decorated couches, reclining on them face to face. They will be waited on by immortal young boys with goblets and ewers and a cup of pure wine that gives no headache nor muddles the mind, and with fruits that are most pleasing, and with the flesh of birds that they desire. In compensation for their past good deeds, they will have houris [heavenly companions of pleasure] with big, dark eyes like pearls peeking from their shells. They will not hear any vain or sinful talk, only the cry, "Peace! Peace!"*

56:27 *The people of the right-hand—Oh! How happy the people of the right-hand will be resting on raised couches amid thornless sidrahs [plum trees] and talh trees [banana trees], thick with fruit, and in extended shade and constantly flowing waters, and abundant fruits, neither forbidden nor out of reach. And We have specially made for them houris, companions, chaste and pure virgins, lovers and friends of equal age with them for the people of the right hand, a large number of the people of old, and a large number of the people of the latter generations.*

56:41 *The people of the left-hand—Oh, how wretched the people of the left-hand will be amid scorching winds and scalding water, and in the shade of black smoke, neither cool nor refreshing. Formerly they were blessed with worldly pleasures, yet they persisted in terrible sin and used to say, "What will be resurrected after we have died and crumbled to bone and dust? What about our fathers, the men of old?"*

56:49 *Say: Yes, the former and the latter. They will all be gathered at the appointed hour.*

56:51 *Then those who denied [Mohammed was a prophet] and erred will certainly eat from the Ez-zakkoum tree [a tree of Hell], and they will gorge themselves with it. Then they will drink scalding water and will drink like a thirsty camel. This will be their feast on the Judgment Day!*

I161 There was added a new element to the religion. Any person who rejected the revelations of Mohammed would be eternally punished. The culture of religious tolerance in Mecca now had a new religion which preached the end of tolerance. Only Islam was acceptable.

I166 Since the word was out, Mohammed began to openly preach his new doctrine. He had been private for three years before he went public.

The first of many parables was given:

> 68:17 *Surely, We have tried them [the Meccans] as We tried the owners of the garden, when they swore they would harvest its fruit in the morning; but added no exception [by saying, "If it is the will of Allah"]. Then an encompassing plague from your Lord swept through it while they slept, and by the morning the garden was barren, as if all its fruit had been cut.* 68:21 *At dawn they called to each other, "Go to your fields early if you want to cut your dates." So they went, quietly whispering to each other, "No poor man will enter your garden today." And so they went out at dawn to their fields with this purpose in mind.*
> 68:26 *But when they saw the garden, they said, "Surely we have gone astray. Indeed, our harvest is destroyed." The best among them said, "Did I not say to you, 'Why do you refuse to praise Allah?'" They said, "Glory to our Lord! Surely we have done wrong."*
> 68:30 *Then they began to blame one another, and they said, "Woe to us! We were insolent! Perhaps our Lord will give us a better garden in exchange. Surely we beg this from our Lord."*
> 68:33 *This has been their punishment, but the punishment of the hereafter is even greater, but they did not know this. Surely the Allah-fearing will be in Gardens of Delight in the presence of their Lord. Should We deal with those who have submitted to Allah like We do those who offend him? What has happened to you [unbelievers] to make you judge as you do? Do you have a Scripture from which you can learn how you can have the things that you choose? Or have you received an oath from Us, binding until Judgment Day, that you will have everything you demand? Ask them [the unbelievers] who will guarantee this? Or do they have other gods? Let them bring their other gods if they are telling the truth.*

The Arabs had always believed in jinns, invisible beings created from fire. Now they appeared in the Koran.

> 114:1 *Say: I seek protection with the Lord of men, the king of men, the judge of men, and from the mischief of gossips, who whisper into the hearts of men tales against the jinn and men.*

> 51:56 *I created jinn and man only to worship me. I need no livelihood from them, and I do not need them to feed me. Truly, Allah is the sole sustainer, the possessor of power, and the unmovable!*

51:59 *Let those who injure you share the fate of the sinners of old. They should not challenge Me to hasten it. Woe to the unbelievers, because of the day they are threatened with.*

The other deities in Mecca were attacked.

53:19 *Do you see Al-Lat and Al-Ozza, and Manat [Arabic deities] the third idol? What? Do you have male children and Allah female children [Arabs called angels the daughters of Allah]? That is an unfair division!*
53:23 *These are mere names. You and your fathers gave them these names. Allah has not acknowledged them. They follow only their own conceits and desires, even though their Lord has already given them guidance.*

53:27 *Surely, the ones who give female names to the angels are the ones who do not believe in the hereafter, but of this they have no knowledge. They are following a guess, and a guess cannot replace the truth.*
53:29 *Stay away from those who turn their backs on Our warnings and desire only the present life. This is all that they know. Truly, your Lord knows everything about those who stray from his path, and He knows everything about those who have accepted his guidance. Whatever is in the heavens and on the earth belongs to Allah. He may reward evildoers according to their own deeds and those who do good will be rewarded with good things.*
53:32 *Surely, your Lord is filled with forgiveness for those who avoid great sins and shameful acts and only commit minor sins. He knew you well when He brought you out of the earth and when you were in your mother's womb. Do not try to justify yourself. He knows the Allah-fearing people the best.*

Mohammed's task in Mecca was difficult.

52:29 *Therefore, continue to warn men. By the grace of your Lord, you are neither insane, nor a soothsayer.*
52:30 *Will people say, "He is a poet! Let us wait until his fortunes turn."? Say: "Wait," because truthfully, I will wait with you.*
52:32 *Is it their dreams that cause them to do this? Or is it because they are a perverse people? Will they say, "He has written it [the Koran] himself?" No! It is because they did not believe. If that is true, let them write a book like it.*
52:35 *Were they created from nothing? Did they create themselves? Did they create the heavens and the earth? No! It is because they have no faith. Do they possess your Lord's treasures? Do they have absolute power? Can they communicate with the angels? If so, let them bring proof.*
52:39 *Does Allah have daughters while you have sons? Do you ask them for a payment so that they are weighed down with debt? Do they have secret knowledge that they can write down? Do they try to set traps for you? The unbelievers are the ones that are ensnared. Do they have any gods besides*

Allah? Glory be to Allah above the false gods they join with Him. If they saw a piece of the sky falling, they would say, "It is only a dense cloud."
52:45 *Ignore them until they meet the day when they will swoon with terror—a day when their tricks will avail them nothing and no help will come their way. Truly, there is another punishment for the evildoers, but most of them do not know it.*
52:48 *Wait patiently for your Lord's Judgment, because you are in Our eye. Sing Allah's praises when you rise up, and give Him praise at night and when the stars are setting.*

The Koran contains encouragement for Mohammed:

94:1 *Did We not open your heart for you [Mohammed] and relieve you of the burden that hurt your back? And did We not improve your reputation? So, certainly, with every hardship there is relief. Certainly, with every hardship there is relief.*
94:7 *When you are through with prayers, you should continue to work. Do everything you can to please your Lord.*

Mohammed spent a great deal of time arguing with the Meccans and telling them that they were doomed to Hell if they rejected him and his message.

84:1 *When the sky is split in half and obeys its Lord, as it must; when the earth is flattened, and has cast out everything it contains and is empty [the graves deliver the dead], and obeys its Lord, as it must; then certainly those who want to meet their Lord will meet Him.*
84:7 *He who receives his book [of life's deeds] in his right hand [saved in Paradise], his account will be taken by a quick and easy reckoning and he will return joyously to his people. But those who receive their book behind their backs [damned to Hell] will invite destruction. They will burn in the Fire. They lived joyously among their people because they did not believe that they would return to Allah, but their Lord is always watching them.*
84:16 *So I do not need to swear by the glow of sunset, and by the night and everything it conceals, and by the moon at its fullest. You will certainly travel from stage to stage.*
84:20 *What is wrong with those who do not believe? When the Koran is read to them, why do they refuse to bow down? The unbelievers call it a lie.*
84:23 *But Allah knows their secrets, so announce to them a painful punishment. Those who believe and do good deeds, they will have a reward that never ends.*

The Meccans said that there was no Day of Doom. The Koran:

> 83:1 *Woe to the cheaters who always demand full measure from others, but skimp when they measure out or weigh to others. What! Do they believe that they will not be resurrected on the great day when all men will stand before the Lord of the worlds? Yes! The register [a record of actions] of the wicked is in Sidjin [a place in Hell where the sinners' records are kept]. And who will make you understand what Sidjin is? It is a complete record.*
>
> 83:10 *Woe on that day to those who deny Our signs, who regard the Judgment Day as a lie! No one regards it as a lie except the transgressor or the criminal, who, when Our signs are recited to him, says, "Old wives tales!" No! Their habits have become like rust on their hearts. Yes, they will be veiled from their Lord's light that day. Then they will be burned in Hell. They will be told, "This is what you called a lie."*
>
> 83:18 *No! But the register of the righteous is in Illiyoun [a place in Paradise where the actions of the righteous are recorded]. And who will make you understand what Illiyoun is? It is a complete record, attested to by the angels nearest Allah.*
>
> 83:22 *Surely, the righteous will live among delights! Seated on bridal couches they will gaze around. You will see the delight in their faces. Fine wines, sealed with musk, will be given them to drink. For those who have aspirations, aspire for wine mixed with the waters of Tasnim, a fountain where those close to Allah drink.*
>
> 83:29 *Sinners used to jeer at the believers and wink at one another when one passed by, and they jested as they returned to their own people. When they see believers, they say, "Those people have gone astray." And yet they were not sent to be the guardians of those people.*
>
> 83:34 *On that day the faithful will mock the unbelievers, while they sit on bridal couches and watch them. Should not the unbelievers be paid back for what they did?*

Not only were the present day Meccans going to Hell if they did not follow Mohammed, history was full of those who were doomed to Hell for ignoring the message of Allah.

> 69:1 *The Inevitable! Who will make you understand what the Inevitable is?*
>
> 69:3 *The people of Thamud and Ad [Ad lay on an old trade route north of Mecca. It was abandoned in Mohammed's day] regarded the Judgment Day as a lie. The people of Thamud were destroyed by crashing thunderbolts. The people of Ad were destroyed by a roaring blast of wind. The wind did Allah's bidding against them for a full week. During that time you could have seen the people laid low, as if they had been the trunks of hollow palms. Could you have seen any of them surviving?*

69:9 *Pharaoh, too, and those who thrived before him, and the overthrown cities, all committed sin, and disobeyed the messenger sent by their Lord. That is why He punished them with an accumulated punishment.*

69:11 *When the flood rose high, We carried you in the ark so We could use that event to warn you and so the hearing ear might hear it. But when one blast is sounded on the trumpet, and the earth and the mountains are shaken, and both are simultaneously crushed into powder, on that day the woe that must come suddenly will come, and the sky will be split in two, because it will be fragile that day. The angels will align on the edges of the sky and over them. Eight will carry up the throne of your Lord.*

69:18 *On that day you will be brought before Him and none of your secrets will remain secret. Those who receive their book in their right hand will say to their friends, "Take my book and read it. I always knew that I would come to my reckoning." And he will have a life of bliss, in a lofty Garden, with clusters of fruit nearby. Eat and drink with satisfaction. This is the reward for the good acts that you performed in the past.*

69:25 *But those who receive their book with their left hand will say, "Oh, I wish that I were never given my book and that I had never heard of my reckoning! I wish that death had been the end of me! My wealth has done me no good! My power has fled from me!"*

69:30 *Take him, and chain him, and cast him into Hell. Then fasten him to a seventy-yard chain, because he did not believe in Allah, the Greatest, and did not help to feed the poor. He will have no friends here that day, no food, only the pus that runs from sores, which only the sinners eat.*

69:38 *I do not need to swear by what you see and by that which you do not see—that this is surely the word of an honored messenger! It is not the word of a poet—you have so little faith! It is also not the word of a soothsayer—you heed little of Our warning! It is a message from the Lord of the worlds.*

69:44 *If he [Mohammed] had invented any of Our revelations, We would have grabbed him by the right hand, and cut his throat, and we would not have protected him from any of you.*

69:48 *But, surely, the Koran is a warning for the Allah-fearing. We know many think it is a lie. But it will cause grief for the unbelievers, because it is the absolute truth.*

69:52 *Praise the name of your Lord, the Greatest.*

I166 The Muslims went to the edge of Mecca to pray in order to be alone. One day a group of the Quraysh came upon them and began to mock them and a fight started. Saad, a Muslim, picked up the jaw bone of a camel and struck one of the Quraysh with it and bloodied him. This violence was the first blood to be shed in Islam.

1167 When Mohammed spoke about his new religion, it did not cause any problems among the Meccans. Then Mohammed began to condemn their religion and rituals and worship. This was a new phenomena. New religions could be added and had been, but not to the detriment to others. The Meccans took offense and resolved to treat him as an enemy. Luckily, he had the protection of his influential uncle, Abu Talib.

1168 Some of the Quraysh went to Abu Talib, Mohammed's tribal protector, and said to him, "Your nephew has cursed our gods, insulted our religion, mocked our way of life, criticized our civilization, attacked our virtues, and said that our forefathers were ignorant and in error. You must stop him, or you must let us stop him. We will rid you of him." Abu Talib gave them a soft reply and sent them away.

1169 The Quraysh saw that Abu Talib would not help. Mohammed continued to preach Islam and attack them and their lives. Mecca was a small town, everybody knew everybody. Islam had split the town of Mecca and divided the ruling and priestly tribe. The Quraysh were attacked at the very ground of their social being.

1170 Things got much worse. Now there was open hostility in the town. Quarrels increased, arguments got very heated. Complete disharmony dominated the town. The tribe started to abuse the recently converted Muslims. But Mohammed's uncle Abu Talib was a respected elder and was able to protect them from real harm.

THE FAIR

Mecca was a town with two sources of money from the outside. The first was trading, and Mohammed had made his money in the caravan trade. The other was the fees from the pilgrims to the shrine of the Kabah. Fairs combined a little of both. All the tribes came for a fair. People would see old acquaintances and buy, sell or trade goods. Since Mecca was one of several sacred or pilgrim sites, rituals for the different tribal gods were performed around the Kabah and Mecca.

1171 It was time for the fair and the Quraysh were in turmoil. They were desperate that the divisions and rancor that had come with Mohammed's preaching not spread to the other clans outside Mecca. So a group of concerned Quraysh talked and decided to meet with Al Walid, a man of respect and influence. He told them that all the visitors would come to them and ask about this man Mohammed and what he was preaching. It was a foregone conclusion that Mohammed would preach and people would ask.

1171 But what could they agree on to tell the visitors so that there could be one voice. What would they call him? Was he possessed? Crazy? A ecstatic poet? A sorcerer? Who was he? What was he? Finally they agreed upon Mohammed being a sorcerer since he separated a son from his father or brother or wife or from his family.

> 68:1 *NUN[1]. By the pen and by what the angels write, by the grace of your Lord, you [Mohammed] are not possessed! Certainly, a limitless reward awaits you, because you have a noble nature, but you will see and they will see, which of you is insane.*

> 53:1 *By the star when it sets, your companion [Mohammed] is not wrong, nor is he misled, and he does not speak out of his own desire.*
> 53:4 *This [the Koran] is a revelation only to him. The Lord of mighty power filled it with wisdom and taught it to him. Allah appeared in a stately form in the highest part of the horizon. He approached and came nearer, at a distance of about two bow-lengths, or even closer, and he gave his revelation to his servant.*
> 53:11 *His heart did not invent what he saw. What! Will you dispute with him what he saw? He had seen Gabriel before, near the Sidrah-tree [a shade tree], which marks the boundary near the Garden of repose. When the Sidrah-tree was mysteriously covered, his eye did not turn away, nor did it wander because he saw his Lord's greatest sign.*

1171 So the Meccans split up and went out on the roadsides of town to speak with the travelers before they even arrived at Mecca.

1171 Mohammed delivered a message from Allah about Al Walid, the leader of the unbelievers. Indeed, many of the rich and powerful, who resisted Mohammed, earned their place in the Koran. The Koran gives such precise details and direct quotes of their arguments that if you were a Meccan of that day, you would know exactly who the person was.

> 96:6 *No, man is certainly stubborn. He sees himself as wealthy. Certainly, all things return to your Lord.*
> 96:9 *What do you think of a man [Abu Jahl] who holds back a servant of Allah [Mohammed] when he prays? Do you think that he is on the right path, or practices piety? Do you think that he treats the truth as a lie and turns his back? Does he not know that Allah sees everything?*
> 96:15 *No! Certainly if he does not stop, We will grab him by the forelock [cutting off or holding by the forelock was a shame in Arabic culture], the lying, sinful forelock! Let him call his comrades [the other Meccans]. We will call the guards of Hell. No, do not obey him, rather, adore and get closer to Allah.*

---

1 These Arabic letters are found in the first verse of several chapters. Their meaning is not known.

74:11 *Let Me deal with My creations, whom I have given great riches and sons to sit by their side, and whose lives I have made smooth and comfortable. And still he [Al Walid] wants me to give him more. No, I say. He is an enemy of Our revelations. I will impose a dreadful punishment on him because he plotted and planned.*

74:19 *Damn him! How he planned. Again, Damn him! How he planned.*

74:21 *Then he looked around and frowned and scowled and turned his back with vain pride and said, "This is nothing but old magic; it is the work of a mere mortal."*

74:26 *We will certainly throw him into Hell.*

74:27 *What will make you realize what Hell is? It leaves nothing, and it spares nothing. It chars the skin.*

74:30 *Nineteen angels oversee it. The angels are the only guardians of Hell, and We have set their number to confuse the unbelievers and to give the believers certain knowledge of the truth of the Koran so the believers will increase their faith. So the believers and the others who have received the Scriptures have no doubts. The weak of heart and the unbelievers will ask, "What does Allah mean by this parable?"*

74:34 *This is how Allah confuses whom He will and how He guides whom He chooses: no one knows the armies of your Lord except Allah himself. This is nothing but a warning to men.*

74:35 *No, by the moon and by the night as it retreats and by the dawn as it breaks, Hell is one of the most dreadful woes filled with warning to men, to any who choose to go forward [believers] or to any who choose to stay behind [unbelievers].*

74:41 *Every soul is pledged for its own deeds except those that stand on Allah's right hand. In their gardens they will ask the wicked: "What has brought you to Hell?"*

74:44 *They will say, "We did not pray, we did not feed the hungry, we argued with the small-minded, and we denied the Judgment Day until our dying day."*

74:49 *No mediation or intercession will help them. What is wrong with them that they reject Our warning like a frightened donkey fleeing a lion? Each of them wants to have everything spelled out, but that cannot be. They do not fear the hereafter.*

74:54 *No! The Koran is warning enough. Anyone who chooses shall be warned. Only if Allah pleases will the people be warned. He is to be feared and often forgiving.*

111:1 *Let the hands of Abu Lahab [Mohammed's uncle and an opponent] die and let him die! His wealth and attainments will not help him. He will be burned in Hell, and his wife will carry the firewood, with a palm fiber rope around her neck.*

1172 The plan of hurting Mohammed by warning the visitors made everyone more curious. When they heard Mohammed's soaring words from the Koran many visitors were impressed. When they left they took all the stories from Mecca, the Quraysh, the new Muslims and then, of course, Mohammed. Soon all of that part of Arabia was talking.

1178 In what would be very fortuitous for Mohammed, the Arabs of Medina were attracted to Mohammed's message. Since half of their town were Jews, the Arabs of Medina were used to the talk of only one god.

PUBLIC TEACHING

CHAPTER 4

> *3:32 Say: Obey Allah and His messenger, but if they reject it,*
> *then truly, Allah does not love those who reject the faith.*

The arguments continued. The Koran condemns those who argue with Mohammed.

> *25:32 Those who disbelieve say, "Why was the Koran not revealed to him all at once?" It was revealed one part at a time so that We might strengthen your heart with it and so that We might rehearse it with you gradually, in slow, well-arranged stages.*
>
> *25:33 They will not come to you with any difficult questions for which We have not provided you the true and best answers. Those who will be gathered together face down in Hell will have the worst place and will be the farthest away from the right path.*

The reaction of the Meccans was with false arguments.

> *18:54 In this Koran We have given to man every kind of example, but man is, in most respects, contentious. Nothing prevents men from believing when guidance comes to them nor from asking their Lord's forgiveness, unless it is that they wish that the same fate which befell the ancients should also befall them—that they come face to face with doom.*
>
> *18:56 We do not send messengers except as bearers of glad tidings and to give warnings. Yet the unbelievers make false contentions so that they may refute the truth. They mock Our signs just like they do Our warnings. Who is more unjust than he who is reminded of His Lord's signs but turns away from them and forgets what His hands have done? Truly We have placed veils over their hearts so that they do not understand, and deafness over their ears. Even if you give them guidance, they will not follow.*
>
> *18:58 Your Lord is most forgiving, the Lord of mercy. If He were to give them what they deserve, He would certainly have hastened their punishment, but they have an appointed time which they cannot escape. The same could be said for the cities. We destroyed them when they behaved wickedly, and We appointed a set time for their destruction.*

The native religions that had been practiced for time out of mind were all false and condemned in every way.

37:11 *Ask the Meccans whether they or the angels are the stronger creation? We created men from clay.*

37:12 *Truly you [Mohammed] are amazed when they mock. When they [the Meccans] are warned, they pay no attention. When they see a sign, they begin to mock and say, "This is obviously magic. What? Will we be resurrected after we are nothing but dust and bones? And what about our ancestors?"*

37:18 *Tell them, "Yes! And you will be disgraced." There will be a single cry, and they will look around and say, "Oh, woe to us!" This is the day of reckoning. This is the Judgment Day that you said was a lie.*

37:22 *Gather together the unjust, their consorts [the demons], and the false gods they worshiped besides Allah and point them down the road to Hell. Stop them because they must be questioned. "What is wrong with you that you do not help each other?"*

37:26 *But on this day, they will submit to Allah and blame one another. They will say, "You [the demons] used to come to us from the right-hand side [the side of a good omen]." But they [the demons] will answer, "No, it was you who did not believe. We had no power over you. No, you were a wicked people. Our Lord's sentence has been passed upon us, and we will surely taste our punishment. We misled you because we were lost." Therefore, they will be partners in punishment that day.*

37:34 *Truly, that is how We deal with the guilty, because when they were told that there is no god but Allah, they swelled with pride and said, "Should we abandon our gods for a crazy poet?"*

37:37 *No! He [Mohammed] comes truthfully and confirms the prophets of old. You will surely taste the painful punishment, and you will be punished for what you have done, all except the sincere servants of Allah! They will have a fixed banquet of fruits; and they will be honored in the Garden of delight, facing one another on couches. A cup filled from a gushing spring will be passed among them, crystal clear and delicious to those who drink. It causes neither pain nor intoxication. And with them are companions [houris] with large eyes and modest glances, fair like a sheltered egg. They will ask one another questions. One of them will say, "I had a close friend who said, 'Are you one of those who accept the truth? What? When we have died, and become dust and bones, will we really be judged?'"*

37:54 *He will say to those around him, "Will you look?" Looking down, he saw his friend in the depths of Hell. And he will say to him, "By Allah, you almost destroyed me. Except for my Lord's favor, I surely would have been one of those who came with you into torment."*

37:58 *"Is it not true that we will not die," say the blessed, "except for our first death and that we have escaped the torment?" Certainly this is the supreme achievement! For something like this, a striver should strive!*

23

37:62 *Is this a better feast than the Zaqqum tree [the tree of Hell]? We have certainly made the tree to torment the wicked. It grows at the bottom of Hell. Its fruit is like the heads of vipers. The damned will certainly eat it until their bellies fill. Then they will drink a mixture of boiling water. Then they will return to the Fire.*
37:69 *The damned knew that the religion of their fathers was wrong, but they still followed the old religion. Even before them, most of the ancients erred, though We had sent messengers to warn them. See what happened to these warned ones except for Allah's true servants?*

21:92 *Truly, this religion of yours is the only religion, and I am your Lord, so worship Me. But they have broken their religion [Christianity] into sects, and yet they will all return to Us. Whoever does good things and believes will not have his efforts denied. We will record everything.*
21:95 *There is a ban on those cities We have destroyed. They will not return until Gog and Magog [barbarians who figure in the Final Days] are let loose and they hurry from every hillside and the true promise draws near. Then the unbelievers will stare in horror and say, "Oh no! We lived in ignorance. No, we were unjust."*
21:98 *Surely you and those you worship besides Allah are nothing but fuel for Hell. You will be sent there. If these were gods, they would not be sent down into it, but all of them will live there forever. There they will do nothing but weep, and that will be the only thing that they hear.*
21:101 *But those for whom We have ordained, good things will be far away. They will not hear the slightest sound from Hell as they live according to their soul's desire. The great Terror [Judgment Day] will cause them no grief. Instead, the angels will greet them every day by saying, "This is your day, the day that you were promised, the day when We roll the heavens up like a scroll. Just as We made the first creation, so We will reproduce it. This is a promise We are bound to. Truly it is something We will fulfill. After the message was given to Our servants We wrote in the Psalms, My righteous servants will inherit the earth." Surely there is a message here for those who worship Allah.*

The Meccans had many leaders who resisted Mohammed.

38:55 *But the evil have a terrible place waiting for them—Hell—where they will be burned. What a wretched bed to lie on! Let them taste boiling water and icy fluid and other vile things. Their leaders will be told, "This group will be thrown head first into the fire with you. There is no welcome for them. They will burn in the fire!"*
38:60 *They will say to those who misled them, "No! There is no welcome for you. You brought this wretched place upon us!" They will say, "Lord, double the punishment for those who brought this upon us." They will say, "Why do we not see the people who we thought were wicked, whom we*

24

mocked? Were we mistaken, or have our eyes missed them?" Truly, that is fitting and just—the mutual accusations of the people of the fire.

38:65 *Say: I am here to warn you. There is no god but Allah, the One, the Almighty! Lord of the heavens and the earth, and everything in between, the mighty, the most forgiving! Say: This is an important message that you turn away from! I had no knowledge of the dispute between those on high. Nothing has been revealed to me except that I am here to warn you.*

I183 Mohammed continued to preach the glory of Allah and condemn the Quraysh religion. He told them their way of life was wrong, their ancestors would burn in Hell, he cursed their gods, he despised their religion and divided the community, setting one tribesman against the others. The Quraysh felt that this was all past bearing. Tolerance had always been their way. Many clans, many gods, many religions. Another religion was fine, why did Mohammed demean them?

25:45 *Have you considered how your Lord makes the shadow grow? If He wished, He could make it stationary. But We have made the sun its guide; then We bring it to Ourselves, a gradual retreat. It is He who makes the night like a covering for you and sleep a repose and makes the day a resurrection.*

25:48 *He sends the winds bearing good news before His mercy, and We send down pure water from heaven so that We may give life to a dead planet and quench the thirst of Our creations, animals and great numbers of people. We distribute it among them so that they celebrate Our praises, but most men refuse to be anything except ungrateful. If We had wished, We could have sent a messenger to every city. So do not listen to the unbelievers, but instead strive against them with all your might.*

25:53 *He let loose the two seas, one sweet and refreshing, the other salty and bitter. Between the two He has set a barrier, an impassible obstruction. He has created man from water and made blood and marriage relationships for him because your Lord is all powerful. And still they worship others besides Allah who can neither help nor hurt them. The unbeliever is Satan's ally against his Lord.*

I183 One day at the Kabah the Meccans were discussing Mohammed and his enmity towards them, when Mohammed arrived. He kissed the Black Stone of the Kabah and started past them as he circumambulated [walk around the Kabah and repeat prayers] the Kabah. Each time he passed by them they insulted him. On the third round, he stopped and said, "Listen to me, by Allah I will bring you slaughter." The Quraysh were stunned at his threat. They said, "Mohammed, you have never been a violent man, go away."

1184 The next day many of the Quraysh were at the Kabah when Mohammed arrived. They crowded around him and said, "Are you the one who condemned our gods and our religion?" Mohammed answered that he was the one. One of them grabbed him and Abu Bakr, Mohammed's chief follower, pressed forward and said, "Would you kill a man for saying that Allah is his Lord?" They let him go. This was worst treatment that Mohammed received in Mecca.

But Mohammed was not afraid. He was on a divine mission.

> 21:107 *We have sent you only to be a mercy for all people. Say: It has been revealed to me that Allah is the only god. Will you submit to Him? If they turn their backs, then say, "I have truthfully warned you alike. I do not know if Judgment Day will come sooner or later. Allah knows what is said openly and what you hide. I only know that you will be tried and that you may enjoy yourself for awhile." Say: My Lord judges with truth. Our Lord is the beneficent Allah Whose help is sought against lies you ascribe to Him.*

He continued to speak of Allah and the Koran. Many times in the Koran we find self-proofs of the validity of the Koran and the proof of Allah.

> 26:1 *TA. SIN. MIN. These are the verses of the Book that make things clear.*
> 26:3 *You may torment yourself [Mohammed] if they do not believe. If We wanted, We could send them a sign from the sky that would force them to humbly bow their heads, but every new warning they receive from Allah is ignored. They have rejected the message, but they will learn the truth of what they mocked! Do they not see the earth and how much of so many noble things We have made there? Truly, there is a sign there, but most do not believe. And surely, your Lord, He is the mighty, the merciful.*
>
> 67:6 *The torment of Hell waits for those who do not believe in their Lord, and the journey there is terrible! When they are thrown in, they will hear the Fire roaring as it boils. It will almost burst with fury. Every time another group is thrown in, its keepers will ask them, "Did someone not warn you?"*
> 67:9 *They will say. Yes. Someone came to warn us, but we rejected him and said, 'Allah has revealed nothing to us. You are deluded.'"*
> 67:10 *They will say, "If we had listened or understood, we would not have been among the prisoners of the Fire." They will acknowledge their sins, but mercy is far away from the prisoners of the Fire.*
> 67:12 *However, forgiveness and a great reward waits for those who secretly fear their Lord. Whether you speak openly or secretly, He knows everything in your heart. Should He not know His creations? He is the subtle, the aware. He smoothed the earth for you, so walk its paths and eat the food He provides. Everything will return to Him after death.*

67:16 *Are you confident that Allah in heaven will not open the earth and swallow you in an earthquake? Are you sure that Allah in heaven will not send a hurricane against you? You will understand My warning then! It is true that your ancestors rejected their prophets. Was not My wrath terrible?*

67:19 *Do they not see the birds above, spreading and folding their wings? Only merciful Allah could keep them aloft. He watches over everything.*

67:20 *Who could help you like an army except merciful Allah? The unbelievers are totally deluded. Who would provide for you if He withheld His provisions? Still, they continue to be proud and reject Him. Is the person groveling along on his face better than those who walk upright on a straight path?*

67:23 *Say: He created you and gave you the gifts of sight, hearing, and feeling. Still, few are grateful. Say: He has sown you in the ground, and He will gather you. And they say, "If you are telling the truth, when will this promise be fulfilled?"*

67:26 *Say: Only Allah has knowledge of the time. I am only sent to publicly warn. But when they see it approach, the faces of the unbelievers will grieve. It will be said, "This is what you have been predicting." Say: What do you think? Whether Allah destroys me and my followers, or grants us mercy, who will protect the unbelievers from a terrible punishment? Say: He is the merciful. We believe in Him and trust Him, and you will learn later who is clearly in error. Say: What do you think? If all water sank into the earth, who would bring you clear running water?*

67:1 *Blessed is He whose hands hold the kingdom and has power over all things; Who created life and death to determine who conducts themselves best; and He is the mighty, the forgiving! He created and raised seven heavens, one above the other. You cannot see one defect in merciful Allah's creation. Do you see a crack in the sky? Look again and again. Your vision will blur from looking, but you will find no defects.*

A TRIBAL CHIEF TRIES TO CUT A DEAL

I186 One day while the Quraysh were in council one of the chiefs, Utba, decided to approach Mohammed and see if he could make a deal that would please everybody. Things were only getting worse about Mohammed and the others said to go and try. So he went to the Kabah and there was Mohammed. "Nephew, you have come to us with an important matter. But you have divided the community, ridiculed our customs, and insulted our forefathers. See if any of my suggestions can help in this matter. If you want money, we will give you money. If you want honor we will make you our king. If you are possessed we will get you a physician."

I186 Mohammed said that he represented the only Allah. His teachings were beautiful, and then he began to recite the glorious poetry and imagery of the Koran. The tribal chief was impressed with the beauty of Mohammed's words and left.

I186 When the tribal chief returned to the Quraysh, he said, "Leave him alone, his words are beautiful. If other Arabs kill him, your problem is solved. If he becomes sovereign over all, you will share in his glory. His power will become your power and you can make money off his success." They replied that Mohammed had bewitched him.

Mohammed spoke beautiful words about Islam.

> 23:49 *And We gave the Book to Moses so that they might be guided.*
> 23:50 *And We made the son of Mary and his mother a sign, and We gave them a lofty abode for shelter, quiet and well provided with meadows and springs.*
> 23:51 *Oh messengers! Eat the things that are good, and do the right thing. I am aware of what you do. And truly your religion is the one religion, and I am your Lord, so fear and obey Me. But mankind has broken religion into sects, each rejoicing at that which they have retained. So leave them in their confusion and ignorance for a while.*
> 23:55 *Do they think that because We have given them an abundance of wealth and sons that We would rush to them with every blessing? No, they do not understand. But those who live in awe for fear of their Lord; and who believe in their Lord's signs; and who accept no other gods with their Lord; and who give charitably with fear in their hearts because they know they will return to their Lord—these will rush for the good things, and they will be the first to attain them.*
> 23:62 *We do not place upon any soul a burden that is beyond its ability, and We possess a record which speaks the truth. They will never be wronged.*
>
> 27:89 *Those who do good deeds will be rewarded beyond their due. They will be safe from terror that day. And if any do evil, they will be thrown face down into the Fire. Should your reward not reflect your actions?*
> 27:91 *Say: I am commanded only to worship the Lord of this land who has made it sacred, and to whom all things belong. I am commanded to be a Muslim, one who has surrendered to Allah, and to recite the Koran. If anyone does good things, they do so only for the good of their souls, and if any go astray, say: I am only here to warn.*
> 27:93 *And say: Praise be to Allah who will soon show you His signs so that you shall know them. Your Lord is not unaware of what you do.*

There were references in the Koran about the Koran.

44:1 *HA. MIM. By the book that makes everything clear!*
44:3 *We revealed it on a blessed night—because We are always warning man—on a night when every command is made clear by Our command. We are always sending Our messengers as a mercy from your Lord. He hears and knows everything.*

20:112 *But those who believe and have done the right things will have no fear of wrong or loss. This is why We sent to you an Arabic Koran and explained in detail Our warnings so that they may fear Allah and heed them. Exalted above all is Allah, the King, the Truth! Do not hurry through its recital before its revelation is made complete to you. Instead say, "Lord, increase my knowledge."*

26:192 *This Book has come down from the Lord of the worlds. The faithful spirit [Gabriel] has come down with it upon your [Mohammed's] heart so that you may warn others in the clear Arabic language. Truly, it is foretold in the ancient scriptures. Is it not a sign that the learned men of the Israelites recognized? If We had revealed it to any of the non-Arabs and he had recited it to them, they would not have believed in it.*
26:200 *This is how We influenced the hearts of the wicked. They will not believe in it until they see the painful punishment. And it will come upon them suddenly when they do not expect it. They will say, "Can we have a reprieve?"*

Mohammed continued to make it clear that not believing the words he brought from Allah would lead to a violent and painful eternity.

76:4 *We have prepared chains, fetters, and a blazing fire for the unbelievers.*
76:5 *The righteous, however, will drink cups filled from a camphor fountain—the fountain Allah's servants drink from—as it flows from place to place rewarding those who perform their vows and fear a day whose evil will spread far and wide. Even when they were hungry they gave their food to the poor, the orphan, and the prisoner. "We feed you for Allah's sake. We are not looking for reward or thanks from you. We are afraid of suffering and punishment from Allah."*
76:11 *But Allah saved them from the evil of that day and brought them happiness and joy. He rewarded their patience with Paradise and silk robes. Reclining on couches, none will suffer from extreme heat or cold. Trees will shade them, and fruit will dangle nearby. Silver cups and crystal goblets will pass among them: silver cups, transparent as glass, their size reflecting the measure of one's deeds. They will be given ginger-flavored wine from the fountain called Salsabil. They will be waited on by eternally young boys. When you look at them you would think they were scattered pearls. When you see it, you will see a vast kingdom of delights. They will*

wear richly brocaded green silk robes with silver bracelets on their arms, and they will quench their thirst with a pure drink given them by their Lord. This will be your reward. Your efforts will not go unnoticed.

76:23 *We have sent the Koran to you in stages to be a revelation. Wait patiently for Allah's command, and do not obey the wicked and the unbelieving. Celebrate your Lord's name in the morning, in the evening, and at night. Adore him and praise him all night long.*

76:27 *But men love the fleeting present and ignore the dreadful day ahead. We have created them, and We built them strong. When We want to, We will make others to replace them. This is certainly a warning. Whoever chooses, will take a straight path to his Lord. But unless Allah wills it, because he is knowing and wise, you will not succeed. You will receive his mercy if he chooses to give it, but he has prepared a terrible punishment for the wicked.*

23:93 *Say: Oh my Lord! If it is your will that I witness what you have promised, then, Oh my Lord, do not place me with the unjust. Certainly, We are able to show you with what We have threatened them. Repel evil with what is the best. We are well aware of what they say about you.*

23:97 *And say: Oh my Lord! I seek refuge with You from the suggestions of the evil ones. And I seek refuge with you, my Lord, from their presence.*

23:99 *When death overtakes one of the wicked, he says, "Lord, send me back again so that I may do the good things that I have left undone." But, no, they are nothing but empty words. There is a barrier around the wicked that will remain until the Judgment Day. When the trumpet is blown, there will be no ties of kinship connecting them, nor will they ask about one another.*

23:102 *Those whose balance is heavy will attain salvation, but those whose balance is light will have lost their souls, and they will abide in Hell. The Fire will burn their faces, and their lips will twitch in pain. It will be said, "Were My signs not recited to you? Did you not reject them?"*

23:106 *They will say, "Lord, misfortune defeated us, and we were led astray. Lord, take us from here. If we return to evil, then surely we are unjust.*

23:108 *Allah will say, "Do not speak to Me, but instead be gone into the flames. Some of My servants would say, 'Lord, we believe. Forgive us and have mercy on us, because you are the most merciful.' But you ridiculed them so much that you forgot My warning while you were mocking them. I have rewarded them for their patience and constancy. They are the blissful."*

23:112 *Allah will ask, "How many years did you stay on earth?"*

23:113 *They will say, "We stayed a day or part of a day. Ask those who keep count."*

23:114 *Allah will say, "You stayed only a little while; if you had only known. Did you think that We had created you in vain and that you would not be brought back to us for judgment?"*

23:116 *Let Allah be exalted, the true king! There is no god but Him, the Lord of the throne of grace. If anyone invokes another god besides Allah, he does so without proof. His reckoning is with Allah, alone. Surely the unbelievers will not succeed.*

23:118 *Say: Oh my Lord! Forgive and have mercy on us, because you are the most merciful.*

18:99 *On that day We shall let them surge against one another like waves. The trumpet will be blown, and We will gather them all together. On that day We shall present Hell for all the unbelievers to see—unbelievers whose eyes were veiled from My signs and who could not even hear. What? Do the unbelievers think that they can take My servants to be guardians besides me? We have prepared Hell to entertain the unbelievers.*

18:103 *Say: Shall We tell you whose actions will make them the biggest losers? Those whose efforts are lost in this world's life even while they thought that they were doing good deeds. These are the people who disbelieve in their Lord's revelations and who do not believe they will meet Him in the afterlife. Their deeds will have been done in vain, and on the Judgment Day, We will not give them any weight. Their reward is Hell, because they disbelieved and mocked Our revelations and Our messengers. As for those who believe and do good deeds, they have the Gardens of Paradise for their entertainment where they will dwell forever, never wishing to leave.*

Mecca was a small town and there were meetings about what to do about Mohammed.

43:68 *My servants, there is no fear for you that day, nor will you grieve, because you have believed in Our signs and surrendered your will to Allah. You and your wives shall enter the Garden rejoicing. Trays and goblets of gold will be passed around to them, and they will have everything they desire. They will dwell there forever. This is the Garden that will be given you because of your good deeds in life. There is an abundance of fruit there for you to enjoy.*

43:74 *The guilty, however, will dwell forever in the torment of Hell. The punishment will not be lightened for them, and they will be overwhelmed with despair. We were not unjust toward them. It was they who were unjust. They will cry, "Malik [an angel who is a keeper of Hell], let your Lord put us out of our misery." He will respond, "No! You will remain here." Surely, We have brought the truth to you, but most of you hate the truth.*

43:79 *Do they make plots against you? We also make plots. Do they think that We do not hear their secrets and their private conversations? We do, and Our messengers are there to record them.*

The Koran records some of the resistance of the Meccans to Mohammed.

38:1 *SAD. I swear by the Koran, full of warning! Truly, the unbelievers must be filled with arrogant pride to oppose you. How many earlier generations did We destroy? In the end, they cried for mercy when there was no time to escape!*

38:4 *They are skeptical that a messenger would come to them from their own people, and the unbelievers say, "This man is a sorcerer and a liar! Has he combined all the gods into one Allah? That is an amazing thing!" And their chiefs [the leaders of the opposition to Mohammed in Mecca] went about and said, "Walk away. Remain faithful to your gods. This is a plot. We have never heard of such a thing in the earlier religion. This is nothing but an invented tale!"*

38:8 *They say, "Why, of all people, has the message been sent to him [Mohammed]?" Yes! They doubt My warnings because they have not tasted My vengeance. Do they possess the blessings of the mighty, your Lord's mercy? Is the kingdom of the heavens and the earth and everything in between in their hands? If so, let them climb up to the heavens if they can! Any allies [Mohammed's opponents] remaining here will be defeated.*

38:12 *Before them the people of Noah and Ad [Ad lay on an old trade route north of Mecca. It was abandoned in Mohammed's day] and Pharaoh, the impaler, rejected their prophets. The people of Thamud [the people of a ruined Nabatean city near Medina] and Lot and the people who lived in the forest also rejected their prophets. They all called My messengers liars; therefore, their punishment was justified.*

38:15 *The unbelievers of Mecca today are only waiting for a single trumpet blast [announcing the Final Day] to happen soon. They will say, "Oh, our Lord, hurry our fate to us. Do not make us wait until the Judgment Day."*

MORE ARGUMENTS WITH THE MECCANS

I188, 189 Another group of Meccans sent for Mohammed to see if they could negotiate away this painful division of the tribes. They went over old ground and again Mohammed refused the money and power that was offered. He said they were the ones who needed to decide whether they wanted to suffer in the next world and he had the only solution. If they rejected him and his message, Allah would tend to them. One of the Quraysh said, "Well, if you speak for and represent the only true god, then perhaps his Allah could do something for them."

"This land is dry. Let his Allah send them a river next to Mecca."

"They were cramped being next to the mountains. Let his Allah open up some space by moving the mountains back."

"Our best members are dead. Let your Allah renew them to life and in particular send back the best leader of our tribe, Qusayy. We will ask Qusayy whether or not you speak truly."

I189 Mohammed said that he was sent as a messenger, not to do such work. They could either accept his message or reject it and be subject to the loss. Then one of them said, "If you won't use your Allah to help us, then let your Allah help you. Send an angel to confirm you and prove to us that we are wrong. As long as the angel was present, let him make Mohammed a garden and fine home and present him with all the gold and silver he needed. If you do this, we will know that you represent Allah and we are wrong." The Quraysh wanted miracles as a proof.

> 15:1 *ALIF. LAM. RA. These are the verses of the Scripture, a recital that makes things clear.*
>
> 15:2 *The unbelievers will often wish they were Muslims. Let them enjoy themselves, and let false hope beguile them. They will eventually learn the truth.*
>
> 15:4 *We never destroy a city whose term was not preordained. No nation can delay or change its destiny. They say: "You [Mohammed] to whom the message was revealed, you are surely insane. If you were telling the truth, why did you not bring angels to us?"*
>
> 15:8 *We do not send the angels without good reason. If We did, the unbelievers would still not understand. Surely, We have sent down the message, and surely, We will guard it. Before your time, We sent apostles to the sects of the ancient peoples, but they mocked every messenger. Similarly, We allow doubt to enter the hearts of the sinners. They do not believe it, even though the example of the ancients has preceded them. Even if We opened a gate into heaven for them the entire time they ascended, they would say, "Our eyes are playing tricks on us. No, we are bewitched."*

I189 Mohammed did not do miracles, because such things were not what Allah had appointed him to do.

I189 Then one of the Quraysh said, "Then let the heavens be dropped on us in pieces as you say your Lord could do. Then if you do not we will not believe." Mohammed said that Allah could do that if Allah wished or he might not if he wished.

I189 They then said, "Did not your Lord know that we would ask you these questions? Then your Lord could have prepared you with better answers. And your Lord could have told you what to tell us if we don't believe. We hear that you are getting this Koran from a man named Al

Rahman from another town. We don't believe in Al Rahman. Our conscience is clear. We must either destroy you or you must destroy us. Bring your angels and we will believe them."

I190 Mohammed turned and left. A cousin chased him and fell in beside him to talk. He said, "Mohammed, your tribe has made you propositions and you have rejected them. First, they asked you for things for themselves that they might see if you are true. Then they would follow you. You did nothing. Then they asked you for things for yourself so they could see your superiority over them and prove your standing with Allah. You did nothing. Then they said to bring on the punishments that your Allah has told you about and you have frightened us with his threats. You did nothing. Personally, I will never believe until you get a ladder up to the sky, you will climb it while I watch, and four angels will come and testify that you are truthful. But you know, even if you did all that, I still don't know if I would believe you."

I190 Mohammed went home and was sad and depressed. He had hoped when they sent for him it was to announce their submission to his Allah and his teachings. Instead, it was resistance and questions.

> 26:204 *What! Do they seek to hasten Our punishment? What do you think? If after giving them their fill for years and their punishment finally comes upon them, how will their pleasures help them? We have never destroyed a city that We did not warn first with a reminder. We did not treat them unjustly.*
>
> 26:210 *The devils were not sent down with the Koran. It does not suit them, and they do not have the power because they are banned from hearing it. Do not call upon any god but Allah, or you will be doomed. Rather, warn your close relatives.*
>
> 26:215 *And be kind to the believers who follow you. If they disobey you, say, "I will not be responsible for your actions." Put your trust in Him who is mighty and merciful, Who sees you when you stand in prayer, and your demeanor among the worshipers, because He hears and knows everything.*
>
> 26:221 *Shall I tell you who Satan will descend upon? He will descend upon every lying, wicked person. They speak of what they hear, but most of them are liars. It is the poets that the erring follow. Do you see how they wander distractedly around every valley, and that they do not practice what they preach? But not so for the believers, who believe, do good works, and remember Allah often, and who defend themselves when unjustly treated. But those who treat them unjustly will find out what a terrible fate awaits them.*

The Koran had advice for Mohammed in these difficult times.

> 15:87 *We have given you seven of the often-repeated verses [Sura 1] and the great Koran. Do not strain your eyes coveting the good things that We have given to some of the unbelievers, and do not grieve for them, but instead take the believers tenderly under your wing. Say: " I am the one who gives plain warning."*

> 25:41 *When they see you, they mock you, saying, "Is this the man whom Allah sends as a messenger? He would have led us far from our gods if we had not been so loyal to them!" When they see the punishment that is waiting, they will soon realize who was more misled. What do you think of someone who worships his own passion like a god? Would you be a guardian for such a person? Or do you think that most of them even hear or understand? They are just like cattle. No, they stray even further from the path.*

I191 Mohammed would come to the Kabah and tell the Meccans what terrible punishments that Allah had delivered to the others in history who had not believed their prophets. That was now one of his constant themes. Allah destroyed others like you who did not listen to men like me.

> 36:1 *YA. SIN. I swear by the wise Koran that you are surely one of the messengers on a straight path, a revelation of the mighty, the merciful, sent to warn a people whose fathers were not warned, and consequently remain heedless.*
>
> 36:7 *Our sentence against them is just because they do not believe. We have bound their necks with chains that reach the chin, forcing their heads up. We have placed barriers in front, behind, and over them, so they cannot see. It does not matter whether you warn them or not, because they will not believe. You can only warn those who follow the message and fear merciful Allah in private. Give them glad tidings of forgiveness and a generous reward. It is true We will give life to the dead and that We record what they will do and what they have done. We have recorded everything in Our perfect ledger.*
>
> 36:13 *Use a parable to tell them the story of the people of the city [Antioch] when the messengers visited. When We first sent two messengers to them, the people rejected them, but We sent a third to strengthen their numbers. They said, "We are messengers sent to you by Allah."*
>
> 36:15 *The people said, "You are merely men just like us. Allah has sent no revelation. You only tell lies."*
>
> 36:16 *The messengers replied, "Our Lord knows that we have been sent to you. Our only duty is to proclaim the clear message."*
>
> 36:18 *They said, "We predict evil from you. If you do not stop, we will certainly stone you and inflict a terrible punishment."*

36:19 *The messengers said, "Your prediction of evil comes from within. Is it because you are warned? No! You are a people in error."*

36:20 *A man [Habib, the carpenter] came running from the outskirts of the city and said, "My people, listen to the messengers! Obey those who do not ask any reward and who follow the right path. It would be unreasonable of me not to serve Him who created me, and to Whom we will all return. Should I worship other gods besides Him? If Allah wished to afflict me their intercession could not help me at all, nor could they save me. If I did worship other gods, I would be in clear error. I believe in your Lord, so listen to me." It was said to him, "Enter the Garden of Paradise." The man replied, "Oh, if only my people knew how gracious Allah has been to me and that He has made me one of the honored ones!"*

36:28 *After the man [Habib] from the outskirts died, We sent no army down from heaven against his people. We did not need to do so. It was nothing more than a single cry, and they were extinct. Oh! The misery that falls upon My servants! Every messenger sent to them has been mocked. Do they not see how many earlier generations We have destroyed? Every one of them will be brought before Us for judgment.*

36:33 *The dead earth is a sign for them. We give it life which produces grain for them to eat. And We have placed gardens of palms and grapes there with springs gushing water so they might enjoy the fruit of Our artistry. Their hands did not make this. Why will they not be grateful?*

According to the Koran the ancient towns of Arabia were destroyed because they did not believe their prophet.

26:141 *The people of Thamud [the people of a ruined Nabatean city near Medina] rejected the messengers. Their brother Salih said to them, "Will you not fear Allah? I am a faithful messenger worthy of all trust. Fear Allah and obey me. I ask for no reward. My reward comes only from the Lord of the worlds. Will you be left safely to enjoy all you have among gardens and fountains and corn-fields and palm-trees, heavy with fruit, and—insolent as you are—your homes carved from the mountain stone? Fear Allah and obey me. Do not obey the bidding of the extravagant who make mischief in the land, and do not reform."*

26:153 *They said, "You are certainly one of the bewitched. You are only a man like us. Give us a sign if you are telling the truth."*

26:155 *He said, "Here is a she-camel. She has a right to drink from the well, and you have a right to drink from the well, each at a scheduled time. But do not harm her, or the punishment of a terrible day will overtake you."*

26:157 *But they hamstrung her, and then regretted it, so the punishment overtook them. Surely, there is a sign here, but most of them do not believe.*

27:45 *Long ago We sent to the Thamud their brother Salih saying, "Worship Allah." But they became two quarreling factions. He said, "My people, why do you embrace evil, rather than good? Why do you not ask Allah's forgiveness so that you may receive mercy?"*

27:47 *They said, "We predict that you and your followers will bring us evil." He said, "The evil that you sense will befall you will come from Allah. You are a people on trial."*

27:48 *In the city there were nine men from one family who made mischief in the land and would not reform. They said, "Swear to one another by Allah that we will attack Salih and his family at night, and we will tell his vengeance-seeking heirs that we did not see the murder of his family, and we will be telling the truth." They plotted and planned, but We also plotted, even though they did not realize. See how their plotting turned out. We destroyed them and their entire people. You may still see their ruined homes which were destroyed because they were wicked. Surely this is a sign for those who understand. We saved those who believed and acted righteously.*

1191 One of the Quraysh, Al Nadr, had been to Persia and had learned many tales and sagas from the storytellers there. The traveler would announce, "I can tell a better tale than Mohammed." Then he would proceed to tell them ancient sagas and stories of Persia. "In what way is Mohammed a better storyteller than me?"

But Mohammed's stories were straight from Allah. Here are stories about David, a king of the Jews:

38:17 *Be patient with what they say, and remember Our servant David, a powerful man, who always looked repentantly to Allah. We made the mountains sing the praises of Allah in unison with him in the morning and the evening, and the birds gathered together; all joined him in praise of Allah. We made his kingdom strong and gave him wisdom and sound Judgment.*

38:21 *Have you heard the story of the two disputing men who climbed the wall of David's private chamber? David was frightened when they entered his room. They said, "Do not be afraid. We have a dispute, and one of us has certainly wronged the other. Judge where the truth lies between us, and do not be unjust, but guide us to the right way. My brother has ninety-nine ewes [female sheep], and I have only one. He pressured me and said, 'Let me have her.'"*

38:24 *David replied, "Certainly he has wronged you by insisting that you give him your ewe. It is true that many partners wrong one another, the exception being those who believe and behave correctly. There are few of those." David realized that We had tried him. He asked forgiveness from his Lord, fell down bowing, and repented.*

38:25 *So We forgave him this sin; truly he is honored and well received by Us and has an excellent place in Paradise. It was said to him, "David, We have indeed made you a vice-regent on earth. Use truth and justice when judging between men, and do not follow your passions because they may cause you to stray from Allah's path. Those who stray from Allah's path will meet a terrible punishment because they have forgotten the Judgment Day.*

Noah

71:1 *We sent Noah to his people and said to him, "Warn your people before a terrible punishment befalls them." He said, "My people, I come to you as a plain-speaking warner. Serve and fear Allah and obey me. He will forgive you your sins and give you respite until the appointed time, because when Allah's appointed time has come, it cannot be delayed. If only you knew this!"*

71:5 *He said, "Lord, I have cried to my people day and night; and my cries only increase their aversion. Whenever I cry to them so that you may forgive them, they cover their ears and cover themselves in their cloaks, and persist stubbornly in their error. Then I called loudly to them. Then I spoke plainly, and I spoke to them privately and I said, 'Beg your Lord for forgiveness because he is ready to forgive. He will open the sky and send down rain in abundance. He will increase your wealth and children and will give you gardens and rivers. What is the matter with you that you refuse to seek goodness from Allah's hand when it was Him who made you in diverse stages?'"*

71:15 *"Do you not see how Allah created the seven heavens and set them one above another? He placed the moon there and made it a light, and made the sun a lamp and placed it there, and Allah caused you to spring out of the earth like a plant. Later he will turn you back into the earth and bring you out again. Allah has spread the earth for you like a carpet so that you may walk there along spacious paths." Noah said, "Lord, they rebel against me and follow those whose wealth and children add only to their troubles."*

71:22 *And they devised a great plot. They said, "Do not forsake your gods; do not forsake Wadd, or Sowah, or Yaghuth nor Yahuk or Nesr [names of Semitic gods]." They have led many astray and have added only error to the ways of the wicked. Because of their sins, they were drowned and forced into the fire, and they discovered that Allah was their only shelter.*

71:26 *And Noah said, "Lord, do not leave one family of unbelievers alive on earth. Because if you do, then they will trick your servants and will only breed more sinners and unbelievers. Lord, forgive me and my parents and every believer that enters my house and all the male and female believers. Give nothing but destruction to the wicked."*

Other Jewish references:

> 38:41 *Do you remember Our servant Job when he cried to his Lord, "Satan has afflicted me with distress and torment." We said to him, "Stamp the ground with your foot. Here is a spring, a cool washing place, and water to drink." And We gave him back his family and doubled their number as an example of Our mercy and as a reminder for men of understanding. We said to him, "Take up in your hand a branch and strike her with it, and do not break your oath.[1]" Truly, We found him to be full of patience and constant. He was an excellent servant, because he constantly turned toward Us in repentance.*
>
> 38:45 *And remember Our servants Abraham, Isaac, and Jacob, men of power and vision. Surely We purified and chose them for a special purpose, proclaiming the message of the afterlife. They were, in Our eyes, truly some of the select and the good.*
>
> 38:48 *And remember Ishmael, Elisha, and Zul-Kifl [Ezekiel]: all of them belong among the chosen.*
>
> 38:49 *This is a reminder, and, surely, the righteous will have an excellent home in the afterlife, the Gardens of Eternity whose doors will always be open for them. They can recline and call at their leisure for abundant fruit and drink. They will have virgins of their own age, who glance modestly. This is what you are promised on the Judgment Day. This is Our gift to you. It will never fail.*

Abraham

> 19:41 *And mention Abraham in the Scripture because he was a man of truth and a prophet. When he said to his father, "Father, why worship something that does not see, hear, or help you in the least? Father, knowledge has come to me that has not come to you. Follow me and I will lead you onto a straight and even path. Father, do not worship Satan because Satan is a rebel against Allah, the merciful. Father, I am afraid that a punishment from Allah, the merciful, will fall upon you and that you will become Satan's slave."*
>
> 19:46 *Abraham's father replied, "Do you reject my gods, Abraham? If you do not stop, I will certainly stone you. Go away from me for a long time."*
>
> 19:47 *Abraham said, "Peace be with you. I will pray to Allah for your forgiveness because He is always gracious to me. But I will turn away from you and the gods you pray to besides Allah. I will call upon my Lord. Perhaps my prayers will not go unanswered."*
>
> 19:49 *When he had separated himself from them and that which they worshiped besides Allah, We gave him Isaac and Jacob and made both of them*

---

1. Job swore to beat his wife with one hundred blows. Later he softened, and, to fulfill his oath, he put one hundred small twigs in his hand and hit her once.

prophets. *In Our mercy, We gave gifts to them and gave them an exalted and true lasting reputation.*

19:51 *And mention Moses in the Scripture because he was a pure man. More than that, he was an apostle and a prophet. We called to him from the right side of the mountain and caused him to come close to Us for a secret conversation. In Our mercy, We gave to him his brother Aaron, a prophet.*

19:54 *And mention Ishmael in the Scripture because he was true to his promise and an apostle and a prophet. He urged his people to pray and give alms and he was pleasing to his Lord. And mention Idris [an uncertain reference] in the Scripture. He was a man of truth and a prophet. We raised him to a lofty station.*

Jonah

37:139 *Jonah was also one of those sent to warn. When he ran away to a laden ship, he agreed to cast lots with them and was condemned, and the fish swallowed him because he had committed wrong. But if he had not been one of those who glorify Allah, he would surely have stayed in its belly until Judgment Day. And We cast him sickly on the naked shore, and We caused a gourd-vine to grow above him, and We sent him to a hundred thousand people or more [in Ninevah, in Syria]. Because they believed, We allowed them to enjoy their lives for a while.*

Solomon

27:15 *In the past We gave knowledge to David and Solomon, and they said, "Praise be to Allah, Who has favored us over many of His believing servants!" Solomon was David's heir, and he said, "People, we have been taught the language of the birds, and have been given everything. This is clearly a blessing from Allah!"*

27:17 *Armies of men, jinns, and birds were gathered together before Solomon and arranged in battle order, and they marched until they reached the Valley of Ants. One ant said, "Ants, go into your homes so Solomon and his armies do not unwittingly crush you underfoot." Solomon smiled at her words and said, "Lord, let me be thankful for your blessings which you have given me; and my parents; and that I should do good things, which are pleasing to you; and include me in the numbers of your righteous servants."*

27:20 *He reviewed the birds and said, "Why do I not see the lapwing [hoopoe]? Is he one of those absent? I will certainly punish him severely or even kill him if he does not have a good excuse." But the lapwing was not far behind, and he said, "I have discovered something you are unaware of, and I come to you from Saba [a kingdom of South Arabia] with good news. I have found out that they are ruled by a woman, and she has been given great wealth and has a mighty throne. I discovered her and her peoples worshiping the sun instead of Allah. Satan has made their actions seem pleasing in their minds and has prevented them from finding the true path so they receive no guidance. They do not worship Allah, Who brings forth what is hidden in the heavens and the earth, and Who knows what you hide and what you admit. There is no god, but Allah! Lord of the glorious throne!"*

27:27 *Solomon said, "We shall soon see whether you are telling the truth, or not. Take and deliver my letter to them; then turn away from them and wait for their answer."*

27:29 *The queen said, "My chiefs, a noble letter has been delivered to me. It is from Solomon and it says, "In the name of Allah, most gracious, most merciful. Do not be arrogant against me, but instead come and submit to me."*

27:32 *She said, "My counselors, give me advice. I never decide an issue without your advice."*

27:33 *They said, "We are strong, willing, and brave, but the power is in your hands. Tell us what you want us to do."*

27:34 *She replied, "Typically, when kings enter a city, they pillage and humiliate its leading citizens. These people will do the same. I will send them a gift and wait until my ambassadors return with their response."*

27:36 *When Sheba's envoy came before Solomon, the king said, "What? Will you try to bribe me with riches? What Allah has given me is better than what He has given to you. You are impressed with your gift, but I am not. Return to your people. You had better believe that we will come to them with forces which they cannot resist, and we will drive them from their land shamed and humbled."*

27:38 *He said to his officers, "My chiefs, which one of you will bring me her throne before they come to me and submit to Allah?"*

27:39 *An evil jinn said, "I will bring it to you before you get out of your chair. I am capable and trustworthy."*

27:40 *But one who knew the Scripture said, "I will bring it to you in the blink of an eye." When Solomon saw it set before him, he said, "This is done by the grace of Allah to see whether or not I would be grateful. If someone is grateful, his gratitude benefits only him. If someone is ungrateful, then he harms only himself. Truly my Lord is self-sufficient, bountiful."*

27:41 *He said, "Disguise her throne so that it is unrecognizable. We will see whether or not she has guidance."*

27:42 *When she arrived, she was asked, "Is this your throne?" She replied, "It seems to be the same." Solomon said, "We received knowledge long before she, and we have submitted to Allah." And he persuaded her from worshiping others besides Allah because she came from a people who had no faith.*

27:44 *It was said to her, "Enter the palace." When she saw it, she thought it was a pool of water, and she pulled up her garment and bared her legs. Solomon said, "It is a palace paved with glass." She said, "Lord, I have sinned against my soul. I submit with Solomon to the Lord of the worlds."*

Adam

20:115 *Long ago We made a pact with Adam, but he forgot it, and We did not find any resolve in him. When We said to the angels, "Fall down and worship Adam," all of them worshiped him except Iblis [Satan] who refused. We said, "Adam, he is truly an enemy to you and your wife. Do not let him drive you from the garden so that you become miserable. There is enough in the garden to provide you with food and clothing forever.*

20:120 *But Satan whispered to him, "Adam, would you like me to show you the tree of immortality and the power that never decreases?" Adam and Eve both ate from the tree, and their nakedness became apparent, so they began to sew clothing made from garden leaves to hide their nakedness. This is how Adam disobeyed Allah and went astray.*

20:122 *Later his Lord chose him and turned toward him again and guided him. And Allah said, "Both of you go down from here enemies to one another. You will receive more guidance from Me later. Whoever follows My guidance will not go wrong and will not be wretched, but whoever turns away from My message will truly have a life of misery. We will resurrect him and the others, blind, on Judgment Day." He will say, "Lord, why have You gathered me here with the others, blind, when before I could see?" He will reply, "Because Our signs came to you and you ignored them, so you will be ignored today." Moses*

20:1 *TA-HA. We did not send the Koran to you to cause you sadness, but as a warning for those who fear Allah. It is a message from Him who made the earth and the heavens above, Allah, the merciful, who sits on His throne. Whatever is in the heavens and the earth, everything in between, and under the ground is His! You do not need to speak loudly, because He knows the most secret whisper and what is even more hidden. Allah! There is no god but Him! He is known by the most beautiful names!*

20:9 *Have you heard the story of Moses? He saw a fire and said to his family, "Wait here. I see a fire. Maybe I can bring an ember from it, or find a guide there."*

20:11 *When he came to it, a voice called out, "Moses! I am your Lord. Take off your shoes. You are in the sacred Tuwa valley. I have chosen you. Listen to what I say. I am Allah. There is no god but Me. Worship Me and observe prayer to celebrate My praise. The Hour [Judgment Day] is certainly coming. I plan to keep it a secret so that all souls may be rewarded for their actions. Therefore do not let those who disbelieve and follow their lusts turn you away from the truth and cause your destruction.*

20:17 *What is that in your right hand, Moses?" He said, "It is my staff. I lean on it and beat the leaves down with it for my sheep, among other things." Allah said, "Throw it down, Moses!" He threw it down, and it turned into a slithering serpent. Allah said, "Grab it and do not be afraid. We will change it back to its former state. Now put your hand under your arm. It will come out white [with leprosy], but unhurt. Another sign so that We may show you Our greatest signs. Go to Pharaoh, because he has exceeded all limits."*

20:25 *Moses said, "My Lord, relieve my mind and make my task easy. Untie my tongue so they can understand what I say. Give me an assistant from my family—Aaron, my brother—add his strength to mine, and make him share my task. We will glorify you without pause, because you are always watching." He said, "Moses, your request is granted. We have shown you favor before. Our message to your mother inspired her saying: 'Put him into a chest and throw it in the river; the river will leave him on the bank where he will be found by an enemy to Me and to him.' But I cast my love down upon you so that you might be raised under my eye."*

20:40 *"Your sister went and said, 'May I bring you someone to nurse him?' Then We returned you to your mother so that her tears would be dried, and so she would not grieve. When you killed a man, We saved you from trouble, and tried you severely. You stayed with the Median [a city on the Red Sea] people for many years, and then you came here by My decree. I have chosen you for Myself. You and your brother go with My signs and do not fail to remember Me. Go to Pharaoh, because he has exceeded all limits, but speak gently to him; hopefully, he will listen or be afraid."*

20:45 *They said, "Lord, we are afraid that he will be arrogant toward us, or try to harm us."*

20:46 *He said, "Do not be afraid, because I am with the both of you. I will listen and watch over you. Go to him and say, 'Surely we have been sent by your Lord. Let the Children of Israel go with us and do not torment them. We bring you a sign from your Lord, and peace to him who follows His guidance. It has been revealed to us that those who reject him and turn away will be punished.'"*

20:49 *And Pharaoh said, "Who is your Lord, Moses?"*

20:50 *Moses said, "Our Lord is the One who created everything and gave it all purpose."*

20:51 *Pharaoh replied, "What is the state of the previous generations?"*

20:52 *Moses said, "That knowledge is with My Lord, recorded in His book. My Lord never errs and He never forgets. He has spread the earth for you* like a carpet and made paths for you to follow. He has sent down the rain from heaven, and from that we produce the various herbs: (Saying) 'Eat and feed your cattle. Surely, there are signs here for a thinking man. We created you from it, we will return you to it, and from it we will raise you a second time.'"

20:56 We showed him all of Our signs, but he rejected and refused them. He said, "Moses, have you come to drive us from our land with your magic? We will surely produce magic to match your own. Let us schedule a contest—which neither of us should miss—in a neutral location."

20:59 Moses said, "Let us meet on the day of the feast. Gather the people together at mid-day."

20:60 So Pharaoh and his magicians made their plans and came to the meeting.

20:61 Moses said to them, "Woe to you! Do not invent a lie against Allah, or He will destroy you with His punishment. A liar is always destroyed."

20:62 The magicians discussed their plans in secret. They said, "These two are expert magicians who plan to drive you from your land with their magic and to destroy your way of life. Make your plans and come and form ranks. Whoever wins today will gain the upper hand." They said, "Moses, will you throw down your rod first, or shall we?" He said, "You cast first." Then, through their magic, their ropes and rods appeared to run, and Moses became afraid.

20:68 We said, "Do not be afraid, you will have the upper hand. Cast down what is in your right hand. It will swallow up what they have made because it is nothing but a magicians trick, and a magician, no matter how good, will not be successful."

20:70 The magicians threw themselves down and worshipped. They said, "We believe in the Lord of Moses and Aaron." Pharaoh said, "Will you believe in him before I give my permission? This must be the master who taught you your magic. I will cut off your hands and feet on opposite sides and crucify you on the trunks of palm trees, and you will surely learn then which of us gives the more terrible and long-lasting punishment."

20:72 They said, "We will never have more regard for you than we do for the clear signs that have been revealed to us, or than we have for our creator. So decree whatever you will decree. Your decrees are only good in this life. We believe in our Lord that He may forgive our sins and magic which you forced upon us. Allah is better and more lasting than you. Hell surely waits for the guilty who come before their Lord. There they will neither live nor die, but lofty positions wait for the believers who come righteously before their Lord! They will dwell in eternal gardens with underground rivers. This is the reward of the pure."

20:77 We revealed to Moses, "Take away My servants and travel by night. Cleave a dry path through the sea for them. Do not be afraid of being *overtaken and have no fear." Pharaoh and his army followed, but the sea overwhelmed them, because he misled his people by not guiding them.*

20:80 *Children of Israel! We saved you from your enemies, and We made a pact with you on the sacred side of the mountain and sent down to you manna and quails. We said, "Eat the good things that We have given you, but not to excess, or My wrath may fall on you, and whoever My wrath falls upon will surely perish. I will surely forgive him who turns to Allah and believes and does good deeds, and listens to guidance."*

20:83 *(Allah said) "Moses, why have you hurried ahead of your people?"*

20:84 *Moses said, "Lord, they are right behind me, but I have hurried to be with you to please you."*

20:85 *He said, "We have tested your people while you were gone, and Samiri [The identity of Samiri is not known] has led them astray."*

20:86 *Moses returned to his people angry and sad. He said, "My People, did your Lord not promise you a good promise? Was I gone from you too long, or did you break your promise with me because you wanted to anger your Lord?"*

20:87 *"We did not want to break our promise with you, but we had to carry the people's ornaments, so Samiri suggested we throw them in the fire." Then he brought out of the fire the image of a lowing calf. They cried, "This is your god and the god of Moses, but he has forgotten."*

20:89 *What! Did they not see that it could not reply to them and could not help or hurt them?*

20:90 *Aaron had already told them, "People, You are being tested. Surely your Lord is the god of Mercy: Follow and obey me."*

20:91 *They said, "We will not stop worshiping it until Moses returns."*

20:92 *Moses said, "Aaron, when you saw that they had gone astray, why did you not come and get me? Did you disobey my order?"*

20:94 *He said, "Son of my mother! Do not grab me by the beard or the head. I was afraid that you would say that I caused a division among the Children of Israel, and did not wait for your word."*

20:95 *Moses said, "Samiri, what was your motive?" He replied, "I saw what they did not. My soul prompted me, so I took a handful of dust from the footprint of Allah's messenger and flung it into the calf."*

20:97 *Moses said, "Go away. Surely your punishment in this life will be to say, 'Do not touch me.' And there is a sentence against you that you cannot avoid. Now look at the god that you are so devoted to. We will certainly burn it to ashes and scatter them on the sea. Your god is Allah. There is no god, but Allah. He knows all things."*

1192 Since Mohammed and the Koran claimed Jewish roots, the Quraysh decided to send their story teller to the Jews in Medina and ask for help. This was not a causal quest, as it took the better part of a month for the trip and questions. So Al Nadr went to Medina and asked the Rabbis what questions to ask Mohammed. He told the Rabbis about Mohammed, what he did, what he said and that he claimed to be a prophet. Since they had prophets they must know more about the subject than the Meccans.

I192 The Rabbis said, "Ask him these three questions. If he knows the answer then he is a prophet, if not then he is a fake."

"What happened to the young men who disappeared in ancient days."

"Ask him about the mighty traveler who reached the ends of the East and the West."

"Ask him, What is the spirit?"

I192 Back in Mecca, they went to Mohammed and asked him the three questions. He said he would get back to them tomorrow. Days went by. Finally, fifteen days had passed. Mohammed waited on Gabriel for the answers. The Meccans began to talk. Mohammed did not know what to do. He had no answers. Finally, he had a vision of Gabriel.

> 19:64 The angels say, "We descend from heaven only by Allah's command. Everything that is before us and everything that is behind us and whatever is in between belongs to Him. And Your Lord never forgets. Lord of the heavens and the earth and everything in between! Worship Him and remain steadfast in your praise of Him. Do you know any that is worthy of the same name?"

The Koran answered all the questions and statements of the Quraysh. With regards to the question about what happened to the young men in ancient times:

> 18:9 Do you believe that the Sleepers of the Cave and the Inscription [an unknown reference] were among Our signs? When the youths [the Sleepers] took refuge in the cave, they said, "Lord, give us Your mercy and cause us to act rightly." We drew a veil over them depriving them of their senses for many years. Then We roused them so that We could know which would best determine the number of years they lived in the cave.
>
> 18:13 We tell you their story truthfully. They were youths who believed in their Lord, and We increased their ability to guide others. We gave strength to their hearts. Recall when they stood up and said, "Our Lord is the Lord of the heaven and the earth. We will worship no other god besides Him. If we did, then we would have certainly said an outrageous thing. Our people have taken other gods to worship besides Allah. Why do they not prove their existence? Who is more wicked than a person who makes up lies about Allah? When will you turn away from them and the things they worship besides Allah? Seek refuge in the cave. Your Lord will extend His mercy to you and cause your affairs to turn out for the best."
>
> 18:17 You may have seen the sun, when it rose, pass to the right of their cave and set to their left while they were in its spacious middle. This is one

of the signs of Allah. Whomever Allah guides is rightly guided. Whomever He allows to stray will not find a friend to guide him.

18:18 *While they were sleeping, you would have thought that they were awake [they slept with their eyes open]. We turned them on their right side and their left side. Their dog lay in the entrance with its paws stretched out. If you had come upon them, you would have certainly run away filled with terror of them. This was their condition before We awakened them so that they might question one another. One of them asked, "How long have you lingered here?" Some said, "We have been here a day or so." Others said, "Your Lord knows exactly how long you have lingered. One of you should take your money into the city to find and buy the best food possible. He should be courteous and should not let anyone know about you. If they should come upon you, they would either kill you or force you to return to their religion, in which case you would never prosper."*

18:21 *We made their existence known to the city so that they would know that Allah's promise is true and that there is no doubt about the Hour of Judgment. The people of the city argued amongst themselves about the affair. Some said, "We should construct a building over them. Their Lord knows all about them." The winners of the debate were those who said, "We will certainly build a temple over them."*

18:22 *Some say, "There were three, the dog being the forth." Others say, "Five, the dog was the sixth." Still others say, "There were seven, and a dog made eight." Say: My Lord knows the exact number. Only a few know the truth. So do not become involved in arguments about them except on matters that are clear, and do not consult any of them about the Sleepers.* 18:23 *And do not say, "I will do it tomorrow," without adding, "Allah willing." Remember your Lord when you forget and say, "I hope that Allah will guide me even closer than this to the right path."*

18:25 *They remained in their cave for three hundred years, though some say three hundred and nine. Say: Allah knows exactly how long they stayed. He knows the secrets of the heavens and the earth. Man has no guardian besides Him. He does not allow any to share His power.*

As to the question about the mighty traveler:

18:83 *They will ask you about Zul-Qarnain [Alexander, the Great]. Say: I will recite to you an account of him. We established his power in the land and gave him the means to achieve any of his aims. So he followed a path, until, when he reached the setting of the sun, he found it setting in a muddy pond. Nearby he found a people. We said, "Zul-Qarnain, you have the authority to either punish them or to show them kindness."* 18:87 *He said, "Whoever does wrong, we will certainly punish. Then he will be returned to his Lord, Who will punish him with a terrible punishment.*

But whoever believes and does good deeds shall be given a wonderful reward, and We will give them easy commands to obey."

18:89 *Then he followed another path, until, when he came to the rising of the sun, he found that it rose upon a people to whom We had given no protection from it. He left them as they were. We knew everything about him. Then he followed another path until, when he reached a place between two mountains, he found a people living in a valley who could scarcely understand a single word. They said, "Zul-Qarnain, the people of Gog and Magog are terrorizing the land. May we pay you tribute so that you will build a strong barrier between us and them?"*

18:95 *He said, "The power which my Lord has given me is better than your tribute. Help me, therefore, with manpower. I will build a strong barrier between you and them. Bring me blocks of iron." Later, when he had filled the gap between the two mountains, he said, "Blow with your bellows!" When it had become as red as fire, he said, "Bring me molten lead to pour over it." So the people of Gog and Magog were unable to climb over the barrier or to go through it. He said, "This is a mercy from my Lord, but when my Lord's promise comes to pass, He will destroy it, because my Lord's promises always come true."*

The question—what is the spirit?

17:85 *They will ask you about the spirit [probably the angel Gabriel]. Say: The spirit is commanded by my Lord, and you are given only a little knowledge about it. If We wished, We could take Our revelations away from you. Then you would find no one to intercede with us on your behalf except as a mercy from your Lord. Surely His kindness to you is great.*

The Quraysh had questions about proof of Mohammed's messages. Here is the Koran's restatement of their questions about angels coming, creating rivers, creating wealth and any other miracle to prove Mohammed's validity. The Koran's response:

17:88 *Say: If men and jinn were assembled to produce something like this Koran, they could not produce its equal, even though they assisted each other. And certainly in this Koran We have explained to man every kind of argument, and yet most men refuse everything except disbelief. They [the Meccans] say, "We will not believe in you until you cause a spring to gush forth from the earth for us; or until you have a garden of date trees and grape vines, and cause rivers to gush abundantly in their midst; or when you cause the sky to fall down in pieces, as you claim will happen; or when you bring us face-to-face with Allah and the angels; or when you have a house of gold; or when you ascend into heaven; and even then we will not believe in your ascension until you bring down a book for us which we may read." Say: Glory be to my Lord! Am I nothing except a man, a messenger?*

17:94 *What keeps men from believing when guidance has come to them but that they say, "Has Allah sent a man like us to be His messenger?" Say: If angels walked the earth, We would have sent down from heaven an angel as Our messenger. Say: Allah is a sufficient witness between you and me. He is well acquainted with His servants and He sees everything.*

17:97 *Whoever Allah guides, he is a follower of the right way, and whoever He causes to err, they shall not find any to assist them but Him. We will gather them together on the Resurrection Day, face down, blind, deaf, and dumb. Hell will be their home. Every time its flames die down, We will add fuel to the Fire. This is their reward because they did not believe Our signs and said, "When we are reduced to bones and dust, will we really be raised up as a new creation?"*

17:99 *Do they not realize that Allah, Who created the heavens and the earth, is able to create the likes of them? He has appointed a duration for them that cannot be denied, but the wicked deny everything except disbelief. Say: If you controlled the treasures of the mercy of my Lord, you would be afraid to spend them because man is miserly.*

As regards to the old Persian stories that are as good as Mohammed's:

25:3 *Still they have worshiped other gods, besides Him, who have created nothing and were themselves created. They are powerless to work good or evil for themselves, nor can they control life or death or resurrection. But the unbelievers say, "This [the Koran] is nothing but a lie which he [Mohammed] has created with the assistance of others producing slander and injustice."*

25:5 *They say, "These are ancient fables that he has written down. They are dictated to him morning and night."*

25:6 *Say: The Koran was revealed by Him who knows the secrets of the heavens and the earth. He is truly forgiving and merciful.*

As for following the religion of their forefathers:

43:21 *Are they clinging to a scripture that We had given them earlier? No! They say, "Our fathers followed a certain religion, and we are guided by their footsteps." And so, whenever We sent a messenger before you to an erring people, their wealthy said, "Our fathers followed a certain religion, and we are guided by their footsteps." The messenger said, "What! Even if I bring you better guidance than your fathers had?" They replied, "We do not believe what you say." So We punished them. Now see what comes to those who reject truth!*

After the Jewish leaders in Medina helped the Meccans with questions to ask Mohammed, the Koran has its first negative comments about the Jews.

27:76 *Surely this Koran explains to the Children of Israel most of the issues upon which they disagree. Certainly it is a guide and a mercy for those who believe. Surely your Lord will use His wisdom to judge between them. He is the mighty and the all-knowing. So put your trust in Allah. Surely, you are on the path to the plain truth.*

27:80 *You cannot make the dead listen or the deaf to hear, when they have turned to flee, nor can you guide the blind from their errors. You cannot make any listen except those who believe our revelations and who have submitted to Islam. When the Word against them is fulfilled, We will send a monster created from the earth to speak to them because mankind did not believe Our signs. One day We will gather together, from all peoples, a group of those who rejected Our signs and organize them into ranks until, when they come before their Lord, He will say, "Did you reject My signs because you could not understand them? What was it that you were doing?" And the Word will be fulfilled against them, because of their wickedness. They will be unable to speak in their own defense.*

THE QURAYSH LISTEN TO MOHAMMED'S READING

I203 Three of the Meccans decided, each on their own, to sit outside Mohammed's house and listen to him recite the Koran and pray. As they left they ran into each other. They said that they should not do it again as someone might think that they cause others to listen. But on the next night they all three did the same thing. And so on the third night as well. They then talked among each other. One said, "I heard things I know and know what was meant by them. And I heard things I don't know and I don't know what was intended by them." The other agreed. The third said that he had always had a competition with one of Mohammed's recent converts. They had both fed the poor and helped the oppressed. They had always been as equals, but now his friendly rival claimed that he had a prophet and his friend did not. Hence, he was now superior. He said, "But I can never believe in this man, Mohammed."

I204 So the next time Mohammed called upon them to submit to Islam, they said, "Our hearts are veiled; we don't understand what you say. There is something in our ears so we can't hear you. A curtain divides us. You go follow your path and we will go ours."

The Koranic response:

17:45 *When you recite the Koran, We place an invisible barrier between you and the unbelievers. We place veils over their hearts and deafness in their ears so that they do not understand it, and when you mention only your Lord, Allah, in the Koran, they turn their backs and flee from the truth. We know absolutely what they listen to when they listen to you, and when they speak privately, the wicked say, "You follow a mad man!" See what they compare you to. But they have gone astray and cannot find the way.*

17:49 *They say, "When we are nothing but bones and dust, will we really be raised up from the dead to be a new creation?" Say: Yes, whether you be stones, or iron, or any other thing which you conceive to be harder to resurrect." When they say, "Who will bring us back to life?" Say: He who created you the first time. They will shake their heads at you and say, "When will this happen?" Say to them, "Perhaps it will be soon—a day when He will call you, and you will answer by praising Him, and you will think that you have waited only a little while!"*

Mohammed's opponents are frequently quoted and paraphrased:

43:29 *I have allowed these men and their fathers to enjoy the pleasurable things of this life until the truth comes to them and a messenger makes things clear.*

43:30 *But when the truth came to them, they said: "This is trickery, and we reject it." And they say, "Why was this Koran not revealed to a great man of one of the two cities [Mecca and Taif]?"*

43:32 *Will they distribute Allah's mercy? We distribute among them their worldly success, and We exalt some of them above the others in ranks, subjecting some to others. Your Lord's mercy is greater than the wealth they amass. And if it were not probable that all humanity might become a single nation of unbelievers, We would have given silver roofs and staircases to everyone, and silver doors for their homes, and silver couches on which to recline, and ornaments of gold, but these are merely luxuries of this world's life. The afterlife with your Lord is for the righteous.*

43:36 *We assign a devil as a companion for those who turn their backs and neglect to remember Allah. Satan will certainly turn man from the way of Allah, even though he believes he is being guided correctly. On the day when man comes before Us, he will say, "Satan, I wish that the distance between east and west separated us." Satan is a wretched companion. But that realization will not help you that day, because you were unjust, and you will share the punishment. Can you make the deaf listen or guide the blind and those clearly in error?*

43:41 *Even if We took you [Mohammed] away, We would surely take vengeance upon them; even though We showed you what We have promised them, We would still have total control over them. So keep a firm hold on the revelation sent to you; surely you are on the right path. The Koran is indeed the message for you and your people, and you shall all be soon brought to account.*

43:45 *And ask Our messengers that We sent before you [Mohammed]: have We ever appointed gods to be worshipped along with the merciful Allah?*

21:1 *Man's final reckoning draws ever closer to him, and yet he heedlessly continues to turn away. Every new warning that comes to him from his Lord is ridiculed. The wicked confer secretly and say, "Is he a man like you, or something more? Will you succumb to witchcraft with your eyes wide open?"*
21:4 *Say: My Lord knows what is spoken in the heavens and on earth. He is the hearer and the knower of all things.*
21:5 *They say, "No, this is nothing but jumbled dreams. He made it up. He is just a crazy poet! We want him to bring us a sign similar to those given to the prophets of the past!" Up to their time, despite Our warnings, not a single city that We destroyed believed. Will these people believe?*
21:7 *Before you, Our messengers were also men to whom We sent a revelation. If you do not know this, you should ask someone who has received the Message. We did not give them bodies that did not need food, and they would not live forever. In the end, We kept Our promise, and We saved whom We pleased and destroyed the sinners. Now We have given you a book [the Koran] that contains the message for you. Now will you understand?*
21:11 *How many wicked cities have We destroyed and replaced with another people? And still, when they sensed Our punishment, they began to run. It was said to them, "Do not run. Return to your homes and easy lives so that you may be called to account for your actions." They said, "Oh no! We were certainly wicked!" This cry of theirs did not stop until We mowed them down and left them like reaped corn.*

The Koran introduces stories about Mary and Jesus.

19:16 *And mention Mary in the Scripture, when she withdrew from her family to a place in the East. She took a veil to screen herself from them. Then We sent Our spirit [Gabriel] to her in the form of a perfect man. She said, "I seek protection from you with Merciful Allah. If you fear Him, then do not come near me."*
19:19 *He said, "I am merely your Lord's messenger. I come to announce to you the gift of a holy son."*
19:20 *She said, "How can I have a son when no man has touched me, and I am chaste?"*
19:21 *He said, "Even so, it will happen. Your Lord says, 'That is easy for Me.' We will make him a sign for all men and a mercy from Us. It is something that is decreed." And she conceived him, and she withdrew with him to a remote place. When the pain of childbirth drove her to the trunk of a palm-tree, she said, "If only I had died before this."*

19:24 *But a voice from below her said, "Do not grieve; your Lord has provided a stream beneath you. Shake the trunk of the palm-tree towards yourself; it will drop fresh ripe dates upon you. So eat and drink and dry your eyes. And if you should see any man, say, 'I have promised a fast to Allah. I will speak to no one today.'"*

19:27 *Later, she brought the baby to her people, carrying him in her arms. They said, "Mary, you have come with an amazing thing. Sister of Aaron, your father was not a wicked man, and your mother was not unchaste." But she merely pointed to the baby. They said, "How can we speak with an infant in a cradle?" The child said, "Surely, I am the servant of Allah. He has given me the Book and has made me a prophet. He has made me blessed wherever I am; and has urged me to pray and give alms, as long as I live; and to be dutiful to my mother; and He has not made me arrogant or miserable. The peace of Allah was on me the day I was born, and will be on me the day that I die; and on the day I will be resurrected."*

19:34 *This was Jesus, the son of Mary; this is a statement of truth about which they [Christians] dispute. It does not befit the majesty of Allah to father a son. Glory be to Him! When He decrees something, He only needs to say, "Be," and it is. Surely, Allah is my Lord and your Lord, so serve Him. That is the right path.*

19:37 *The sects differ among themselves about Jesus. Woe to the unbelievers because of the upcoming Judgment of a momentous day. They will see and hear clearly on the day they come before Us. But today the unjust are clearly in error. Warn them of the day of distress when the matter is decided. They are negligent, and they do not believe. We will inherit the earth and everyone on it, and they will be returned to Us.*

The Koranic view of Christianity:

43:81 *Say to the Christians: If Allah, the most gracious, had a son, I would be the first to worship. Glory to the Lord of the heavens and the earth, the Lord of the throne! He is free from the things attributed to Him! So leave them to chatter on and play with words until they meet the day they are promised.*

43:84 *Allah rules the heavens and the earth. He is the wise, the knowing. Blessed is He whose kingdom is the heavens and the earth and everything in between. He has knowledge of the Hour of Judgment, and you will be returned to Him.*

43:86 *Those whom they invoke for protection besides Allah have no power to intercede. Only He who bears witness to the truth may do that, and they know Him. If you asked them who their creator is, they would certainly say, "Allah." Then, how are they turned from the truth? And the Prophet will cry, "My Lord, truly these are people who do not believe." So turn away from them and say, "Peace." They will soon find out.*

The Koran continued to teach about the spirit world of Satan (Iblis) and the jinns.

15:26 *We created man from potter's clay, from black mud molded into shape. We earlier created the jinn from a blazing fire. Remember, your Lord said to the angels, "I will create man from dry clay, from black mud molded into shape. When I have fashioned him and breathed My spirit into him, you must fall down and worship him."*

15:31 *And the angels bowed down together to worship him, except Iblis. He refused to bow down.*

15:32 *Allah said, "Iblis, why did you not bow down and worship with the others?"*

15:33 *He said, "I am not the kind to bow down and worship man, whom you have created from clay, from shaped mud."*

15:34 *Allah said, "Then get out of here, because you are cursed, and you will remain cursed until the Judgment Day."*

15:36 *He said, "Allah, give me a reprieve until the day man is raised from the dead."*

15:37 *Allah said, "You are granted a reprieve until the preordained time."*

15:39 *He said, "Because You have led me astray, I will make evil seem to be fair to those on the earth, and I will mislead all of them, except those who are Your devoted servants."*

15:41 *Allah said, "This way leads straight to Me. You will have no power over My servants, except those wrongdoers who will follow you." Surely, Hell is the promised place for all of them. It has seven gates, and each of those gates has an assigned group.*

15:45: *The righteous will live among gardens and fountains. They will be told: "You may enter in peace and security." We will remove all rancor from their hearts, and they will sit together like brothers, facing each other on couches. Fatigue will not touch them there, and they will never be asked to leave. Tell My servants that I am forgiving and merciful, and My punishment is the most terrible punishment.*

67:5 *We adorned the sky with lights. We will use them as missiles [shooting stars] against the evil ones [jinns who try to listen to the words of heaven]. We have prepared a torment of Fire for them.*

Now verses in the Koran began to form the basis of the legal system (the Sharia) of Islam.

23:1 *The successful ones will be the believers, who are humble in their prayers, who avoid vain conversation, who contribute to the needy, and who abstain from sex (except with their wives or slaves [slaves are bought or taken in battle], in which case they are free from blame, but those who exceed these limits are sinners). Those who honor their promises and contracts and who pay strict attention to their prayers will inherit Paradise. They will dwell there forever.*

17:25 *Your Lord knows everything in your souls. He knows if you are righteous. He is forgiving to those who frequently turn to Him. Render to your kin their due rights and also to the needy and the traveler. Do not squander your wealth wastefully. The wasteful are brothers of the evil ones, [satans] and the evil ones are always ungrateful to their Lord. And if you turn away from them seeking your Lord's mercy, which you hope for, speak kindly to them. Do not let your hand be tied to your neck like a miser, and do not stretch it out to its limits so that you become rebuked and destitute. Surely, your Lord will abundantly provide sustenance for whom He pleases, and He provides in a just measure. He is always aware of His servants.*

17:31 *Do not kill your children because you fear poverty. We will provide for them as well as for you. Surely, killing them is a terrible sin.*

17:32 *Have nothing to do with adultery. It is a shameful act and an evil path that leads to other evils.*

17:33 *Do not kill anyone whom Allah has forbidden to be slain [a Muslim] unless it is for a just cause [apostasy, retribution for a killing]. Whoever is unjustly slain, We have given their heirs the authority to either forgive or demand retribution, but do not allow him to exceed limits in slaying because he will be helped by the law.*

17:34 *Do not use the property of the orphan, except to improve it, until he reaches maturity. Fulfill your promise because every promise will be investigated.*

17:35 *Give full measure when you measure, and weigh with an honest scale. This is fair and much better in the end. Do not follow that of which you have no knowledge. Every act of hearing, seeing, or feeling will be investigated on the Day of Reckoning.*

17:37 *Do not walk arrogantly upon the earth because you cannot split the earth in two, and you cannot become as tall as the mountains. All of this is evil and hateful in the sight of your Lord. This is part of the wisdom that your Lord has revealed to you [Mohammed]. Do not worship another god with Allah, or you will be thrown into Hell, condemned and abandoned.*

16:98 *When you recite the Koran, seek refuge in Allah from the accursed Satan. He has no authority over those who believe and put their trust in their Lord. Satan has authority only over those who befriend him and those who worship others besides Allah.*

7:204 *And when the Koran is read, listen to it with attention and hold your peace that mercy may be shown to you. Remember the Lord humbly within yourself in a low voice in the mornings and the evenings [prayer]. Do not be one of the neglectful ones. Those who are with the Lord are not too proud to serve Him. They celebrate His praises and prostrate themselves before Him.*

16:104 *Allah will not guide those who do not believe, and they will have a painful punishment. Those who do not believe in Allah's revelations forge lies. They are the liars.*
16:106 *Those who disbelieve in Allah after having believed [became apostates], who open their hearts to disbelief, will feel the wrath of Allah and will have a terrible punishment. (But there is no punishment for anyone who is compelled by force to deny Allah in words, but whose heart is faithful) This is because they love the life in this world more than the afterlife and because Allah does not guide unbelievers. Allah has sealed the hearts, ears, and eyes of those people, and so they are heedless. Undoubtedly, they will be the losers in the afterlife.*

STRUGGLES

CHAPTER 5

8:20 *Believers! Be obedient to Allah and His messenger, and do not turn your backs now that you know the truth. Do not be like the ones who say, "We hear," but do not obey.*

I217 Each of the clans of the Quraysh began to persecute those Muslims that they had any power over. If Mohammed attacked them, they would attack him through his converts. One slave, Bilal (to become famous later) was physically abused by being placed in the hot sun with a huge rock on his chest and being told to deny Islam. He refused. This was repeated until Abu Bakr, a chief Muslim, took notice and asked how long the owner would abuse him. The owner said, "You are one of those who corrupted him, you save him." So Abu Bakr offered to trade a stronger black, non-Muslim slave for Bilal. Then Abu Bakr freed Bilal. Abu Bakr did this with six other Muslim slaves as well.

MIGRATION TO ETHIOPIA

I208 Since the Quraysh were resisting Islam and being harsh to the Muslims, Mohammed decided to send many of his followers to Ethiopia as the Christian king there would not bother them. So eighty to ninety Muslims left Arabia to cross the Red Sea to Ethiopia.

In these times of stress, the Koran has advice for Mohammed.

7:157 *Those who follow the Messenger—the Prophet who neither reads nor writes, whom they shall find described in the Torah and the Gospel, who commands good and forbids evil; allows the pure and healthful and prohibits the impure; releases them from the burdens and shackles that were upon them—those who believe in him, honor and help him and follow the light [the Koran] that was sent down with him, they are the successful. 7:158 Say: Oh, people, I am sent to you as the messenger of Allah, whose kingdom is the heavens and the earth. There is no god but He. He gives both life and death. So believe in Allah and His messenger, the unlettered Prophet, who believes in Allah and His word. Follow Him so that you may be led aright.*

34:39 *Say: My Lord will be liberal or sparing in supplies with whom He pleases of his servants, and whatever you spend for good, He will replace it; He is the best provider. One day He will gather His angels all together, and He will say, "Did these men worship you?" They will say, "Glory to you. You are our guardian, not them. No, they worshipped the jinn. Most of them believed in them." So on this day they will not have power over one another for profit or harm, and We will say to the evildoers, "Taste the torment of the Fire, which you called a lie."*

34:43 *For when Our clear signs are recited to them, they say, "This is merely a man who would turn you away from your father's religion." They say, "This (Koran) is only a lie." And when they hear the truth, the unbelievers say, "This is nothing but clear sorcery." Yet We did not give them any books to study deeply, nor have We sent them a messenger with warnings. Those before them rejected the truth, but they have not given Us a tenth of what We have given to them. When they rejected My messengers, My vengeance was terrible.*

34:46 *Say: I advise you in one thing: that you stand up before Allah and reflect. There is no madness in your fellow citizen [Mohammed]. He is only your warner before a severe punishment.*

34:47 *Say: I do not ask any reward from you. Keep it for yourselves. My reward is from Allah alone. He is witness to all things. Say: Truly my Lord sends the truth. He knows the unseen. Say: The truth has come, and falsehood will vanish and not return. Say: If I am wrong, it will cost my own soul. If I am guided, it is because of what my Lord reveals to me for He Hears all things and is near.*

34:51 *If you could see them when they are seized with terror. There will be no escape, and they will be taken from their graves. And they will say, "We believe in the truth," but how can they reach faith in this life? They rejected faith before, and they aimed slanders at the mysteries. A barrier will be placed between them and their desires as was done with those who doubted.*

I235 A Meccan met Mohammed and said, "Mohammed, you stop cursing our gods or we will start cursing your Allah." So Mohammed stopped cursing the Meccan gods. An ongoing theme of Mohammed's was of ancient civilizations who did not listen to their prophets and the terrible downfall of that country.

11:50 *We sent their brother Hud to the Ad [an ancient people of southern Arabia] people. He said, "Oh, my people, worship Allah. You have no god beside Him. You only invent your other gods. Oh, my people, I ask you for no payment for this message. My reward is only with Him who made me. Will you not understand? Oh, my people, ask pardon of your Lord. Turn to Him and repent. He will send clouds with ample rain and will give you additional strength. Do not turn back with deeds of evil."*

11:53 They said, "Oh, Hud, you have not brought us clear proofs of your mission. We will not abandon our gods at your word because we do not believe you."

11:54 They said, "We can only say that some of our gods may have seized you with evil."

11:55 Hud said, "With Allah as my witness and you as witnesses also, I am innocent of your joining other gods to Allah. So conspire against me all of you, and do not grant me a delay. I trust in Allah, my Lord and yours. There is not a single beast that He does not hold by the hairs on its head. My Lord is truly on the right path. If you turn back, at least I have already delivered my message to you. My Lord will put another people in your place. You cannot hurt Him. My Lord is guardian over all things." When We inflicted Our doom, We rescued Hud and those who believed with Him by Our special mercy. We rescued them from a severe penalty.

11:59 The men of Ad rejected signs of their Lord, rebelled against His messengers, and followed the bidding of every proud, defiant person. They were cursed in this world, and on Resurrection Day it will be said to them, "Did Ad not reject their Lord?" The people of Ad were cast far away.

11:84 We sent their brother Shuaib to Midian. He said, "Oh, my people, worship Allah. You have no other god than He. Do not give short weight and measure. I see you are prosperous, but I fear you will receive the punishment of the all-encompassing day. "Oh, my people, give to others their due in full weight and measure; do not withhold from people what is rightly theirs, and do not commit injustice on the earth causing corruption. "That which Allah leaves with you is better for you if you are believers. But I am not your keeper."

11:87 They said to him, "Oh, Shuaib, does your religion of prayer command that we leave the gods our fathers worshipped or that we should not do what we please with our property? You are the patient one, the right-minded."

11:88 He said, "Oh, my people, see if I have a clear revelation from my Lord and if He supplies me in abundance. I do not desire to do what I forbid you to do; I seek only your betterment. My sole help is Allah. In Him I trust, and to Him I turn. "Oh, my people, do not let your opposition to me cause you to sin so you suffer a similar fate to that of the people of Noah, or the people of Hud, or the people of Salih, and the people of Lot are not too distant from you. Ask forgiveness of your Lord and turn to Him. Surely, my Lord is merciful and loving."

11:91 They said, "Oh, Shuaib, we do not understand much of what you say, and we clearly see that you are powerless among us. If it were not for your family, we surely would have stoned you, and you could not have prevailed against us."

11:92 *He said, "Oh, my people, do you think more highly of my family than Allah? Do you put Him behind you, neglected? My Lord surrounds you. And, Oh, my people, do whatever you have the power to do. I will do my part, too, and soon you will know who will receive the penalty that will disgrace him and who is the liar. Watch, and I, too am watching with you."*

Lot, his wife and family:

14:5 *We sent Moses with Our signs saying to him, "Bring your people out from the darkness into the light, and remind them of the days of Allah's favors." There are signs here for every patient and grateful person.*

14:6 *Remind them that Moses said to his people, "Remember Allah's kindness to you when He freed you from the tyranny of the family of Pharaoh. They afflicted you with severe torments and slaughtered your male children while they spared your females." This was a great trial from your Lord. Remember. Your Lord made it known: "If you give thanks, then I will surely give you more and more, but if you are thankless, my chastisement is terrible." And Moses said, "If you and all who are on the earth are thankless, still Allah is self-sufficient and worthy of all praise."*

14:9 *Has the story not reached you of those who came before you, the people of Noah, and Ad [an ancient people of southern Arabia], and Thamud [Thamud was a trade town in ruins north of Mecca], and of those who lived after them? No one knows them but Allah. Their messengers came to them with clear proofs of their mission, but they put their hands on their mouths and said, "We do not believe in your mission, and we doubt what you say."*

14:10 *Their messengers said, "Is there any doubt about Allah, maker of the heavens and of the earth? It is He who invites you so that He may pardon your sins and give you a reprieve until an appointed time." They said, "You are just men like us. If you desire to turn us away from our fathers' worship, then bring us some clear proof."*

14:11 *Their messengers said to them, "Yes, we are only men like you, but Allah gives His favors to whom He pleases. It is not in our power to bring you any special proof except by the permission of Allah. Let the believers put their trust in Allah. What reason do we have for not putting our trust in Allah since He has already guided us in our ways? We will certainly bear with patience the harm you would do to us. Let the trusting put their trust in Allah."*

14:13 *And those who did not believe said to their messengers, "We will surely drive you from our land unless you return to the religion of our ancestors." Then their Lord revealed to them, "We will certainly destroy the unjust. We will certainly cause you to dwell in the land after them. This for him who dreads the time he will stand at My judgment-seat and who dreads My threats!" They sought a decision that moment, and every rebellious unbeliever perished.*

14:16 *Hell is before him, and for drink he will have boiling, stinking water. He will drink it in gulps, but he will not swallow it because he detests it. Death will come at him from every side, but he cannot die. Before him will be an unrelenting doom.*

1235 A story teller boasted that he could tell better old stories and would tell them in competition with Mohammed. But the story teller was an unbeliever and the Koran condemned him, as well as all unbelievers.

31:6 *There are men who engage in idle tales [A Persian story-teller in Mecca said that his stories were better than Mohammed's] without knowing, and they mislead others from the way of Allah and turn it to scorn. There will be a shameful punishment for them. When Our signs are revealed to him, he turns away in arrogance as if he had not heard them, as though there were deafness in his ears. Give him tidings of a terrible punishment. Those who will believe and do good works, will enjoy the Gardens of Bliss, where they will abide forever. It is Allah's true promise, and He is mighty and wise.*

31:10 *He created the heavens without pillars that can be seen and put mountains firmly on the earth so that they would not move. He scattered over it animals of every sort. He sent down rain from the heavens and caused every kind of noble plant to grow. This is the creation of Allah. Now show me what others beside Him have created. The wrongdoers are in obvious error.*

42:35 *Those who argue about Our signs should know that there will be no escape for them. Whatever you receive is but a passing comfort for this life. What is better with Allah and more enduring for those who believe and put their trust in their Lord is to avoid greater crimes and shameful deeds, and when they are angered, forgive.*

42:38 *Those who listen to their Lord and observe regular prayer are those whose affairs are guided by mutual counsel, who spend from what We have given them, and who, when a wrong is done them, defend themselves. Let the punishment for evil be equal to the evil, but he who forgives and is reconciled will be rewarded by Allah himself for He does not love those who act unjustly.*

42:41 *Whoever defends himself after being wronged will bear no blame against him. The blame is only against those who unjustly wrong others and rebel on earth disregarding justice. These will have a grievous punishment. Whoever bears wrongs and is patient and forgiving shows courage in their acts.*

42:44 *Whomever Allah sends astray will no longer have a protector. And you will see the wrongdoers when they see the doom saying, "Is there any way to return?" And you will see them brought before the Fire made humble by disgrace, and looking with stealthy glances. The believers will say, "Truly, they are losers who have lost themselves and their families on Resurrection Day. Now the wrongdoers will be in lasting torment." They have no protectors other than Allah, and there is no road for him whom Allah causes to err.*

42:47 Listen to your Lord before the day comes when you cannot turn back. You will have no refuge on that day, nor will you be able to deny your sins.

42:48 If they turn aside from your [Mohammed's] message, We have not sent you to guard over them. Your duty is only to deliver the message. When we cause man to taste Our gifts of mercy, he will rejoice in it, but if evil afflicts him for deeds he has done, then man is ungrateful.

1238 A Meccan took an old bone to Mohammed, crumbled it up and blew the dust towards Mohammed. He asked, "Will your Allah revive this bone?" Mohammed said, "Yes, I do say that. Allah will resurrect this bone and you will die. Then Allah will send you to Hell!"

The Koran gives the details of Judgment Day and Hell.

40:45 So Allah preserved him from the evils they plotted while a dreadful punishment overtook the Pharaoh's people. They will be brought in front of the Fire morning and evening, and on Judgment Day, when the hour comes to pass, it will be said, "Cast Pharaoh's people into the severest punishment."

40:47 When they will argue with each other in the Fire, the weak ones will say to those who were so arrogant, "We were only following you. Will you take a larger share of the Fire?"

40:48 And the arrogant ones will say, "We are all in this Fire; for now, Allah has judged between his servants."

40:49 Those in the Fire will say to the keepers of Hell, "Entreat your Lord to relieve us of one day of this torment."

40:50 They shall say, "Did your messengers not bring you clear signs?" "Yes," they will reply. They shall say, "Then pray for help," but the prayers of the unbelievers will be in vain.

40:51 Assuredly, We will help Our messengers and the believers in this present life, and on the day when the witnesses arise, the day on which their excuses will not profit them, they will only have a curse and the woe of a home in Hell.

40:53 We did, of old, give Moses the guidance—a guidance and warning to men of understanding—and We made the Children of Israel the inheritors of the Book. Then patiently persevere for the promise of Allah is true. Seek pardon for your faults, and celebrate the praises of your Lord at evening and at morning.

40:56 *As to those who dispute the signs of Allah without authority having reached them, there is nothing in their hearts but a desire to become great, which they will never attain. So take refuge in Allah for He is the hearer, the beholder.*

40:57 *Greater surely than the creation of man is the creation of the heavens and of the earth, but most men do not know it. The blind man and the seer are not alike, and neither is the evildoer equal with the believer who does things that are right. How few think of this. The Hour will surely come. There is no doubt of it, but most men do not believe it.*

40:60 *And your Lord says, "Call on me, and I will answer your prayer, but those who are too arrogant to serve Me will enter Hell with shame."*

The Koran gives the qualities of Allah.

40:61 *Allah made the night so you could rest and the day to give you light for seeing. Allah is rich in bounties to men, but most men do not give thanks. Such is Allah your Lord, creator of all things. There is no god but Allah. Why then are you turned from the truth? Those who deny the signs of Allah are turned aside.*

40:64 *Allah made the earth for you as a resting place and built up the heavens over it. He formed you and made your forms beautiful, and provided you with good things. This is Allah your Lord. Blessed be Allah, Lord of the worlds. He is the living one. There is no god but Allah. Call on Him with sincere devotion. Praise be to Allah, Lord of the worlds.*

40:66 *Say: I am forbidden to worship any beside Allah after the clear signs that have come to me from my Lord, and I am commanded to submit to the Lord of the worlds.*

40:67 *It is He who created you from dust, then from a drop of sperm, then a clot. That you may understand, He brought you forth as a child, let you reach your full strength, let you become an old man (but some die first), and then you reach the appointed term. It is He who gives life and death, and when He decrees a thing, He only says of it, "Be," and it is.*

40:69 *Do you not see those who dispute the signs of Allah and how are they turned aside?*

40:70 *Those who reject the Book and the revelations with which We have sent our messengers will soon know the truth. When the yokes and the chains are on their necks, they will be dragged into the boiling waters then they will be thrust into the Fire and burned. Then it will be said to them, "Where are the ones whom you made partners with Allah?" They will say, "They have gone away from us. Before, we did not call on anyone." This is how Allah leads the unbelievers astray. This is because you rejoiced in other things than the truth on the earth. Enter the gates of Hell to live there forever. Evil is the abode of the arrogant ones.*

40:77 *Have patience, for the promise of Allah is true. Whether We let you [Mohammed] see part of the woes We promise them, or We cause you to die first, they will all return to Us. We have already sent messengers before you. We have told you the stories of some of them, and of others We have told you nothing. But no messenger had the power to work a miracle unless by the permission of Allah. When the command of Allah comes, judgment is given with truth. Those who treat it as a lie perish.*

40:79 *It is Allah who gave you the cattle. On some of them you may ride, and of some you may eat. There are other advantages in them. You may carry burdens. And on ships and on cattle you are carried. He shows you His signs. Which of the signs of Allah will you deny?*

40:82 *Have they not traveled in this land and seen what was the end of those who came before them? They were more numerous than these and mightier in power and in the fortifications they left on the land, yet all they accomplished was no profit to them. When their messengers came to them with clear signs, they exulted in the knowledge they possessed, but the very wrath that they mocked encompassed them. And when they saw Our vengeance they said, "We believe in Allah alone, and we reject the partners we once associated with Him."*

40:85 *But their professions of faith, when they had seen our vengeance, did not profit them. Such has been the procedure of Allah with regard to his servants. Then the unbelievers perished.*

I239 Some Meccans approached Mohammed and said, "Let us worship what you worship. Then you worship what we worship. If what you worship is better than what we worship, then we will take a share of your worship. And if what we worship is better, then you can take a share of that." The Koran's reply:

10:94 *If you are in doubt as to what We have revealed to you, ask those who have read the Scriptures [Jews, Christians] before you. The truth has come to you from your Lord. Do not be one of those who doubts. And do not be one of those who rejects the signs of Allah, or you will be one of those who will perish. Those against whom the decree of your Lord is pronounced shall not believe until they see the painful doom, though every kind of sign was brought to them. Why were the people of Jonah the only city that believed when We warned them? When they believed, We delivered them from the penalty of shame in this world and gave them comfort for a while.*

10:99 *But if the Lord had pleased, all men on earth would have believed together. Would you compel men to become believers? No soul can believe without the permission of Allah, and He will place doubt on those who do not understand. Say: Consider whatever is in the heavens and on the earth, but neither signs nor warners profit those who do not believe.*

10:102 *What do they expect, then, but what happened in the days of men who passed before them? Say: Wait. I, too, will wait with you. We save Our messengers and those who believe. It is binding on Us to deliver the faithful. Say: Oh, men, if you are in doubt of my religion, I do not worship whom you worship beside Allah, but I worship Allah who will cause you to die. I am commanded to be a believer.*

10:105 *And set your face toward the true religion, sound in faith, and do not be of those who revere other gods besides Allah. Do not call on gods besides Allah who cannot help or hurt you. If you do this, you will be one of the wrongdoers. And if Allah afflicts you with harm, there is no one who can remove it but Him, and if He intends good for you, no one can hold it back. He strikes whichever servant He pleases, and He is the gracious and the merciful.*

10:108 *Say: Oh, men, now truth has reached you from your Lord. He who receives the guidance will be guided only for his own soul, and he who strays does so at his own loss, and I am not your guardian. Follow what is revealed to you, and be patient until Allah judges for He is the best of judges.*

Islam means submission and that is what all must do. The only religion in Allah's eyes is Islam.

41:47 *He alone has knowledge of the Hour. No fruit grows, nor does any female conceive or deliver without His knowledge. On the day when He calls men to return to Him saying, "Where are the other gods?" they will say, "We confess that none of us can testify for them." The gods they used to worship will fail them, and they will realize that there is no escape for them.*

41:49 *Man never tires of praying for good, but if evil touches him, he becomes despondent and hopeless. If We show mercy after some affliction touches him, he will surely say, "This is due to my own virtues. I do not believe that the Hour of Judgment will ever occur, but if I am returned to my Lord, I will certainly receive my highest good." But We will show the unbelievers everything that they have done, and We will give them a taste of a terrible punishment. When We show favor to man, he turns away and withdraws from Allah, but when evil touches him, he becomes full of long prayers.*

41:52 *What do you think? If this Book is really from Allah and you deny it, who will have done a greater wrong than he who openly rejects Allah? We will show them Our signs all over the earth and in their own souls, until it becomes clear to them that it is the truth. Is it not enough that your Lord is a witness to all things? Do they doubt that they will meet their Lord? Does He not encompass all things?*

6:21 *And who is more unjust than he who conceives a lie concerning Allah or who rejects Our signs? The wrongdoers will not prosper.*

6:22 *On the Day We will gather them all together, We will say to those who praised other gods than Allah, "Where are those make-believe gods of yours?" Then they will have no other excuse but to say, "By Allah, our Lord, we were not unbelievers." See how they lie against themselves, and the gods they invented failed them!*

6:25 *Some among them listen to you [Mohammed], but We have cast veils over their hearts and a heaviness to their ears so that they cannot understand our signs [the Koran]. If they see every sign, they will not have faith in them, but when they come to you, they will dispute with you, and the unbelievers will say, "This is only the fables of the old ones."*

6:26 *And they prohibit others from it [the Koran] and depart from it themselves, but they only destroy their own souls, while they do not perceive it. If you could see when they will be set over the Fire. They will say, "Oh, if we could return we would not deny the signs of the Lord, and we would be one of the believers." Yes, they will clearly see what they had concealed from themselves, but if they returned, they would return to forbidden things, for surely they are liars.*

6:29 *And they say, "There is only our life in this world, and we will not be raised up again." If you could see them when they will stand before their Lord. He will say to them, "Is this not the truth [the Resurrection and Judgment]?" They will say, "Yes, by our Lord!" He will say, "Taste then the punishment because you rejected faith."*

6:31 *They are lost who deny that they will meet with Allah until, suddenly, the Hour comes upon them, and they cry "Oh, woe to us that we neglected it." They shall bear their evil burdens on their backs. Life in this world is but a pastime and amusement, but best is the mansion in Paradise for those who do their duty! Do you not understand?*

THE SATANIC VERSES

T1192[1] Mohammed was always thinking of how he could persuade all the Meccans. It came to him that the three gods of the Quraysh could intercede with Allah. Mohammed said, "These are the exalted high flying cranes whose intercession is approved." The Meccans were delighted and happy. When Mohammed lead prayers at the Kabah, all the Meccans, Muslim and non-Muslim, took part. The Quraysh hung about after the combined service and remarked how happy they were. The tribe had been unified in worship, as before Islam.

T1192 When the news reached Ethiopia, some of the Muslims started for home. But then, trouble. The Koran revealed that Mohammed was

---

1.   The T references are to Al Tabari's *History of Prophets and Kings*

wrong. Meccan gods could have no part in his religion. Satan had made him say those terrible words about how the other gods could help Allah. The retraction by Mohammed made the relations between Islam and the Meccans far worse than it had ever been.

> 22:52 *Never have We sent a prophet or messenger before you whom Satan did not tempt with evil desires, but Allah will bring Satan's temptations to nothing. Allah will affirm His revelations, for He is knowing and wise. He makes Satan's suggestions a temptation for those whose hearts are diseased or for those whose hearts are hardened. Truly, this is why the unbelievers are in great opposition so that those who have been given knowledge will know that the Koran is the truth from their Lord and so that they may believe in it and humbly submit to Him. Allah will truly guide the believers to the right path.*
>
> 22:55 *But the unbelievers will never stop doubting until the Hour of Judgment comes upon them unaware or until the punishment of a disastrous day. On that day Allah's rule will be absolute. He will judge between them. And those who believed and did good works will be led into Gardens of delight. As for the unbelievers who treated Our signs as lies, they will receive a shameful punishment.*

THE POET'S SUBMISSION

1252 Al Dausi was a poet of some standing in Arabia and when he visited Mecca he was warned to stay away from Mohammed. Mohammed had hurt the Quraysh and broken the harmony of the tribe. He was warned that Mohammed could bring such divisions to his own family. But Al Dausi went to the mosque and there was Mohammed. Since he had been warned about Mohammed this made Al Dausi more curious to hear what Mohammed said when he prayed. He liked what he heard and followed Mohammed home. They spoke for some time and Al Dausi decided to submit to Islam.

1253 He returned home. His father was old and came to greet his son. Al Dausi said to him, "Go away father, for I want nothing to do with you or you with me." His father said, "Why, my son?" Al Dausi said, "I have become a Muslim." The father replied, "Well, then I shall do so as well."

1253 He then entered his home and told his wife, "Leave me, I want nothing to do with you." She cried, "Why?" Al Dausi said, "Islam has divided us and I now follow Mohammed." She replied, "Then your religion is my religion." He then instructed her in Islam.

The Koran is constant in its admonitions about whom a Muslim should be friends with.

9:23 *Oh, Believers, do not make friends of your fathers or your brothers if they love unbelief above Islam. He who makes them his friends does wrong. Say: If your fathers, and your sons, and your brothers, and your wives, and your kin-folks, and the wealth which you have gained, and the merchandise that you fear you will not sell, and the dwellings in which you delight—if all are dearer to you than Allah and His Messenger and efforts on His Path, then wait until Allah's command comes to pass. Allah does not guide the impious.*

3:28 *Believers should not take unbelievers as friends in preference to other believers. Those who do this will have none of Allah's protection and will only have themselves as guards. Allah warns you to fear Him for all will return to Him.*

3:118 *Believers! Do not become friends with anyone except your own people. The unbelievers will not rest until they have corrupted you. They wish nothing but your ruin. Their hatred of you is made clear by their words, but even greater hatred is hidden within their hearts. We have made Our signs clear to you. Therefore, do your best to comprehend them.*

5:57 *Oh, you who believe, do not take those who have received the Scriptures [Jews and Christians] before you, who have scoffed and jested at your religion, or who are unbelievers for your friends. Fear Allah if you are true believers. When you call to prayer, they make it a mockery and a joke. This is because they are a people who do not understand.*

I260 There was one Christian in Mecca in whom Mohammed took an interest. In the market there was a Christian slave who ran a booth. Mohammed would go and speak with him at length. This led to the Quraysh saying that what Mohammed said in the Koran, came from the Christian slave. The Koran's response:

16:101 *When We exchange one verse for another, and Allah knows best what He reveals, they say, "You are making this up." Most of them do not understand.*

16:102 *Say: The Holy Spirit [Gabriel] has truthfully revealed it from your Lord so that it may confirm the faith of those who believe and be a guide and good news for those who submit. We know that they say, "It is a man that teaches him." The man [his name is uncertain] they point to speaks a foreign language while this is clear Arabic.*

11:12 *You may feel like abandoning part of what was revealed to you, and you will be distressed at heart for fear of them, saying, "Why has there not been a treasure or an angel sent down with him?" You are there only to warn. Allah has all things in his charge. Or they might say, "He invented the Koran." Say: Then invent ten Suras of your own, and call whomever you can to help you besides Allah if you are men of truth. If your false gods do not answer you, then know that this has been sent to you with the awareness of Allah and that there is no Allah but He. Will you submit to Islam, then?*

32:1 *ALIF. LAM. MIM. This Book is without a doubt a revelation sent down from the Lord of the worlds. Do they say, "He [Mohammed] has made it up"? No. It is the truth sent from your Lord so that you may warn a people who have not yet been warned so that they may be guided.*

THE NIGHT JOURNEY

17:1 *Glory to Allah, Who took His servant on a night time journey from the Sacred Mosque in Mecca to the furthest Mosque, whose neighborhood We have blessed so that We might show him Our signs: He, and only He, hears and sees all things.*

1264 One night as he lay sleeping, Mohammed said that the angel nudged him with his foot. He awoke, saw nothing, and went back to sleep. This happened again. Then it happened a third time. Mohammed awoke, saw Gabriel and took his arm. They went out the door and found a white animal, half mule and half donkey. Its feet had wings and could move to the horizon at one step. Gabriel put Mohammed on the white animal and off they went to Jerusalem to the site of the Temple.

1264 There at the temple were Jesus, Abraham, Moses, and other prophets. Mohammed led them in prayer. Gabriel brought Mohammed two bowls. One was filled with wine and the other was filled with milk. Mohammed took the one with milk and drank it. That was the right choice.

1265 When Mohammed told this story at the Kabah, the Quraysh hooted at the absurdity of it. Actually, some of the Muslims found it too hard to believe and left Islam. One of them went to Abu Bakr and told him that Mohammed had gone to Jerusalem the night before. Bakr said they were lying. They told him to go and hear for himself. Mohammed was at the mosque telling of his story. Abu Bakr said, "If he says it, then it is true. He tells me of communication with Allah that comes to him at all hours of the day and night. I believe him."

1265 Aisha, Mohammed's favorite wife, said that Mohammed never left the bed that night, however, his spirit soared.

1266 Mohammed reported that Abraham looked exactly like him. Moses was a ruddy faced man, tall, thin, and with curly hair. Jesus was light skinned with reddish complexion and freckles and lank hair.

1268 After the prayers had been done in Jerusalem, Gabriel brought a fine ladder. Mohammed and Gabriel climbed the ladder until they came to one of the gates of heaven, called Gate of the Watchers. An angel was in charge there and had under his command 12,000 angels. And each of those 12,000 angels had 12,000 angels under them. The guardian angel asked Gabriel who Mohammed was. When Gabriel said it was Mohammed, the angel wished Mohammed well.

1268 All the angels who greeted Mohammed, smiled and wished him well, except for one. Mohammed asked Gabriel who was the unsmiling angel. The unsmiling angel was Malik, the Keeper of Hell. Mohammed asked Gabriel to ask Malik if he would show him Hell. So Malik removed the lid to Hell and flames blazed into the air. Mohammed quickly ask for the lid to be put back on Hell.

1269 At the lowest heaven, a man sat with the spirits of men passing in front of him. To one he would say, "A good spirit from a good body." And to another spirit he would say, "An evil spirit from an evil body." Mohammed asked who the man was. It was Adam reviewing the spirits of his children. The spirit of a believer excited him and the spirit of an infidel disgusted him.

1269 Mohammed saw men with lips like a camel. In their hands were flaming hot coals. They would shove the coals into their mouths and the burning coals came out of their ass. These were those who had stolen the wealth of orphans. Then he saw the family of the Pharaoh with huge bellies. Then he saw women hanging from their breasts. These women had fathered bastards on their husbands. Mohammed said that Allah hates women who birth bastards. They deprive the true sons of their portion and learn the secrets of the harem.

1270 Then Mohammed was taken up to the second heaven and saw Jesus and his cousin, John, son of Zechariah. In the third heaven he saw Joseph, son of Jacob. In the fourth heaven, Mohammed saw Idris. In the fifth heaven was a man with a long beard and white hair. He was a very handsome man who was Aaron, son of Imran. In the sixth heaven was a dark man with a hooked nose. This was Moses. In the seventh heaven was a man sitting on a throne in front of a mansion. Every day 70,000 angels went into the mansion, not to come out until the day of resurrection. The man on the throne looked just like Mohammed; it was Abraham. Abraham took Mohammed into Paradise and there was a beautiful woman with red lips. Mohammed ask who she belonged to, for she was very attractive to him. She belonged to Zaid. When he got back, Mohammed told him of this.

1271 When Gabriel took Mohammed to each of the heavens and asked permission to enter he had to say who he had brought and whether they had a mission. They would then say, "Allah grant him life, brother and friend." When Mohammed got to the seventh heaven his Lord gave him the duty of fifty prayers a day. When he returned past Moses, Moses asked him how many prayers Allah had given him. When Moses heard that it was fifty, he said, "Prayer is a weighty matter and your people are weak. Go back and ask your Lord to reduce the number for you and your community. Mohammed went back and got the number reduced to forty. When he passed Moses, the same conversation took place. And so on until Allah reduced the number to five. Moses tried to get Mohammed to go back and get the number reduced even further, but Mohammed felt ashamed to ask for more.

In the Night Journey we see Mohammed as the successor to the Jewish prophets.

More stories from the Torah:

> 12:3 *We reveal to you [Mohammed] one of the most beautiful stories in this Koran, though before this, you were one of those who did not know.*
> 12:4 *When Joseph said to his Father [Jacob], "Oh, my Father, I saw in a dream eleven stars and the sun and the moon, and I saw them prostrate themselves to me."*
> 12:5 *He said, "Oh, my son, do not tell your brothers of your vision unless they conspire in a plot against you, for Satan is an open enemy of man. So your Lord will choose you and will teach you the interpretation of stories and will perfect His favors to you and to the family of Jacob, even as He perfected it for your fathers Abraham and Isaac. The Lord is knowing, wise."*
> 12:7 *Surely in Joseph and his brothers are signs for the seekers of truth. [Jacob had twelve sons out of two wives and two slaves. Rachel was the mother of Joseph and Benjamin.] They [the other ten brothers] said, "Joseph and his brother [Benjamin] are better loved by our Father than we, but we are more in number. Our father is wrong. Let us kill Joseph or drive him to some other land so that your father's favor will be for you alone. After that you can live as upright persons."*
> 12:10 *One of them said, "Do not kill Joseph, but cast him down to the bottom of the well, if you must, so some travelers will take him up."*
> 12:11 *They said, "Oh, our Father, why do you not trust us with Joseph since we are his sincere friends? Send him with us tomorrow so he may enjoy himself and play. We will guard him well."*
> 12:13 *Jacob said, "It grieves me that you will take him away, and I fear that the wolf may devour him while you are not paying attention."*
> 12:14 *They said, "If the wolf were to devour him with so many of us there and when we are so strong, we would have perished first."*

12:15 *When they went away with him, they agreed to place him at the bottom of the well, and We revealed to Joseph, "You will tell them of this deed when they shall not know you." And they came weeping to their father at nightfall. They said, "Oh, our Father, truthfully, we went to run races, and we left Joseph with our things, and the wolf devoured him, but you will not believe us even though we speak the truth." They brought his shirt with fake blood upon it. Jacob said, "No, you have arranged this affair, but patience is good, and I will pray for the help of Allah so I may bear what you tell me."*

12:19 *There came a caravan of travelers, and they sent their water-carrier for water, and he let down his bucket. He said, "Ah, there, good news; this is a fine youth." They hid him like a treasure to make merchandise of him, but Allah knew what they did. They sold him for a small price, a few pieces of silver. They attached no value to him. An Egyptian who bought him said to his wife, "Treat him hospitably. He may be useful to us, or we may adopt him as a son." This is how We settled Joseph in the land [Egypt], and We instructed him in the interpretation of stories, for Allah is master of His affairs, but most men do not know it. When Joseph had reached full maturity, We gave him wisdom and knowledge, for this is how We reward the well doers.*

12:23 *The mistress of his home developed a passion for Joseph, and she shut the doors and said, "Come here." He said, "Allah keep me! Your husband has given me a good home and treated me honorably no good comes to wrongdoers." Still, she desired him, and he would have longed for her if he had not seen the signs from his Lord. So We ordered that We might turn him away from all evil and indecency for he was one of Our sincere servants.*

12:25 *They both raced to the door, and she tore his shirt from behind, and they met her husband at the door. She said, "What is the punishment to him who would do evil to your wife? Prison or a painful doom?"*

12:26 *Joseph said, "It was she who asked me to commit an evil act." One from her own family bore witness: "If his shirt is torn in front, then she speaks truth, and he is a liar. But if his shirt be torn behind, she lies and he is true."*

12:28 *So when his lord saw his shirt torn behind, he said, "This is a device of you women. Your devices are great, "Joseph, leave this affair. Wife, ask pardon for your crime, for you have sinned."*

12:30 *The women in the city said, "The wife of the Prince is trying to seduce her servant. He has inspired her with his love, but we clearly see she is going astray." And when she heard of their spiteful talk, she sent for them and prepared a banquet for them and gave each one of them a knife. She said, "Joseph, show yourself." When they saw him, they were amazed and cut their hands and said, "Allah keep us. This is no man. This is a noble angel."*

She said, "This is the man about whom you blamed me. I tried to seduce him from his true self, but he stood firm. Now, if he does not obey my command, he will surely be cast into prison and become one of the despised."

12:33 He said, "Oh, my Lord, I prefer the prison to that which they invite me, but unless you turn away their snares from me, I will feel inclined to play the youth with them and become one of the foolish." So his Lord heard him and turned aside their snares from him for he is the hearer and the knower.

12:35 It occurred to the men, even after they had seen the signs of his innocence, to imprison him for a time. And two youths entered into the prison with him. One of them said, "I had a dream that I was pressing grapes." The other said, "I dreamed that I was carrying bread on my head that the birds did eat. Tell us what this means, for we see you are good to all."

12:37 Joseph said, "Before any food comes to feed either of you, I will acquaint you with the truth and meaning of your dreams. This is a part of what my Lord has taught me, for I have abandoned the religion of those who do not believe Allah and who deny the life to come. I follow the religion of my fathers, Abraham, Isaac, and Jacob. We could never join false gods with Allah. This is because of Allah's bounty towards us and towards mankind, but most men do not give thanks. Oh, my two fellow prisoners, are various lords best or Allah, the one, the mighty? Those you worship beside Him are mere names that you and your fathers have named without authority. This decision is for Allah, alone. He has commanded that you worship none but Him. This is the right faith, but most men do not know it. 12:41 "Oh, my two fellow prisoners, one of you will pour wine for his Lord to drink, but the other will be crucified, and the birds will eat from his head. So the matter is decreed concerning your question." Joseph said to the one whom he judged would be released, "Mention me in the presence of your lord, " but Satan caused him to forget to mention Joseph to his lord, so he stayed in prison a few years.

12:43 The King of Egypt said, "I saw seven fat cows in a dream being eaten by seven lean cows, and seven green ears of corn and seven others withered. Oh, nobles, explain to me my dream if you are able to explain dreams."

12:44 They said, "They are confused and mixed dreams, and we do not interpret dreams."

12:45 Then Joseph's freed prisoner companion said, "I will tell you the interpretation. Let me try." He went to Joseph in prison and said, "Joseph, truthful one, explain to us the dream of the seven fat cows which seven lean ones devoured, and of the seven green ears with the others withered that I may return to the men and that they may be informed."

12:47 He said, "You will sow seven years as usual, and the corn you reap you will leave in its ear except a little of which you will eat. After that will come seven grievous years when you will eat what you have stored except that which you will have kept. A year after this, men will have rain, and they will press wine and oil."

12:50 The King said, "Bring him to me." And when the messenger returned, Joseph said, "Go back to your lord, and ask him what is the case of the women who cut their hands, for my lord well knows the snare they laid."

12:51 The King sent for the women and asked, "What happened when you tried to seduce Joseph?" They said, "Allah keep us. We do not know any evil against him." The wife said, "Now the truth appears. It was I who tried to seduce him. He is most surely one of the truthful ones."

12:52 Joseph said, "I asked for this so that my lord may know that I was not false in his absence, and that Allah does not guide the snares of the false ones. Yet I do not absolve myself, for the human heart is prone to evil except that my Lord has mercy on us, for my Lord is forgiving and merciful."

12:54 So the King said, "Bring him to me. I will take him for my special service." And when he had spoken with Joseph he said, "Be assured that from this day you will be with us, confirmed in rank and trusted."

12:55 Joseph said, "Set me over the granaries of the land, and I will guard over them wisely." So We gave Joseph power in the land. He was the owner of it as he pleased. We give our favors to those We will, and We will guard the reward of the righteous. The reward of the life to come is better for those who have believed and feared Allah.

12:58 Joseph's brothers came before him. He knew them, but they did not know him. And when he had provided them with their provision, he said, "Bring me your brother [Benjamin] from your father. Do you not see that I fill the measure and am the best of hosts? If you do not bring him to me, there will be no measure of corn for you from me, nor will you come near me."

12:61 They said, "We will try to obtain him from his father [Jacob], and we will surely do it."

12:62 Joseph told his servants, "Put their money into their camel-packs so they will see it when they have returned to their family so they will come back to us."

12:63 When they returned to their father, they said, "Oh, our father, the grain has been denied us unless we return with our brother [Benjamin], so send our brother with us, and we will have our measure. We will guard him well."

12:64 He said, "Should I trust you with him as I trusted you before with his brother? Allah is the best guardian, and He shows the most compassion of the compassionate."

12:65 When they opened their goods, they found their money had been returned to them. They said, "Oh, our father, what more can we desire? Our *money has been returned to us. We will provide corn for our families and will take care of our brother and will receive a camel's burden of more corn. What we bring now is a light quantity."*

12:66 He said, "I will not send him with you but on your oath before Allah that you will bring him back to me unless you are surrounded." When they had given him their pledge, he said, "Allah is witness of what we say."

12:67 And he said, "Oh, my sons! Do not enter by one gate, but enter by different gates. Yet I cannot help you against anything decreed by Allah. Judgment belongs to Allah, alone. I put my trust in Him, and let all who trust put their trust in him."

12:68 And when they entered as their father commanded, it did not protect them from anything decreed by Allah. It was a desire of Jacob's soul, which he satisfied. He was possessed of knowledge, which we had taught him, but most men do not know. When they came to Joseph, he took his brother to him. He said, "I am your brother, so do not grieve at what they did." When he had provided them with their provisions, he placed his drinking cup in his brother's camel-pack. Then a crier cried after them, "Oh, travelers, you are surely thieves."

12:71 They turned back to them and said, "What is that you are missing?"

12:72 "We miss," they said, "the King's cup. Whoever finds it will receive a camel's load of corn. We are bound by that promise."

12:73 The brothers said, "By Allah, you know certainly that we did not come to make mischief in the land and are not thieves."

12:74 "What," said the Egyptians, "will be the penalty for this if you are found to be liars?"

12:75 They said, "The penalty will be on the one in whose camel-pack it will be found, he will be given up to you in satisfaction for it. This is how we punish the unjust."

12:76 Joseph began to search their sacks before he came to the sack of his brother [Benjamin]. From the sack of his brother he drew out the cup. We planned this for Joseph. By the King's law, he had no power to seize his brother if Allah had not willed it. We uplift whomever we please, but above every one else is the all-knowing.

12:77 They said, "If he steals, a brother of his has stolen before," but Joseph kept his secret, and did not reveal it to them. He said, "You are in the worse condition, and Allah knows what you allege."

12:78 They said, "Oh, Prince, he has a very aged father, who will grieve him. Take one of us instead, for we see that you are a generous person."

12:79 He said, "Allah forbids that we take someone other than him with whom our property was found, for then we should be acting unjustly."

12:80 When they saw that Joseph was unyielding, they privately conferred. The eldest of them said [to Benjamin], "Do you not know that your father took a pledge from you in Allah's name and how you failed in duty with regard to Joseph? So I will not leave this land until my father permits me, or Allah decides for me for He is the best. Return to your father and say, 'Oh, our father, your son has stolen. We bear witness to what we know. We could not guard against the unforeseen. Ask for yourself in the city where we have been and of the caravan with which we have arrived. You will find we are telling the truth.'

12:83 Jacob said, "No, you have arranged all this among yourselves. Patience is most fitting for me, and Allah may bring them back to me together for he is the knowing, the wise."

12:84 He turned away from them and said, "Oh, how I am grieved for Joseph!" and his eyes became white with grief for he bore a silent sorrow.

12:85 They said, "By Allah, will you never cease to think of Joseph until you are at the point of death, or dead?"

12:86 He said, "I only plead my grief and my sorrow to Allah, but I know from Allah what you do not know. Go, my sons, and seek tidings of Joseph and his brother, and do not give up hope of Allah's mercy for only the unbelievers despair of the mercy of Allah."

12:88 And when they came in to Joseph, they said, "Oh, Prince, distress has reached us and our family, and we have poor merchandise, so give us full measure, and be charitable to us for Allah will repay the alms givers."

12:89 Joseph said, "Do you know what you did to Joseph and his brother in your ignorance?"

12:90 They said, "Are you indeed Joseph?" He said, "I am Joseph, and this is my brother. Allah has been gracious to us. For he who guards against evil and is patient will be rewarded. Allah will not allow the reward of the righteous to be lost!"

12:91 They said, "By Allah, now Allah has chosen you above us, and we have indeed been sinners!"

12:92 He said, "No blame will be on you this day. Allah may forgive you for He is the most merciful of those who show mercy. Go with this shirt of mine, and lay it on my father's face, and he will recover his sight, and come to me with all your family."

12:94 When the caravan departed from Egypt, their father said, "I surely perceive the smell of Joseph. Do not think I am feeble."

12:95 They said, "By Allah, it is your old mistake." Then when the bearer of good tidings came, he cast the shirt on his father's face, and Jacob's eyesight returned. Then he said, "Did I not tell you that I knew from Allah what you did not know?"

12:97 They said, "Oh, Our father, ask pardon for our crimes for us for we have truly been sinners."

12:98 He said, "I will ask your pardon of my Lord for He is forgiving and merciful."

12:99 *When they came to Joseph, he took his family to him, and said, "Enter Egypt in safety if Allah wills."*

12:100 *And he raised his parents onto the throne, and they fell down bowing themselves unto him. Then he said, "Oh, my father, this is the meaning of my dream of old. My Lord has now made it true, and He has surely been gracious to me since He took me from the prison and has brought you up out of the desert, even after Satan stirred up strife between me and my brothers. My Lord is gracious to whom He will for He is knowing and wise.*

12:101 *"Oh, my Lord, you have given me some power and have taught me to interpret dreams. Maker of the heavens and of the earth, You are my guardian in this world and in the next. Cause me to die a Muslim, and join me with the just."*

12:102 *This is one of the secret stories, which We reveal to you. You were not with Joseph's brothers when they conceived their design and laid their plot. And though you try, the greater part of men will not believe you. You will not ask them for any reward for this message. It is simply a reminder for all mankind.*

Noah

10:71 *Tell them the history of Noah when he said to his people, "Oh, my people, if my stay and my reminding you of the signs of Allah are grievous to you, I still trust Allah. So choose a course of action—you and your false gods. Do not let your plans be uncertain to you. Then come to some decision about me, and do not delay. If you turn your backs on me, I ask no reward from you. My reward is with Allah alone, and I am commanded to submit to Allah's will." But they treated him as a liar, and We rescued him and those with him in the ark, and We made them to inherit the earth while We drowned those who rejected Our signs. See what was the end of those who were warned?*

10:74 *Then after him, We sent messengers to their peoples, and they brought them clear signs, but they would not believe in what they had denied earlier. So We seal up the hearts of the transgressors. After them We sent Moses and Aaron with Our signs to Pharaoh and his nobles, but they were arrogant and a guilty people. When the truth came to them from Us, they said, "This is clear sorcery."*

10:77 *Moses said, "What do you say of the truth when it has come to you, 'Is this sorcery?' but sorcerers will not prosper."*

10:78 *They said, "Have you come to us to turn us away from the faith of our fathers so that you and your brother will have greatness in this land? We are not going to believe in you."*

10:79 *Pharaoh said, "Fetch me every skilled magician." When the magicians arrived, Moses said to them, "Cast down what you have to cast."*

10:81 *And when they had cast them down, Moses said, "What you have brought is sorcery, and Allah will render them vain. Allah does not uphold the work of mischief-makers. Allah will verify the truth by his words, though the guilty may be averse to it." And none believed in Moses except some of the children of his people because they feared that Pharaoh and his nobles would persecute them. Pharaoh was a tyrant in the land and one who committed excesses.*

10:84 *And Moses said, "Oh, my people, if you believe in Allah, put your trust in Him and submit."*

10:85 *They said, "In Allah we put our trust. Oh, our Lord, do not make us subject to the persecution of unjust people, and deliver us by Your mercy from the unbelieving people."*

10:87 *Then We revealed to Moses and to his brother this message: "Provide houses for your people in Egypt, and in your houses, places of worship and proclaim good tidings to the believers."*

10:88 *And Moses said, "Oh, our Lord, You have given the Pharaoh and his nobles splendor and riches in this present life. Oh, our Lord, they do lead people astray from Your way. Oh, our Lord, destroy their riches, and harden their hearts so they do not believe until they have seen the painful doom."*

10:89 *Allah said, "Your prayer is heard, Moses and Aaron. Keep to the straight path, and do not follow the path of those who have no knowledge."*

10:90 *We led the Children of Israel through the sea, and, due to spite and tyranny, Pharaoh and his hosts followed them until they drowned. Pharaoh said, "I believe there is no god but He in whom the Children of Israel believe, and I submit to Him."*

10:91 *"Yes now, but just a little while before you were rebellious and one of the wrongdoers. But this day We will rescue you and your body so that you may be a sign to those who will come after you, but truly, most men disregard Our signs."*

10:93 *We settled the Children of Israel in a beautiful home and provided them with good things, but they fell into disagreements when the knowledge (the Law) came to them. The Lord will decide between them on Resurrection Day concerning their differences.*

Mohammed is the final prophet and the Koran is pure and perfect, whereas the Jewish and Christian scripture have been corrupted. Jews and Christians must submit to Islam. The Koran continues and perfects the Scriptures.

28:48 *Yet when the truth came to them [the Meccans] from Us they said, "Why is he not given what was given to Moses?" Did they not reject what was given to Moses? They said, "Two works of sorcery [the Torah and the Koran] that helped each other, and we disbelieve them both."*

28:49 *Say: Then bring a Book from Allah that will be a better guide than this so I may follow it if you speak the truth. If they do not answer you, then know that they are following their own lusts. Who is more widely astray than he who follows his own desires without guidance from Allah? Allah does not guide the wicked. And now We have caused our word to reach them so they may be warned. Those [some of the Jews] to whom We gave the Scriptures before do believe in it [the Koran]. When it is recited to them they say, "We believe in it for it is the truth from Our Lord. We were Muslims before it came."*

28:54 *They will receive their reward twice because they suffered with patience, repelled evil with good, and gave to charity out of that which We provided them.*

It is Islam that defines the Jews and Christians.

45:16 *Long ago we gave to the Children of Israel the Torah and the wisdom and the gift of prophecy, and We provided them with the good things. We favored them over all nations. We gave them clear commandments, but after they received knowledge, they began to differ amongst themselves because of envy. Your Lord will judge between them on the Day of Reckoning concerning these issues which separated them.*

7:159 *And among the people of Moses there is a certain number who guide others with truth and establish justice. And We divided them into twelve tribes, or nations, and We inspired Moses when the people asked for drink, saying, "Strike the rock with thy staff," and from there gushed twelve springs, and each tribe knew its own place for water. We gave them clouds to shade them, and sent manna [food from heaven] and the quails to them. "Eat the good things We have provided you." They did no harm to Us, but they did injure themselves [when they stored the manna instead of trusting that more would be furnished the next day].*

7:161 *When it was said to them.. "Live in this town and eat wherever you wish and speak with humility and enter the gate in humility. We will forgive your wrongs, and We will give more to those who do good." But those who did wrong among them changed that word [the Jews made a pun and changed hittat, absolution, to habbat, corn] into another that had been told to them, so We sent them a plague for their wrongdoings.*

7:163 *Ask them about the town that stood by the sea, how the Jews broke the Sabbath. Their fish came to them on their Sabbath day appearing on the surface of the water. But during the work week there were no fish to catch. So We made a trial of them for they were evildoers. And when some of them said, "Why do you preach to those whom Allah is about to destroy or chastise with awful doom?" They said, "To do our duty for the Lord so that they may be able to ward off evil."*

7:165 *When they disregarded the warnings that had been given to them [not to work on the Sabbath], We rescued those who had forbidden wrongdoing, and We punished the wrongdoers for their transgressions. But when they persisted in what they had been forbidden, We said to them, "Be as apes, despised and loathed." [The Jews were changed into apes.]*

7:167 *Then the Lord declared that until Resurrection Day, He would use others to punish the Jews, for the Lord is quick to punish, and most surely is He forgiving and merciful. And We sent them out on the land as separate nations. Some of them were righteous and some were not. We have tried them with prosperity and adversity in order that they might return to Us.*

7:169 *After them came an evil generation. They inherited the Scriptures [the Torah], but they chose the pleasures of this world saying, "Everything will be forgiven us." If similar vanities came to them again, they would seize them again. But did they not accept a promise through the Scripture that they would not speak anything of Allah but the truth? And they have studied what is in the Book [Koran], but the home in the hereafter is for those who fear Allah. Do you not understand? And for those who keep the Scriptures and keep regular prayer, We will not waste the reward of the righteous. When We shook the mountain over them, as if it were a covering, and they thought it was going to fall on them, We said "Hold fast to what We have given you, and remember what is in it so you may guard against evil."*

The Koran mentions a Jew who converted to Islam.

46:4 *What are you thinking when you worship other gods? Show me which part of earth or heaven they created. Bring me their revelations if you are telling the truth. And who is more mistaken than he who calls on gods who will have no answers until the Resurrection? And on Judgment Day he will become enemies with them [his false gods] and deny that he worshipped them.*

46:7 *And when We clearly reveal the truth to the unbelievers, they say it is surely magic and sorcery. Or they say "He has invented it." Say: If I have invented it, then you will obtain not one blessing for me from Allah. He knows what is between me and you, and He is forgiving and merciful.*

46:9 *I am not Allah's first messenger, nor do I know what He will do with me and you. I follow what is revealed to me through inspiration, and my charge is to warn you [the Meccans]. What do you think? This Scripture is from Allah, and you reject it, and a witness [a Jew, bin Salama] from the Children of Israel testifies that he has seen earlier scripture like it and believes it, while you proudly show scorn. Surely, Allah does not guide the unjust.*

46:11 *But the unbelievers say, "If the believers' scriptures were true, we would have had them first." And they refuse the scriptures; they say they are a legend, a lie.*

46:12 *Before this Book [the Koran] was the book of Moses, a rule and a mercy. This book confirms in Arabic the warning to the unjust and the good tidings to the just.*

1272 Mohammed continued to preach Islam and condemn the old Arabic religions. There were those of the Quraysh who defended their culture and religion and argued with him. Mohammed called them mockers and cursed one of them, "Oh Allah, blind him and kill his son." The Koran records the Meccan's resistance as plots and schemes.

6:124 *So We have placed wicked ringleaders in every city to scheme there, but they only plot against themselves, and they do not realize it. And when a sign comes to them they say, "We will not believe until we receive one like those that Allah's messengers received." Allah knows best where to place His message. The unbelievers will be disgraced when they receive their punishment for their scheming.*

6:125 *For those whom Allah intends to guide, He will open their hearts to Islam. But for those whom He intends to mislead, He will make their hearts closed and hard, as though they had to climb up to the heavens. Thus does Allah penalize the unbelievers. And this is the right way of your Lord. We have detailed Our signs for those who will listen and see. They shall have an abode of peace with their Lord. He will be their protecting friend because of their works.*

6:128 *One day He will gather them all together and say, "Oh, jinns, you took away a great part of mankind." And their friends among men will say, "Oh, Lord, some of us profited by others, but we have arrived at our appointed term, which You had set for us." He will say, "The Fire is your home where you will abide forever, as long as Allah wills." The Lord is wise and knowing. So We let the wrongdoers turn to each other because of their works.*

6:130 *Oh, race of jinn and mankind, were there not messengers among you giving you my warning of the meeting of this your day? They shall say, "We testify against ourselves." This world's life deceived them, and they will testify against themselves that they were unbelievers.*

6:131 *The messengers were sent because the Lord would not destroy the unbelievers' cities until they were warned of their negligence.*

7:189 *It is Allah Who created you from a single person [Adam] and Who brought forth his wife that he might dwell with her. When they are united, she carries a light burden, which goes unnoticed until it becomes heavy. Then they cry to Allah saying, "If You give us a goodly child we vow we will be forever grateful."*

7:190 *Yet when Allah gives them a goodly child, they praise idols for what Allah has given to them. Allah is exalted above the idols they prefer to Him. Do they truly venerate others who create nothing, while they themselves were created by Him? These others can give no aid nor can they help themselves. If you call them to guidance, they will not obey. It is the same whether you call them or keep silent.*

7:194 *Those you call on besides Allah are His servants like you are. Call on them then, and let them answer you if you are truthful. Do they have feet to walk with? Do they have hands to hold with? Do they have eyes to see with? Do they have ears to hear with? Say: Call on these god-partners of yours. Then plot against me. Do not delay. My Lord is Allah who revealed the Scripture. He befriends the good. Whoever you call on besides Allah is not able to help you nor can they help themselves. If you call them to guidance, they will not hear you. You see them look towards you, but they do not see. Keep to forgiveness, command what is right, and turn away from the ignorant. And if a suggestion from Satan afflicts you, seek refuge with Allah. He hears and knows all things. Those who guard against evil when thoughts from Satan assault them remember Allah's guidance, and they see clearly. Their brethren plunge them deeper in error and do not cease in their efforts.*

7:203 *If you do not bring a revelation, they [the Meccans] say, "Why do you not have one?" Say: I only follow that which is inspired by my Lord These are clear proofs from your Lord and guidance and mercy for those who have faith. And when the Koran is read, listen to it with attention and hold your peace that mercy may be shown to you. Remember the Lord humbly within yourself in a low voice in the mornings and the evenings [prayer]. Do not be one of the neglectful ones. Those who are with the Lord are not too proud to serve Him. They celebrate His praises and prostrate themselves before Him.*

The Meccans keep saying that if Mohammed were right about the Judgment Day, then let them see it, now.

32:4 *It is Allah Who created the heavens and the earth and everything in between in six days before ascending His throne. You have no one besides Allah to protect you. Will you not think about this? He governs all things in the heavens and on earth. At the end of this world, all things will return to Him on a day that will seem to last a thousand years.*

32:6 *This is He Who knows all things—seen and unseen. He is mighty and merciful and has created all good things. He began creating man from clay then made his seed from a worthless fluid. He shaped him and breathed his Spirit into him and gave him the senses of sight, sound, and understanding. Small thanks do you give.*

32:10 *And they say, "What? When we have been buried in the ground, shall we really be resurrected?" Yes, but they deny that they will meet their Lord. Say: The angel of death has been put in charge of you and will take your lives. You will be returned to your Lord. If you could only see when the wicked shall hang their heads before their Lord, and say, "Lord, We have seen and heard. Return us to life. We will act righteously because now we are convinced."*

32:13 *If We had wished, We could have given guidance to every soul. My word will come true: "I will fill Hell with jinns and men together. So taste the evil of your deeds. You forgot that you would have a meeting on Judgment Day. We will forget you. Taste the eternal punishment because of your actions.*

32:15 *Only they believe in Our signs, who, when they are recited to them, fall down in adoration and celebrate the praises of their Lord, and they are not scornful. They shun their beds to pray to their Lord in fear and hope, and spend charitably from what We have given them.*

32:17 *No soul knows the hidden delights that are reserved for the righteous. There is a reward for their good deeds. Is the man who believes no better than the man who does not believe? They are not the same. As a reward for their behavior there are Gardens of repose waiting for those who believe and do good works.*

32:20 *The wicked will live in the Fire. Whenever they try to leave, they shall be forced back, and it will be said to them, "Taste the torment of the Fire, that you used to deny." Certainly, We will cause them to taste the lesser penalty in this life before tasting the supreme penalty so that they may repent and return. And who is more wrong than he who is reminded of the signs of his Lord and who then turns away from them? We will certainly punish the guilty.*

And if Mohammed were actually a prophet, why not show them something other than words. Why not do a miracle?

13:27 *The unbelievers say: Why does his Lord not send a sign down to him? Say: Allah will truly mislead whom he chooses and will guide to Himself those who turn to Him. They believe and their hearts find rest in remembering Allah. Without a doubt all hearts find rest in the remembrance of Allah. Those who believe and do what is right will be blessed and find joy in the end.*

13:30 *Therefore, We have sent you to a nation before which other nations have passed away so that you may recite Our revelations to them. Nevertheless they deny the merciful Allah. Say: He is my Lord; there is no god but Him. I put my trust in Him, and to Him I will return.*

13:31 *If there were a Koran that could move mountains, tear the earth apart, or make the dead speak, this would be it! Allah is in command of all things! Do the believers not know that if it had been Allah's will, He could have guided all the people? Disaster will never cease to afflict the unbelievers for their wrongful deeds or to come into their homes until Allah's will is fulfilled. Allah will not fail to keep His promise.*

13:32 Many messengers who came before you were mocked. For a long time We allowed the unbelievers to go unpunished, but finally We punished them. Then how terrible was Our punishment!

13:33 Who is it that watches over every soul and knows all its actions? And yet they worship gods other than Allah. Say: Then name them! Would you inform Him of something on the earth that is unknown to Him? Or are these merely meaningless words? Certainly, their lies seem to make sense to the unbelievers because they are kept from the right path. No one can help those whom Allah has sent astray. They will receive punishment in this life, but what is worse is their punishment in the life to come, and they will have no protector against Allah.

13:35 Paradise is promised to those who fear Allah. It is a land watered by flowing rivers where food is plentiful and shade is perpetual. This is the reward for those who fear Allah. But the end of the unbelievers is the Fire. And those to whom We have given the Scriptures [Jews] rejoice in what has been revealed to you, although some groups among you deny a part of it. Say: I am commanded to worship Allah alone and not to regard any as His equal. I call on Him, and to Him I will return. Therefore, We have revealed this judgment of authority in Arabic. If you were to follow their desires after having received this knowledge, then you would find neither a guardian nor a defender in Allah.

13:38 Messengers were sent before you and were given wives and children, but none of them was able to perform a miracle without the permission of Allah. For every time period there is a Book revealed. Allah will destroy and build up what He pleases for He is the source of revelation.

13:40 Whether We allow you to see the fulfillment of part of our threats or We cause you to die before it takes place, your part is only to spread the message while it is Our part to give out the punishment. Do they not recognize that We take control of their lands and invade its diminishing borders? When Allah makes a decree, nothing can be done to change it, and He is quick at His reckoning. Those who lived before them devised plots as well, but Allah is the master of all plotting. He knows every soul. The unbelievers will come to know for whom the heavenly home is destined. The unbelievers will say, "You are not a messenger of Allah." Say: Allah and whoever has knowledge of the Scriptures is a sufficient witness between you and me.

If Judgment Day were to come, then the Meccans asked Mohammed to tell Allah to bring it here this day and prove Mohammed was a true prophet.

29:44 *Allah created the heavens and the earth in truth. This is a sign to those who believe.*

29:47 *So it is that We have sent down the Book [Koran] to you [Mohammed]. Those [the Jews] to whom We have given the Book of the law believe in it, and some other Arabians there believe in it. None, save the unbelievers, reject our signs.*

29:48 *You [Mohammed] were not a reader of the Scripture before this book came, nor did you write one with your right hand. Then the critics could have treated it as a vain thing and doubted it. But it is a clear sign in the hearts of those whom knowledge has reached. None but the unjust reject Our signs. They say, "Why are the signs not sent down to him from his Lord?" Say: The signs are in the power of Allah alone. I am only a plain warner. Is it not enough for them that We have revealed to you the Book to be recited to them? This is a mercy and a warning to those who believe. Say: Allah is witness enough between me and you. He knows all that is in the heavens and the earth. Those who believe in the falsehood and reject Allah—these will be the lost ones.*

29:53 *They will challenge you to hasten the punishment. If there had not been a season fixed for it, the punishment would have already come upon them. It will come on them suddenly when they are not looking for it. They will ask you to hasten the punishment, but Hell will encompass the unbelievers. One day the punishment shall wrap around them, both from above them and from below them, and Allah will say, "Taste your own doings."*

29:56 *Oh, My servants who believe, My earth is vast; therefore, serve Me. Every soul will have a taste of death. Then to Us you will return. Those who believe and serve righteousness, We will house in Gardens with palaces, beneath which the rivers flow. They will abide there forever. How good the reward of the workers, those who patiently endure and put their trust in their Lord.*

7:179 *We have created many of the jinn and men for Hell. They have hearts with which they cannot understand, eyes with which they cannot see, and ears with which they cannot hear. They are like cattle—no, even worse, for they are neglectful.*

7:180 *The most beautiful names belong to Allah. So call Him by them, and avoid those who use His name profanely for they will suffer for what they do.*

7:181 *Among those whom We have created are a people who guide others with truth and do justice. As for those who reject Our signs as lies, We draw them to destruction in ways they will not see. They have been granted a delay, but My scheme is certain. Have they not considered that their companion [Mohammed] is not mad? He is only a plain warner. Have they not considered the kingdoms of heaven and of the earth and all the things that Allah created? Do they not see that their own term may be drawing near? What message will they believe after this? If you are rejected from the guidance of Allah, you will have no other guide. He leaves them to wander blindly in distraction.*

7:187 *They will ask you [Mohammed] about the fixed time of the final Hour. Say: That knowledge is only with my Lord. He alone will reveal it at its proper time. It weighs heavily on jinns and men. It will suddenly come to you. Say: The knowledge of it is only with Allah. Most men do not know.*

7:188 *Say: I have no power over any good or harm to myself except as Allah wills. If I had knowledge of his secrets, I would multiply the good, and evil would not touch me. I am only a warner, a bearer of glad tidings to those who believe.*

And after Judgment Day comes Paradise and Hell.

7:35 *Oh, children of Adam, if messengers come to you from among yourselves relating My signs to you, then those who refrain from evil and mend their ways will have no fear or grieving. But they who reject Our signs and scorn them will be companions of the Fire and will abide there forever.*

7:37 *Who does greater wrong than one who invents a lie against Allah or rejects His signs? To them shall a portion here below be assigned in accordance with the Book of our decrees until the time when our messengers arrive to take their souls and say, "Where are they whom you used to call beside Allah?" They will say, "They are gone from us." And they will testify against themselves that they were unbelievers.*

7:38 *He shall say, "Enter into the company of those who passed before you into the Fire, the generations of jinn and men. Every time a fresh generation enters, it will curse its sister peoples until all have followed each other into the Fire, and the last comers will say to the former, 'Oh, our Lord, these are the ones who led us astray. Give them a double torment of Fire.'" He will say, "You all will have double," but you do not understand this.*

7:39 *And the former of them will say to the latter, "You have no advantage over us, so taste the punishment that you earned." There will be no openings at the gates of heaven for those who have rejected Our signs and scorned them nor will they enter Paradise until the camel passes through the eye of the needle. This is Our reward to the guilty. They will make their bed in Hell, and sheets of Fire will cover them. This is how we will reward the evildoers.*

7:42 *But as for those who believe and do good works, no burden do We place on any soul but that which it can bear. They are the rightful owners of the Garden and will dwell there forever. And We will remove whatever ill feeling is in their bosoms. Rivers will roll beneath them, and they will say, "Praise to Allah who guided us here. We would never have been guided if it had not been for Allah. The messengers of the Lord truly brought us the truth." And they will hear the cry, "This is Paradise. You inherit it for your righteous deeds." And the dwellers of Paradise shall cry to the dwellers of the Fire, "We have found the promise of our Lord to be true. Have you also found what your Lord promised you to be true?" They shall answer, "Yes," and a herald shall proclaim between them, "The curse of Allah is on the evildoers."*

7:45 Whoever would turn men from the path of Allah and seek to make it crooked, they were those who did not believe in the life to come. Between them is a veil, and on the Heights are men [men whose good and bad deeds balance each other] who know all by their markings [the men of Hell will have blackened faces and those of Paradise will have white shining faces], and they shall cry to the inmates of Paradise, "Peace be to you," but they will not enter, though they will hope. And when their eyes are turned towards the inmates of the Fire, they shall say, "Oh, our Lord, do not send us to the place of the wrongdoers." And the men on the Heights will cry to those whom they will know by their markings [darkened faces], "How did you profit from your wealth and your pride?" [Turning to the blessed, the men on the Heights say:] "Are not these the men to whom you swore Allah would show no mercy? Enter Paradise. You will have no fear, nor grief."

7:50 The dwellers of the Fire will cry to the dwellers of Paradise, "Pour some of the water on us or anything that Allah gives you." They shall say, "Allah forbids these things to unbelievers." For those who made their religion a sport and pastime and who were deceived by the life of the world, this will be the day We forget them as they forgot the meeting of this day and as they did deny Our signs. We have brought them the Book, which We explained in detail as a guide and a mercy to all who believe.

7:53 Are they waiting for its fulfillment [the Koran's promises of rewards and punishments]? On this day those who disregarded it will say, "The Messengers of our Lord did bring the truth. Do we have any intercessor to intercede for us, or could we return to life on earth? Then we could act differently than we have acted." But they have lost their souls, and the gods of their own devising have fled from them.

The Koran records the actual quotes of Mohammed's opponents.

34:3 The unbelievers say, "The Hour will never come on us." Say: By my Lord, it will surely come on you. He knows the unseen, and not the smallest atom in heaven or earth escapes him nor anything smaller or larger, but it is clearly in the book [of deeds]."

34:4 Allah will reward those who believe and do good things with a pardon and rich reward for them. For those who strive against Our signs, there will be a penalty, a painful doom of wrath. And those to whom knowledge has been given will see that what has been sent from the Lord is the truth, and that it leads to the path of the mighty, the praised.

34:7 *The unbelievers say, "Should we show you a man who will tell you that when you are scattered in dust with the most complete disintegration, you will be created anew? He has invented a lie about Allah, or is a jinn [a creature made of fire who can help or hurt humans] in him?" No, those who do not believe in the next life are doomed by their mistakes. Do they not consider what is before them and behind them in heaven and earth? If We desired, We could cause the earth to swallow them up or cause the sky to fall on them. There is a Sign in this for every servant who returns to Allah.*

Mohammed continued to tell about older Arabian cultures that had refused to listen to their prophets. In every case, Allah smote them with a terrible scourge.

41:3 *The Book brings good news and a warning. Still, most of them will turn away and not hear. They say, "Our hearts are concealed under veils from your teachings. We are deaf and there is a barrier between us and you. Do what you wish. We will do as We wish."*

41:6 *Say: I am only a man like you. It has been revealed to me that your Allah is the only god. Go straight to Him and ask His forgiveness. Woe to those who join gods with Allah, those who do not pay the poor tax, and those who do not believe in the afterlife. As for those who believe and do the right things, they will have a never ending reward.*

41:9 *Say: Do you really deny Him Who created the world in two days, and do you believe He has equals with Him? He is the Lord of all the worlds. In four days He placed the towering, strong mountains upon the earth. He blessed it and placed food throughout to meet the needs of everyone. He then turned His attention to heaven which was a vapor, and said to it and the earth, "Both of you come, either willingly or unwillingly." They both said, "We will come willingly." So in two days He created the seven heavens, and He assigned to each heaven its mandate. He adorned the lower heaven with stars and left it guarded. That was the decree of the mighty, the all-knowing.*

41:13 *But if they turn away, say to them, "I have warned you of a disaster like the scourge that punished Ad [Ad lay on an old trade route north of Mecca. It was abandoned in Mohammed's day] and Thamud [the people of a ruined Nabatean city near Medina]."*

41:14 *When their messengers came from all directions saying, "Serve only Allah," they answered, "If our Lord had wished, He would have sent angels down to us, so we do not believe the message you carry."*

41:15 *As for the people of Ad, they were unjustly arrogant throughout the land, and they said, "Who has more power than us?" Could they not see that Allah, Who created them, was more powerful than themselves? Still, they continued to reject Our signs! So we sent a furious wind against them during days of disaster so that We might make them taste the penalty of disgrace in this life. The penalty of the afterlife will be even more disgraceful. They will not be helped.*

41:17 *We showed the people of Thamud [the people of a ruined Nabatean city near Medina] the right way, but they preferred blindness to guidance. So the scourge of humiliation overtook them because that was what they earned. However, We saved those who believed and acted righteously. On the day when the enemies of Allah are gathered to face the Fire, they will be marched together in groups. When they reach the Fire, their ears, eyes, and skin will bear witness against them for what they have done.*

41:21 *They will say to their skins, "Why do you testify against us?" And their reply will be, "Allah, Who has given speech to all things, has made us speak. He created you originally, and you will be returned to Him. You did not try to hide yourselves so that your ears, eyes, and skins could testify against you. You thought that Allah was unaware of most of the things that you did. But this evil thought of yours [that there are other gods] has brought you to destruction, and now you are one of the lost."*

41:24 *And though they are resigned, the Fire will still be their home. If they ask for goodwill, they will not receive it. We have given them companions in this world who made their present and past seem good to them. They deserve the fate of the past generations of jinns and men. They are certainly losers.*

1272 One day Mohammed stood with the angel, Gabriel, as the Quraysh performed the rituals of their religion. Among them were the leaders who defended their native culture and religion and opposed Mohammed. When the first leader passed by Gabriel, Gabriel threw a leaf in his face and blinded him. Gabriel then caused the second one to get dropsy which killed him. The third man Gabriel caused him to develop an infection which killed him. The fourth man was caused later to step on a thorn which killed him. Gabriel killed the last man who dared not to worship Allah with a brain disease.

MOHAMMED'S PROTECTOR AND WIFE BOTH DIE

1278 Mohammed's protector was his uncle, Abu Talib. When Abu Talib fell ill, some of the leaders of the Quraysh came to his bedside. They said to him, "You are one of our leaders and are near dying. Why don't you call Mohammed and let's see if we can't work out some solution to the pain and division in our tribe? Why doesn't he leave us alone, not bother us and we will not bother him? We will have our religion and he can have his."

1278 So Abu Talib called Mohammed to his side. "Nephew, these men have come so that you can give them something and they can give you something." Mohammed said, "If they will give me one word, they can rule the Persians and the Arabs. And they must accept Allah as their Lord and renounce their gods."

1278 The Quraysh said, "He will give us no agreement. Let Allah judge between us." And they left.

1278 Mohammed turned his attention to his dying uncle. He asked him to become a Muslim and then Mohammed could intercede for him on judgment day. His uncle told him, "The Quraysh would say that I only accept Islam because I fear death. But I should say it just to give you pleasure." He drifted off, but as he died, his lips moved. His brother put his head close to Abu Talib and listened. He then said, "Nephew, my brother said what you wished him to say." Mohammed's reply was, "I did not hear him." Mohammed left.

Abu Talib had taken the orphan Mohammed into his home and raised him. He took Mohammed on caravan trading missions to Syria and taught him how to be a businessman. Abu Talib was the clan chief who protected Mohammed's life when the rest of Mecca wanted to harm him. Abu Talib was Mohammed's life and security, but he was damned to Hell, he was not a Muslim and no amount of friendship could prevent that.

After Abu Talib's death, the pressure on Mohammed was greater. It reached the point where one of the Quraysh threw dust at Mohammed. This was the worst that happened.

The death of his wife had no political effect, but it was a blow to Mohammed. His wife was his chief confidant, and she consoled him.

MARRIAGE

M113[1] About three months after the death of Khadija Mohammed married Sauda, a widow and a Muslim.

M113 Abu Bakr had a daughter, Aisha, who was six years old. Soon after marrying Sauda Mohammed was betrothed to Aisha, who was to become his favorite wife. The consummation would not take place until she turned nine.

---

1.   The reference is to Muir's *Life of Mohammed*

M031, 5977[2] *Aisha reported Mohammed having said: I saw you in a dream for three nights when an angel brought you to me in a silk cloth and he said: Here is your wife, and when I removed (the cloth) from your face, lo, it was yourself, so I said: If this is from Allah, let Him carry it out.*

---

2.   An M reference with a comma is to Muslim's Hadith, *Sahih Muslim*

POLITICAL BEGINNINGS

CHAPTER 6

24:52 It is such as obey Allah and His Apostle, and fear Allah and do right, that will win (in the end).

1279 With Abu Talib's death, Mohammed needed political allies. Mohammed went to the city of Taif, about fifty miles away, with one servant. In Taif he met with three brothers who were politically powerful. Mohammed called them to Islam and asked them to help him in his struggles with those who would defend their native religions.

1279 One brother said that if Mohammed were the representative of Allah, then the brother would go and rip off the covering of the Kabah, Allah's shrine.

1279 The second brother said, "Couldn't Allah have found someone better than Mohammed to be a prophet?"

1279 The third brother said, "Don't let me even speak to you. If you are the prophet of Allah as you say you are, then you are too important for me to speak with. And if you are not, then you are lying. And it is not right to speak with liars."

1280 Since they could not agree, Mohammed asked them to keep their meeting private. But Taif was a small town and within days everyone knew of Mohammed's presence. Taif was a very religious town in the old ways of the Arabs. Mohammed kept condemning them and their kind, until one day a mob gathered and drove him out of town, pelting him with stones.

1281 Half way back to Mecca, he spent the night. When he arose for his night prayer, the Koran says that jinns came to hear him pray.

> *46:29 We sent a company of jinn so that they might hear the Koran. When the reading was finished, they returned to their people with warnings. They said, "Oh, people! We have heard a scripture sent down since the days of Moses verifying previous scriptures, a guide to the truth and the straight path. Oh, people! Hear the Messenger of Allah and believe Him that He will forgive your faults and protect you from tormenting punishment."*
>
> *46:32 Those who do not respond to Allah's messenger cannot defeat His plan on earth, and he will have no protectors beside Him. Such men are in flagrant error. Have they not seen that Allah, who created the heavens and*

the earth and was not wearied by their creation, can give life to the dead? Yes, He has power over all things.

46:34 *On the day the unbelievers are set before the Fire and are asked, "Is this not the truth?" they will say, "Yes, by Our Lord!" He will say, "Then taste the punishment because you did not believe." Then be patient, as the messengers had patience and firmness, and do not try to hasten their doom. When they see what has been promised them, it will be as if they had waited but one hour. Will any perish except those who have transgressed?*

The Koran speaks further about Satan:

7:8 *The weighing on that day will be just [a balance will be used to weigh the good and bad deeds of life], and those who weigh heavy in good deeds will be happy. And those who weigh light, their souls will suffer because they rejected Our signs.*

7:10 *And We have given mankind authority on earth and given you the means for a livelihood. How little are the thanks you give. We created you, then fashioned you, then said to the angels, "Fall prostrate to Adam, and they obeyed in worship, save Iblis. He refused to fall prostrate."*

7:12 *Allah said, "What prevented you from prostrating in worship when I asked?" Iblis said, "I am nobler than Adam and You created me from fire, while You created him from clay."*

7:13 *Allah said, "Then go down from here. Paradise is no place for pride. Get out! You are of the degraded ones."*

7:14 *He said, "Give me a reprieve until the day when mankind will be raised from the dead."*

7:15 *Allah said, "You will be of the reprieved."*

7:16 *He [Satan] said, "Because you have thrown me out, I will lie in wait for them in your straight path. Then I will assault them from before and from behind, and from their right hand and from their left, and You will not find most of them to be thankful."*

7:18 *Allah said, "Get out of here, disgraced and banished! If any of them follow you, I will fill Hell with you all."*

7:19 *"Oh, Adam! You and your wife will dwell in Paradise and eat where you will, but do not come to this tree, or you will become one of the wrongdoers."*

7:20 *Then Satan whispered to them, telling them of their hidden and evil inclinations. He said, "Your Lord has forbidden you from this tree fearing that you might become angels or one of the immortals." And he swore to both of them, "I am a friend to you." So he used deceit to cause their fall, and when they had tasted of the tree, they knew their shame and began to hide themselves sewing together leaves of the garden for clothing. And their Lord called to them, "Did I not forbid you this tree, and did I not say to you, 'Satan is your open enemy'?"*

7:23 *They said, "Oh, our Lord! We have wronged ourselves; if you will not forgive us and have mercy on us, we will surely be lost."*
7:24 *Allah said, "Get out. Your descendants will be enemies of each other. Earth will be home and your livelihood for a time. There you will live, there you will die, and from there you will be raised."*

PREACHING BACK IN MECCA

1282 When the fairs returned to Mecca, Mohammed went out to the crowd of visitors and told them he was the prophet of Allah and brought them the Koran. They should abandon their ancient religions and follow him.

16:93 *If Allah wished, He could make mankind one nation, but He causes some to err and some to be guided as he pleases. You will certainly be questioned about what you did.*
16:94 *Do not use your oaths to practice deceit between you or a foot that was firmly planted may slip, and you might have to taste the evil consequences of having kept men from the path of Allah. A terrible punishment would befall you. Do not exchange the covenant of Allah for a small price. What Allah gives is better for you if you only knew it.*
16:96 *The things you have are temporary while what Allah has is eternal. Truly, We will give to those who are patient a reward that corresponds with their best actions. Whoever does good, whether male or female, and believes, We will certainly give a happy life, and We will certainly give them their reward for the best of their actions.*
16:116 *Do not say while describing something, "This is lawful, and this is forbidden," in order to invent a lie against Allah. Those who invent lies against Allah will never prosper. Such lies may bring a momentary pleasure, but they will certainly have a painful punishment. The things which We have mentioned to you before are also forbidden to the Jews. We did them no injustice; they were unjust to themselves. Your Lord is forgiving and merciful toward those who do wrong in ignorance but who later repent and make amends.*
16:120 *Abraham was an example of someone who was obedient to Allah, upright, and who did not worship others besides Allah. He was grateful for Allah's favors. Allah had chosen him and guided him on the right path. We gave him good in this world. In the afterlife, he will be among the righteous.*
16:123 *We revealed to you this message, "Follow the ways of Abraham, the upright. He did not worship false gods alongside Allah.*
16:124 *The Sabbath was commanded only for those who disagreed about it. Allah will judge between them on Judgment Day about their differences.*
16:125 *Use your wisdom and beautiful preaching to call everyone to the way of your Lord. Reason with them in the best way that you can. Surely your*

Lord knows best who strays from His path and who follows the right way. If you make reprisals, then punish in the same manner in which you were afflicted. But if you show patience, it is the best for those who are patient. Be patient; your patience comes from Allah. Do not grieve for them, and do not be distressed because of their plots. Allah is with those who guard against evil and those who do good.

30:28 *He gave you a parable that relates to yourselves: Do you equally share your wealth with any slave you own? Would you fear your slave as you would fear a free man? This is how We explain Our signs to those who understand. No, you do not. The wicked, without knowledge, pursue their base desires. But who can guide those whom Allah has allowed to go astray? There will be no one to help them.*

30:30 *Set your resolve as a true convert to the religion that Allah has created, and for which He has created man. Allah's creation cannot be changed. This is the right religion, but most people do not know. Turn to Him in repentance; observe your prayers; and do not be one of those who join other gods with Allah, those who split up their religion into sects, and where every division rejoices in its own tenets.*

30:33 *When men are touched by troubles, they turn to their Lord and pray to Him: but when He has given them a taste of His mercy, suddenly some of them begin to worship other gods, as if to show their ingratitude for the favors that We have shown them. Enjoy yourselves for a little while. In the end you will know how foolish you have been. Have We given them any evidence that says that there are other gods that may be worshiped along with Allah?*

30:36 *When We give men a taste of mercy they rejoice, but if evil comes to them as a result of their actions, they despair. Do they not see that Allah gives generously or sparingly to whomever He chooses? Truly, there are signs here for those who believe.*

11:111 *And truly your Lord will repay everyone according to their deeds for He is well aware of what they do.*

11:112 *Continue on the right path as you have been commanded—you and those who have turned to Allah with you—and do no wrong. He knows what you do. Do not depend on the evildoers for fear that the Fire will seize you. You have no protector beside Allah, and you will not be helped against Him. Observe prayer at early morning, at the close of the day, and at the approach of night, for good deeds drive away evil deeds. This is a warning for the mindful. Be patient, for Allah will not let the reward of the righteous perish.*

11:116 *Why were there not men with virtue, who were not corrupt, in the generations before you except the few whom we saved from harm? The evildoers enjoyed the selfish pleasures of earthly life, and became sinners.*

Your Lord would not destroy cities unjustly while its people were doing right.

11:118 *If the Lord pleased, He could have made mankind of one nation, but only those to whom your Lord has granted His mercy will cease to differ. For this He created them, for the word of your Lord will be fulfilled: "I will completely fill Hell with jinn and men together."*

11:120 *All that We relate to you of the stories of these messengers is to make your heart firm. The truth has reached you through them, and this is the truth, a warning, and a reminder to those who believe.*

11:121 *To those who do not believe say, "Do whatever you can. We will do our part. Wait. We too will wait."*

11:123 *To Allah belong the secrets of the heavens and earth, and all things return to Him, so worship Him and put your trust in Him. Your Lord is not unmindful of your doings.*

Mohammed spoke of the greatness of Allah to the Meccans and the visitors.

16:65 *Allah sends rain down from the clouds and with it gives life to the earth. Truly there is a sign here for people who will listen. In cattle there is a lesson to you. We give you pure milk; it is easy and tasty for those who drink it. From the fruit of the date-palm and the grapevine, you obtain things to drink and eat. Truly, there is a sign here for people who are wise.*

16:68 *Your Lord taught the bee to make hives in the mountains, in trees, and in buildings. They feed on fruits and submissively follow Allah's path. Honey comes from their bellies which is therapeutic for mankind. Truly, there is a sign here for people who reflect.*

16:70 *Allah creates you and causes you to die, and some of you will be brought back to the worst part of life so that after attaining knowledge, they do not know anything. Allah is knowing and powerful.*

16:71 *Allah has given more of His gifts of material things to some rather than others. In the same manner, those who have more do not give an equal share to their slaves so that they would share equally. Would they then deny the favors of Allah?*

16:72 *Allah has given you wives from among your own people and sons and grandsons from your wives. He has given you many good things. Do they believe in lies and deny the grace of Allah? The others they worship besides Allah do not have the ability to provide anything in the heavens and the earth and have no power at all. Do not make likenesses of what you think Allah looks like. Allah knows and you do not.*

16:75 *Allah gives you a parable. One man is a slave to another; he has no power. Another man has received many favors from Allah, and he spends from his wealth secretly and openly. Are the two men equal? Praise be to Allah. However, most do not understand. Allah gives another parable of* two men. One man is dumb with no power. He is a tiresome burden to his master; no good comes from anything he is directed to do. Is he equal to the man who commands justice and walks the right path?

16:77 *The mysteries of the heavens and the earth belong to Allah. The decision of the Hour of Judgment is as fast as the blink of an eye or even quicker. Allah has power over all things. Allah has brought you from your mother's womb knowing nothing and has given you hearing, sight, intelligence, and emotions so that you may give thanks.*

16:79 *Do they not look at the birds poised in mid-air? Nothing holds them up except Allah. Truly there are signs here for people who believe.*

16:80 *Allah has given you houses to live in and has given you the hides of animals so you may make tents, which you may carry with you on journeys. And He has given you their wool, fur, and hair, which you make useful and comfortable things from.*

16:81 *Allah has given you shelter from the sun and has given you mountain retreats and garments that ward off the cold and armor that protects against violence. He does this to complete his favor to you so that you may submit to His Will.*

42:1 *HA. MIM. AIN. SIN. KAF. Allah sends inspiration to you as He did to those before you. He is mighty and wise. All that is in the heavens and all that is in the earth is His. He is the High, the Great.*

42:5 *The heavens are almost split apart while the angels celebrate praise of their Lord and ask forgiveness for those on earth. Allah is indulgent and merciful. But those who take protectors besides Him—Allah watches them, but you have no charge over them.*

42:7 *So We have revealed to you an Arabic Koran so that you may warn the mother-city [Mecca] and all around it, and warn them of that day of the gathering, of which there is no doubt, when some will be in Paradise and some in the Flame.*

42:8 *If Allah had desired, He could have made them one people and of one creed, but He brings whom He will into His mercy. As for the evildoers, they will have no friend or helper. Have they taken other patrons than Him? Allah is the protecting friend. He gives life to the dead, and He is mighty over all things.*

42:10 *Whatever your differences may be, the decision rests with Allah. This is Allah, my Lord. I trust in Him and turn to Him. He is the Creator of the heavens and of the earth, and He gave you mates from among yourselves and mates for cattle, too. This is how He multiplies you. There is nothing else like Him. He is the hearer and the seer. He holds the keys of the heavens and of the earth. He gives open-handedly or He gives sparingly to whomever He desires. He knows all things.*

1283 One of the chiefs of a visiting tribe was taken with the power of Mohammed. He said, "By Allah, if I could take this man from the Quraysh, I could eat up the Arabs with him." He asked Mohammed, "If I give allegiance to you and Allah gives you victory over your enemies, will we have authority over you?" Mohammed replied that Allah gave authority where he pleased. The chief said back, "So we protect you with our arms and lives and you will reap the benefit! Thanks, but no thanks."

THE BEGINNING OF POWER AND JIHAD IN MEDINA

Medina was about a ten-day journey from Mecca, but since ancient times the Medinans had come to Mecca for the fairs. Medina was half Jewish and half Arabian, and there was an ongoing tension between the two. The Jews worked as farmers and craftsmen and were literate. They were the wealthy class, but their power was slowly waning. In times past the Arabs had raided and stolen from the Jews who retaliated by saying that one day a prophet would come and lead them to victory over the Arabs. In spite of the tensions, the Arab tribe of Khazraj were allies with them.

1286 So when the members of the Khazraj met Mohammed, they said among themselves, "This is the prophet the Jews spoke of. Let us join ranks with him before the Jews do." They became Muslims, and their tribe was rancorous and divided. They hoped that Islam could unite them, and soon every house in Medina had heard of Islam.

1289 The next year when the Medinan Muslims returned to Mecca, they took an oath to Mohammed. They returned to Medina, and soon many of Medinans submitted to Islam.

1294 At the next fair in Mecca, many of the new Muslims from Medina showed up. During the early part of the night about seventy of them left the caravan to meet with Mohammed. He recited the Koran and said, "I invite your allegiance on the basis that you protect me as you would your children." The Medinans gave their oath. After the oath, one of them asked about their now severed ties to the Jews of Medina. If they helped Mohammed with arms and they were successful would he go back to Mecca? Mohammed smiled and said, "No, blood is blood, and blood not to be paid for is blood not to be paid for." Blood revenge and its obligation were common to them. "I will war against them that war against you and be at peace with those at peace with you."

1299 One of the Medinans said to those who made the pledge, "Do you realize to what your are committing yourselves in pledging your support to this man? It is war against all. If you think that if you lose your property and your best are killed, and then you would give him up, then quit now.

But if you think that you will be loyal to your oath if you lose your property and your best are killed, then take him, for it will profit you now and in Paradise." They asked what they would receive for their oath, Mohammed promised them Paradise. They all shook hands on the deal.

1301 In the morning the leaders of the Quraysh came to the caravan. They had heard that the Medinans had come to invite Mohammed to Medina and had pledged themselves to war against the Quraysh. The Quraysh wanted no part of war with the Medinans. Those Medinans in the caravan who were not Muslims were puzzled by all of this since they had no idea about the pledge in the night.

The Koran is clear that the proper relationship between humanity and Allah is fear.

> 39:8 *When trouble touches a man, he cries to his Lord and repents, yet no sooner does He grant a favor than he forgets what he cried for and praises other gods than Allah and misleads others from Allah's path. Say: Enjoy your ungratefulness for a little while for surely you will be a companion to the Fire.*
>
> 39:9 *Is he equal to an unbeliever who worships devoutly in the hours of the night, prostrate or standing in devotion, mindful of the life to come, and hoping for the mercy of his Lord? Say: Are those who know equal with those who do not know? Only men of understanding will take the warning.*
>
> 39:10 *Say: Oh, My servants who believe, fear your Lord. For those who do good in this world, good awaits. Allah's earth is spacious. Those who are patient will be rewarded in full measure.*
>
> 39:11 *Say: I am commanded that I serve Allah with sincere devotion. I am commanded to be the first of those who submit. Say: If I should disobey my Lord, I fear the penalty of a grievous day. Say: I serve Allah being sincere in my obedience.*
>
> 39:15 *Worship what you will besides Him. Say: The losers will be those who will lose their own souls and their families on the day of resurrection. Surely, this is a clear loss. They will be covered by Fire from above and below. With this Allah stirs fear in His servants, so fear Me, My servants.*

1304 Back in Medina the Muslims now practiced their new religion openly. But most of the Arabs still practiced their ancient tribal religions. The Muslims would desecrate the old shrines and ritual objects. They would even break into houses and steal the ritual objects and throw them into the latrines. On one occasion they killed a dog and tied the dog's body to the ritual object and thew it into the latrine.

THE OPENING WORDS OF WAR

1313 Up to now the main tension in the division in the Quraysh tribe over the new religion had been resolved by words. Curses and insults had been exchanged. Mohammed condemned the ancient religion and customs on an almost daily basis. The Quraysh had mocked Mohammed and abused lower class converts. What blood had been drawn had been in the equivalent of a brawl. Dust had been thrown, but no real violence. No one had died.

IMMIGRATION

1314 The Muslim Medinans had pledged Mohammed support in war and to help the Muslims from Mecca. The Muslims in Mecca left and went to Medina. The Muslims from both Mecca and Medina were about to be tested.

> 29:1 ELIF. LAM. MIM. Do men think that they will be left alone when they say, "We believe," and that they will not be tested? We tested those who lived before them, so Allah will surely know who is sincere and who is false. Do the ones who work evil think that they will escape Us? Their judgment is evil.
>
> 29:5 Whoever hopes to meet Allah, the set time will surely come. He hears and knows. Whoever makes efforts for the faith makes them for his own good only. Allah is independent of His creatures. As for those who believe and do good works, We will blot out all evil from them, and We will reward them according to their best actions.
>
> 29:8 We have commanded that men show kindness to their parents, but if they try to make you worship others besides Me, do not obey them. You will all return to Me, and I will tell you what you did. And those who believe and do the things that are right, We will admit them to the company of the righteous.
>
> 29:10 Some men say, "We believe in Allah," yet when they meet with sufferings in the cause of Allah, they regard trouble from man as if it were the wrath of Allah. If help comes from Allah, they are sure to say, "We were on your side!" Does Allah not know what is in the hearts of His creatures? Yes, and Allah knows those who believe, and He well knows the hypocrites.

THE KORAN OF MEDINA

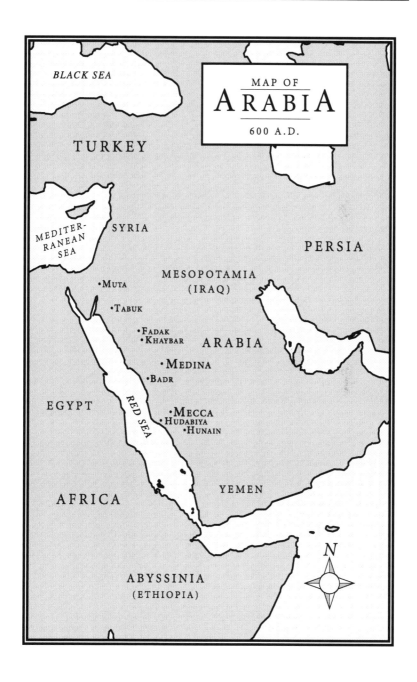

BLACK SEA

MAP OF
ARABIA
600 A.D.

TURKEY

MEDITER-
RANEAN
SEA

SYRIA

PERSIA

MESOPOTAMIA
(IRAQ)

•MUTA

•TABUK

•FADAK
•KHAYBAR

ARABIA

•MEDINA
•BADR

EGYPT

RED SEA

•MECCA
•HUDABIYA
•HUNAIN

AFRICA

YEMEN

N

ABYSSINIA
(ETHIOPIA)

THE HYPOCRITES

CHAPTER 7

47:33 Believers! Obey Allah and the messenger,
and do not let your effort be in vain.

THE HYPOCRITES

1351 Before Mohammed arrived, the Arabs who practiced their ancient religions were content with their religion and tolerant of others. Many Arabs became Muslims due to a pressure to join Islam. But in secret they were hypocrites who allied themselves with the Jews because they thought Mohammed was deluded.

1365 The Koran gives an analogy about the hypocrites:

> 2:8 And some of the people [the Jews] say, "We believe in Allah and the Day," although they do not really believe. They wish to deceive Allah and His believers, but they fool no one but themselves although they do not know it. Their hearts are diseased, and Allah has increased their suffering. They will suffer an excruciating doom because of their lies.
>
> 2:11 And when they are told, "Do not make evil in the earth," they say, "We are only trying to make peace." But they truly are the evil-doers even though they do not realize it. When it is said to them, "Believe as others have believed," they say, "Should we believe as the fools believe?" They are the fools, if only they knew it! And when they meet with the faithful they say, "We believe too." But when they are alone with their fellow devils [Jews and Christians] they say, "Really, we are with you. We were only mocking them." Allah will throw their mockery back on them and leave them to wander alone in their blindness.

1355 One of the Medinans became a Muslim and later began to doubt the truth of Mohammed and said, "If this man is right, we are worse than donkeys." His best friend had converted and told Mohammed of his friend's doubts. Allegiance to Islam comes before family, nation, or friend. When Mohammed confronted him about his remarks and doubts, he denied it. The Koran's comments:

> 9:74 They swear by Allah that they said nothing wrong, yet they spoke blasphemy, and some Muslims became unbelievers. They planned what they could not carry out [a plan against Mohammed], and only

disapproved of it because Allah and His Messenger had enriched them by His bounty [the resistance to Mohammed decreased when the money from the spoils of war came into the Medinan economy]. If they repent, it will be better for them, but if they fall back into their sin, Allah will afflict them with a painful doom in this world and the next. On earth, they will have neither friend nor protector.

1356 Ironically, the friend who reported the doubts to Mohammed later turned against him, killed two Muslims during battle, and fled to Mecca. Mohammed ordered him killed, but he escaped. Again the Koran says:

3:86 *How will Allah guide the people who fall into disbelief after having been believers and having acknowledged the messenger as true and after having received clear signs? Allah does not guide those that do evil. As for these, they will receive Allah's curse, as well as the curse of His angels and of all mankind, and they will live under it forever. Their punishment will not be lightened nor will they be forgiven except for those who repent and change their ways. Allah is forgiving and merciful.*

1357 Mohammed used to say about one of the hypocrites that he had the same face as Satan. The man used to sit and listen to Mohammed and then take back to the hypocrites what he said. He said of Mohammed, "Mohammed is all ears. If anyone tells him anything, he will believe it." The Koran speaks of him and other hypocrites:

9:61 *There are some of them who injure the Messenger and say, "He is only a hearer." Say: He is a hearer of good for you. He believes in Allah and believes in the faithful. He is a mercy to those of you who believe, but those who injure the Messenger of Allah will suffer a painful doom. They swear to you by Allah to please you, but Allah and His Messenger are worthier, so they should please Him if they are believers.*
9:63 *Do they not know that whoever opposes Allah and His Messenger will abide in the Fire of Hell, where they will remain forever? This is the great shame.*
9:64 *The hypocrites are afraid that a sura [chapter] would be sent down about them telling plainly what is in their hearts. Say: Go on mocking, but Allah will bring to light all that you fear.*

1358 One of the hypocrites excused his criticism by saying that he was only talking and jesting. No criticism was too small to be unnoticed.

9:65 *If you ask them, they will surely say, "We were only talking idly and jesting." Say: Do you mock Allah, His signs, and His Messenger? Make no excuse. You have rejected faith after you accepted it. If we forgive some of you, we will punish others because they are evildoers. Hypocritical men and women have an understanding with one another. They command what is evil, forbid what is just, and do not pay the poor tax. They have forgotten Allah, and He has forgotten them. The hypocrites are the rebellious wrongdoers. Allah promises the hypocritical men and women and the unbelievers the Fire of Hell, and they will abide there; it is enough for them. Allah has cursed them, and an eternal torment will be theirs.*

1365 The hypocrites change their faces depending upon who they are with. When they are with the Muslims, they believe. But when they are with the evil ones (the Jews) they say they are with the Jews. It is the Jews who order them to deny the truth and contradict Mohammed.

2:16 *It is these who have bought error at the price of guidance. Their purchase is profitless, and they have lost the right direction. They are like the ones who lit a fire, and when it shed its light all around them, Allah took it away and left them in total darkness where they were unable to see. Deaf, dumb and blind, they will never turn back to the right path.*

2:19 *Or like the ones who, standing beneath a storm cloud dark with thunder and lightning, put their fingers in their ears to keep out the sound, fearing death. Allah surrounds the unbelievers. The lightning nearly takes their sight away. Each time the lightning flashes on them, they walk around, but when the darkness comes, they stand still. If Allah willed it, He could destroy their hearing and sight because Allah has power over everything.*

The Koran argues against the hypocrites.

57:12 *The day will come when you will see true believers, men and women, with their light stretching out before them and on their right hands, and they will hear it said to them, "Good news comes to you today of Gardens watered by flowing rivers where you will live forever." This is the ultimate victory!*

57:13 *On that day the hypocritical men and women will say to the believers, "Wait for us so that we kindle our lights from yours," but they will say to them, "Go back and find your own light!" A wall with a gate will be in between them, and those receiving mercy will be on the inside, and those on the outside in front of it will receive the torment of Hell. They will cry out to them and say, "Were we not with you?" and they will reply, "Yes, but you allowed yourselves to be led into temptation, you hesitated, and you doubted. Your lowly desires deceived you until Allah's punishment arrived. The deceiver tricked you about Allah. No ransom will be accepted from you today or from the faithless. The Fire will be your home for that is the proper place for you, and a wretched doom it is!*

Not all Muslims in Mecca left for Medina. They were to have the same fate as the hypocrites.

4:97 *When the angels take the souls of the unbelievers back [Muslims in Mecca who did not immigrate with Mohammed and reverted to their native religions. These unbelievers fought against Mohammed at Badr], they will ask, "What have you been doing?" The unbelievers will reply, "We were weak and oppressed in the earth." The angels will say, "Was Allah's earth not big enough for you to flee and seek asylum in?" It will be these who will have Hell as their home and a terrible journey to it.*

4:98 *As for the men, women, and children who were too weak to escape and were not shown the way, Allah will forgive them, for Allah is forgiving and gracious.*

4:138 *Warn the hypocrites that torturous punishment awaits them. The hypocrites take unbelievers as friends rather than believers. Do they look for honor at their hands? Truly all honor belongs to Allah.*

4:140 *He has already sent down to you in the Book that when you hear Allah's revelations rejected and mocked by unbelievers you should not sit and listen to them until they talk about something else, for if you stayed you would become like them. Truly Allah will gather all the hypocrites and unbelievers together in Hell. These are the ones who watch you closely, and if you are successful they say, "Did not we stand with you?" And if the unbelievers are successful they say, "Did we not gain power over you, and did we not defend you from the believers?" Allah will judge between the two of you on the Day of Resurrection, and Allah will not allow the unbelievers to be victorious over the believers.*

4:142 *The hypocrites wish to deceive Allah, but He will deceive them. When they stand for prayer, they rise slowly so as to be seen by others, and they hardly remember Allah. They go back and forth being neither a part of one group or the other. You will not be able to guide anyone Allah leads astray.*

4:145 *The hypocrites will be thrown into the lowest abyss of the Fire, and there will be no one to help them. Except for those who ask for forgiveness and change their ways, who hold tightly to Allah and are sincere in their dedication to Allah, they will be counted with the believers, and Allah will give the believers a great reward. Why should Allah inflict punishment on you if you are grateful and believe? Allah will reward you for your works, for He knows all things.*

4:148 *Allah does not love harsh words to be spoken in public, unless by someone who has been wronged. Allah is all-hearing and all-knowing. Whether you do good in public or in private, whether you pardon a wrong, truly Allah is forgiving and all-powerful!*

THE JEWS

CHAPTER 8

9:63 Do they not know that whoever opposes Allah
and His Messenger will abide in the Fire of Hell, where
they will remain forever? This is the great shame.

When Mohammed came to Medina about half the town were Jews. There were three tribes of Jews and two tribes of Arabs. Almost none of the Jews had Hebrew names. They were Arabs to some degree. At the same time many of the Arabs' religious practice had elements of Judaism. The Jews were farmers and tradesmen and lived in their own fortified quarters. In general they were better educated and more prosperous than the Arabs.

Before Mohammed arrived, there had been bad blood and killing among the tribes. The last battle had been fought by the two Arab tribes, but each of the Jewish tribes had joined the battle with their particular Arab allies. In addition to that tension between the two Arab tribes, there was a tension between the Jews and the Arabs. The division of the Jews and fighting on different sides was condemned by Mohammed. The Torah preached that the Jews should be unified, and they failed in this.

All of these quarrelsome tribal relationships were one reason that Mohammed was invited to Medina. But the result was further polarization, not unity. The new split was between Islam and those Arabs and their Jewish partners who resisted Islam.

I351 About this time, the leaders of the Jews spoke out against Mohammed. The rabbis began to ask him difficult questions. Doubts and questions about his doctrine were about Allah. Doubts about Allah were evil. However, two of the Jewish Arabs joined with Mohammed as Muslims. They believed him when he said that he was the prophet that came to fulfill the Torah.

THE REAL TORAH IS IN THE KORAN

Mohammed said repeatedly that the Jews and Christians corrupted their sacred texts in order to conceal the fact that he was prophesied in their scriptures. The stories in the Koran are similar to those of the Jew's scriptures, but they make different points. In the Koran, all of the stories found in Jewish scripture indicated that Allah destroyed those cultures that did not listen to their messengers. According to Mohammed, the scriptures of the Jews have been changed to hide the fact that Islam is the true religion.

1364 But the Jews did not believe that Mohammed was a prophet. As a result, they are in error and cursed by Allah. And by denying his prophethood they conspired against him and Islam.

1367 Mohammed is the final prophet. His coming was in the original Torah. Allah has blessed the Jews and protected them and now they refuse to believe the final and perfect prophet. The Jews are not ignorant, but deceitful. The Jews know the truth of Mohammed and cover the truth and hide the truth with lies.

> 2:6 *As for the unbelievers, whether you warn them or not, they will not believe. Their hearts and ears are sealed up by Allah, and their eyes are covered as well. There will be a dreadful doom awaiting them.*

> 2:40 *Children of Israel! Remember the favor I have given you, and keep your covenant with Me. I will keep My covenant with you. Fear My power. Believe in what I reveal [the Koran], which confirms your Scriptures, and do not be the first to disbelieve it. Do not part with My revelations for a petty price. Fear Me alone. Do not mix up the truth with lies or knowingly hide the truth [Mohammed said the Jews hid their scriptures that foretold Mohammed would be the final prophet]. Be committed to your prayers, give to charity regularly, and bow down with those who bow down. Would you instruct others to be righteous and forget to attend to your own duties? You read the Scriptures! Do you not have sense? Seek guidance with patience and prayer; this is indeed a hard duty, but not for the humble who remember that they will have to meet their Lord and will return to Him.*

1367 The Koran repeats the many favors that Allah has done for the Jews—they were the chosen people, delivered from slavery under the pharaoh, given the sacred Torah and all they have ever done is to sin. They have been forgiven many times by Allah, and still, they are as hard as rocks and refuse to believe Mohammed. They have perverted the Torah after understanding it.

> 2:75 *Can you believers then hope that the Jews will believe you even though they heard the Word of Allah and purposefully altered it [Mohammed said the Jews hid their scriptures that foretold Mohammed would be the final prophet] after they understood its meaning? And when they are among the believers they say, "We believe too," but when they are alone with one another they say, "Will you tell them what Allah has revealed to you so that they can argue with you about it in the presence of your Lord?" Do you not*

have any sense? Do they not realize that Allah knows what they hide as well as what they reveal?

2:78 *There are illiterate people among them who do not know the Scriptures but only lies and unclear conjectures. Wretchedness will come to those who write their own scriptures and then claim, "This is from Allah," so that they can sell it for a pitiful price. They will have a mournful fate because of what they have written and for what they have earned by their actions.*

2:80 *And they say, "The Fire will not touch us except for a few days." Say: Did you receive such a promise from Allah because Allah will not break his promise, or do you merely speak of Allah what you do not know? Surely those who do evil and become surrounded by sin will be prisoners of the Fire where they will live forever. Those who believe and do good deeds are the rightful owners of the Garden where they will live forever.*

1369 The Jews' sins are so great that Allah has changed them into apes. Still they will not learn and refuse to admit that Mohammed is their prophet. They know full well the truth and hide and confuse others. Even when they say to Mohammed they believe, they conceal their resistance.

2:63 *And remember, Children of Israel, when We made a covenant with you and raised Mount Sinai before you saying, "Hold tightly to what We have revealed to you and keep it in mind so that you may guard against evil." But then you turned away, and if it had not been for Allah's grace and mercy, you surely would have been among the lost. And you know those among you who sinned on the Sabbath. We said to them, "You will be transformed into despised apes." So we used them as a warning to their people and to the following generations, as well as a lesson for the Allah-fearing.*

1370 The Jews have understood the truth of Mohammed and then changed their scriptures to avoid admitting that Mohammed is right.

5:59 *Say: Oh, people of the Book [Jews and Christians], do you not reject us only because we believe in Allah, in what He has sent down to us, in what He has sent before us, and because most of you are wrongdoers? Say: Can I tell you of retribution worse than this that awaits them with Allah? It is for those who incurred the curse of Allah and His anger; those whom He changed into apes [Jews] and swine [Christians]; those who worship evil are in a worse place, and have gone far astray from the right path.*

5:61 *When they presented themselves to you, they said, "We believe," but they came as unbelievers to you, and as unbelievers they left. Allah well knew what they concealed. You will see many of them striving with one another to hurry sin, to exceed limits, and to eat unlawful things. What they do is evil. Why do their doctors and rabbis not forbid them from the* habit of uttering wickedness and eating unlawful food? Certainly, their works are evil.

5:64 *The Jews say, "The hand of Allah is chained up." Their own hands will be chained up [on the Last Day, the Jews will have their right hand chained to their necks], and they will be cursed for what they say. No, both His hands are outstretched. He bestows His gifts at His own pleasure. That which has been sent down to you from your Lord will surely increase the rebellion and unbelief of many of them. We have put animosity and hatred between them that will last until Resurrection Day. Every time they kindle a fire for war, Allah will extinguish it. Their aim will be to assist mischief on the earth, but Allah does not love those who assist mischief.*

5:65 *If only the people of the Scriptures [Jews and Christians] will believe and guard against evil, we will surely take their sins away from them and will bring them into Gardens of delight. If they will observe the Law and the Gospel and what was sent down to them from their Lord, they will surely be nourished from above them and from beneath their feet. Some of them are on the right course, but many of them do evil.*

5:67 *Oh, Messenger, deliver what has been sent down to you from your Lord. If you do not, you will not have delivered His message. Allah will protect you from evil men, for Allah does not guide unbelievers. Say: Oh, people of the Book [Jews and Christians], you have no ground to stand on until you observe the Law and the Gospel and that which was sent down to you from your Lord. The Book [the Koran] that was sent down from your Lord will certainly increase the rebellion and unbelief of many of them, but do not be grieved for the unbelievers.*

5:69 *Those who believe and those who are Jews, Sabers [unknown, but perhaps a sect of Christians in Iraq], and Christians–whoever believes in Allah and in the last day–does what is right. They will have no fear, nor will they be put to grief.*

5:70 *We made the covenant of old with the Children of Israel, and We sent messengers to them. Whenever there was a messenger with news that they did not desire, they became rebellious, and some of them they treated as liars, and some they killed. They thought no harm would come of it, so they became blind and deaf. Then Allah turned to them in mercy. Then again many of them became blind and deaf, but Allah sees what they do.*

2:174 *Those [the Jews] who conceal any part of the Scriptures which Allah has revealed in order to gain a small profit shall ingest nothing but Fire in their stomachs. Allah will not speak to them on the Day of Resurrection, and they will pay a painful penalty. They are the ones who buy error at the price of guidance and torture at the price of forgiveness; how intently they seek the Fire!*

MOHAMMED TRULY FOLLOWS THE RELIGION OF ABRAHAM

1381 Christians and Jews argued with Mohammed that if he wished to have salvation, then he would have to convert. But Mohammed is the one who truly follows the religion of Abraham. Mohammed is the true Jew with the true Torah.

> 2:135 *They say, "Become a Christian or a Jew, and you will be rightly guided to salvation." Say: No! We follow the religion of Abraham, the upright, and he was no idol worshiper. Say: We believe in Allah and in that which has been revealed to us, and to Abraham, Ishmael, Isaac, Jacob, and the tribes, and in that given to Moses and Jesus and all other messengers by our Lord. We make no distinction between any of them, and we bow down to Allah.*
> 2:137 *If they believe as you do, they will be on the right path, but if they turn against it, they are only cutting themselves off from you, and Allah will be a more than adequate defender against them. He is all-hearing and all-knowing. We take on Allah's own dye. And who has a better dye than Allah? It is Him we worship.*
> 2:139 *Say: Will you [the Jews] argue with us about Allah, knowing that He is both your Lord and ours? We are responsible for our actions as you are for yours, and we are devoted to Him alone. Will you say, "Truly Abraham, Ishmael, Isaac, Jacob, and the tribes, were all either Jews or Christians"? Say: Do you know best, or does Allah? Who is more evil than one who receives a testimony from Allah and hides it? Allah is never unaware of what you do. Those are a people who have passed away. They have received what they deserved and you will receive what you deserve. You will not be asked to answer for what they did.*

1383 Mohammed entered a Jewish school and called the Jews to Islam. One asked him, "What is your religion, Mohammed?"

"The religion of Abraham."

"But Abraham was a Jew."

"Then let the Torah judge between us." He meant the Torah of the Koran.

> 3:66 *Abraham was neither a Jew nor a Christian, but a righteous man, a Muslim, not an idol worshiper. Doubtless the ones who follow Abraham are the closest to him, along with this messenger and the believers. Allah is protector of the faithful. Some of the People of the Book try to lead you astray, but they only mislead themselves, although they may not realize it.*
> 3:70 *People of the Book [Jews and Christians]! Why do you reject Allah's revelations when you have witnessed their truth? People of the Book! Why do you cover up the truth with lies when you know that you hide the truth?*

1397 Three Jews came to Mohammed and said, "Do you not allege that you follow the religion of Abraham and believe in the Torah which we have and testify that it is the truth from Allah?" He replied, "Certainly, but you have sinned and broken the covenant contained therein and concealed what you were ordered to make plain to men. I disassociate myself from your sin [the Jews' concealing the part of the Torah that prophesied the coming of Ahmed (a variation of the name Mohammed)]".

1399 Jews came to Mohammed and said, "Is it true that what you have brought to us is from Allah? For our part we cannot see that it is arranged as the Torah is." He replied, "You know quite well that it is from Allah. You will find it written in the Torah which you have." By this he meant the real Torah that they concealed.

AN OMINOUS CHANGE

1381 In Mecca Mohammed spoke well of the Jews, who were very few. In Medina there were many Jews and his relations were tense. Up to now Mohammed had lead prayer in the direction of Jerusalem. Now the kiblah, direction of prayer, was changed to the Kabah in Mecca. Some of the Jews came to him and asked why he had changed the direction of prayer. After all, he said that he followed the religion of Abraham. The Koran responded:

> 2:142 *The foolish ones will say, "What makes them turn from the kiblah [the direction they faced during Islamic prayer]?" Say: Both the east and the west belong to Allah. He will guide whom He likes to the right path. We have made you [Muslims] the best of nations so that you can be witnesses over the world and so that the messenger may be a witness for you. We appointed the former kiblah towards Jerusalem and now Mecca so that We could identify the messenger's true followers and those who would turn their backs on him. It was truly a hard test, but not for those whom Allah guided. It was not Allah's purpose that your faith should be in vain, for Allah is full of pity and merciful toward mankind. We have seen you [Mohammed] turn your face to every part of Heaven for guidance, and now We will have you turn to a kiblah that pleases you. So turn your face towards the direction of the sacred Mosque, and wherever the believers are, they will turn their faces toward it. The People of the Book know that this is the truth from their Lord, and Allah is not unaware of what they do. Even if you were to give the People of the Book [Jews] every sign, they would not accept your kiblah, nor would you accept theirs. None of them will accept the kiblah of the others. If you should follow their way after receiving the knowledge you possess, then you will certainly be a part of the unrighteous.*

2:146 *Those to whom we gave the Scriptures know Our messenger as they do their own sons [Jews who were secretly convinced of the truth of Mohammed], although some of them knowingly conceal the truth. This is the truth from your Lord; therefore, do not doubt it at all.*

1382 Mohammed summoned the Jews to Islam and made it attractive and warned them of Allah's punishment and vengeance. The Jews said that they would follow the religion of their fathers. The Koran:

2:168 *All people! Eat that which is lawful and wholesome in the earth and do not follow Satan's footsteps for he is your declared enemy. He commands you to commit evil and shameful acts and urges you say words about Allah when you know nothing. When it is said to them, "Follow what Allah has revealed," they say, "No, we follow the practices of our ancestors." What? Even though their ancestors were ignorant and without guidance? The unbelievers can be compared to animals who only respond to a shout or a cry. They are deaf, dumb, and blind, understanding nothing.*

Since Islam is the successor to Judaism, Allah was the successor to Jehovah. It was actually Allah who had been the deity of the Jews and the Jews had deliberately hidden this fact by corrupted scriptures. For this the Jews will be cursed.

2:159 *Those who conceal the clear signs and guidance [Mohammed said that the Jews corrupted the Scriptures that predicted his prophecy] that We have sent down after We have made them clear in the Scriptures for mankind, will receive Allah's curse and the curse of those who damn them. But for those who repent, change their ways, and proclaim the truth, I will relent. I am relenting and merciful. Those who reject Me and die unbelievers will receive the curse of Allah and of the angels and of mankind. They will remain under the curse forever with no lightening of their punishment and no reprieve. Your Allah is the one god. There is no god but Him. He is compassionate and merciful.*

62:5 *Those to whom the Torah [the first five books of the Old Testament] was given and do not follow it can be compared to a donkey who is made to carry a load of books but is unable to understand them. Those who reject Allah's revelations are a sorry example. Allah does not guide those who do wrong.*
62:6 *Say: You Jews! If you believe that you are Allah's favorite people, set apart, then wish that you will die if you are telling the truth! But they will never wish to die because of their previous actions that have been sent on before them. Allah knows the evil-doers.*

62:8 *Say: The death from which you flee will certainly find you, and then you will return to the knower of things done in secret and in the open, and He will tell you everything you have ever done.*

4:44 *Have you not thought about those [Jews] to whom a part of the Scripture was given? They buy error for themselves and wish to see you go astray from the right path. But Allah knows your enemies best. Allah is sufficient as your protector, and Allah is sufficient as your helper. Some among the Jews take words out of the context of the Scriptures and say, "We have heard, and we disobey. We hear as one who does not hear. Look at us!" in this way twisting the phrase and defiling the faith. But if they said, "We hear and obey. Hear us and look at us!" it would be better for them and more righteous. But Allah has cursed them for their disbelief; only a few of them have faith!*

4:47 *To those of you [Jews and Christians] to whom the Scriptures were given: Believe in what We have sent down confirming the Scriptures you already possess before We destroy your faces and twist your heads around backwards, or curse you as We did those [the Jews] who broke the Sabbath, for Allah's commandments will be carried out.*

THE CHRISTIANS

CHAPTER 9

*33:21 You have an excellent example in Allah's Messenger
for those of you who put your hope in Allah and the
Last Day and who praise Allah continually.*

1404 While some Christians were in Medina, they argued religion with Mohammed. They held forth with the doctrine of the Trinity and the divinity of Christ. Mohammed later laid out the Islamic doctrine of the Christian doctrine. The Koran tells in detail the real story of Jesus, who is just another of Allah's prophets, and that the Trinity of the Christians is Allah, Jesus and Mary.

1406 No one has power except through Allah. Allah gave the prophet Jesus the power of raising the dead, healing the sick, making birds of clay and having them fly away. Allah gave Jesus these signs as a mark of his being a prophet. But Allah did not give the powers of appointing kings, the ability to change night to day. These lacks of power show that Jesus was a man, not part of a Trinity. If he were part of God, then all powers would have been in his command. Then he would not have to have been under the dominion of kings.

> 3:20 *If they argue with you, then say: I have surrendered myself entirely to Allah, as have my followers. Say to the People of the Book and to the ignorant: "Do you surrender to Allah?" If they become Muslims, then they will be guided to the right path, but if they reject it, then your job is only to warn them. Allah watches over all His servants.*
> 3:21 *Warn those who do not believe in Allah's revelations, and who unjustly kill the messengers and those who teach justice, of the excruciating punishment they will receive. Their works will be meaningless in this world and in the world to come, and they will have no one to help them!*
> 3:23 *Consider those who have received part of the Scriptures. When they are called to accept the Book of Allah, some of them turn away and are opposed to it. This is because they say, "We will only have to endure the Fire for a few days." They have created their own lies regarding their religion. How will they react when We gather them together on the assured day, and every soul will receive what it has earned, and they will not be dealt with unjustly?*

3:26 *Say: Allah! Lord of heaven and earth, you give power to whom you choose and take it away from whom you chose. You lift up whom you choose, and You bring down whom you choose. All that is good lies within your hand. You have power to do all things. You cause the night to turn into day, and the day to turn into night. You bring the living out of the dead, and the dead out of the living, and You give generously to whom you please.*

I407-8 Christ spoke in the cradle and then spoke to men as a grown man. Speaking from the cradle is a sign of his being a prophet. Christ's prophethood was confirmed by making clay birds fly. By Allah Christ healed the blind, the lepers, and raised the dead.

5:109 *One day Allah will assemble the messengers and say, "What response did you receive from mankind?" They will say, "We have no knowledge. You are the knower of secrets." Then Allah will say, "Oh Jesus, Son of Mary, remember my favor to you and your mother when I strengthened you with the Holy Spirit [Gabriel] so that you would speak to men alike in childhood and when grown. I taught you the Scripture, wisdom, the Torah, and the Gospel, and you created the figure of a bird with clay, by my permission, and breathed into it. With My permission it became a bird. You also healed the blind and the leper, with My permission. With My permission you raised the dead. I restrained the Children of Israel from harming you when you went to them with clear signs, and the unbelievers said, "This is nothing but plain sorcery."*
5:111 *When I revealed to the disciples, "Believe in Me and the One I sent," they said, "We believe and bear witness to You that we are Muslims."*

I408 Christ only comes through Allah. Christ's signs of being a prophet come only from Allah. Jesus enjoins others to worship Allah, not him. But people refused to hear him, the Disciples came forth to help him with his mission. The Disciples were servants of Allah and were Muslims just like Christ.

3:44 *This is one of the secret revelations revealed to you, Mohammed. You were not there when they cast their lots to see who would have guardianship of Mary, nor were you there when they argued about her. And remember when the angels said to Mary, "Allah brings you good news of His Word. His name will be Messiah, Jesus, Son of Mary, worthy of honor in this world and the world to come, one who is near to Allah. He will speak to the people when in the cradle and as a man. He will live a righteous life." She said, "My Lord! How can I have a son when no man has ever touched me?" He said, "It will be so. Allah creates what He will, and when He decrees a plan, all He must do is say, 'Be' and it is!" Allah will teach him the Scriptures and Wisdom, the Law, and the Gospel. He will be sent out as a messenger to the Children of Israel saying, "I have come to you with a sign from your Lord. I will make a figure of a bird out of clay and then, by Allah's will, I will breathe life into it. By Allah's permission I cause the blind to see, heal the lepers, and bring the dead back to life. I will tell you what you should eat and what you should store up in your houses. This will be a sign for those who truly believe. I have come to fulfill the Law which came before me and to give you permission to do certain things which were once unlawful. I come to you with a sign from your Lord, so fear Allah and obey me. Allah is my Lord and yours, so worship Him. That is the right path."*

3:52 When Jesus saw that they did not believe, he said, "Who will be my helpers for Allah?" The disciples replied, "We will be Allah's helpers! We believe in Allah and witness our submission to Him. Lord! We believe in what you have revealed and we follow Your messenger; therefore, record us as Your witnesses."

1409 Christ was not crucified. When the Jews plotted against Christ, they found Allah to be the best plotter. Allah took Jesus up directly to him and will refute those who say he was crucified and was resurrected. On the final day, the Day of Resurrection, those who follow Christ but do not believe in his divinity will be blessed. Those who insist that Christ is God, part of the Trinity, and reject true faith will be punished in Hell.

3:54 So the Jews plotted and Allah plotted, but Allah is the best of plotters. And Allah said, "Jesus! I am going to end your life on earth and lift you up to Me. [Jesus did not die on the cross. He was taken to Allah. He will return to kill the anti-Christ and then die a natural death.] I will send the unbelievers away from you and lift up those who believe above all others until the Day of Resurrection. Then all will return to Me and I will judge their disputes. As for the unbelievers, they will be punished with excruciating agony in this world and the world to come. They will have no one to help them. As for the believers who do good works, He will fully reward them. Allah does not love those who do wrong. These signs and this wise warning We bring to you."

3:59 Truly, Jesus is like Adam [neither had a father] in Allah's sight. He created him from the dust and said to him, "Be!" and he was.

Although the Koran says less about Christians than Jews, it does address them.

4:171 People of the Book [Christians]! Do not overstep the boundaries of your religion and speak only what is true about Allah. The Messiah, Jesus, the son of Mary, is only Allah's messenger and his Word which he sent into Mary was a spirit from Him. Therefore, believe in Allah and His messengers and do not say, "Trinity." Hold back and it will be better for you. Allah is only one god. Far be it from Allah to have a son! All in the heavens and earth are His. Allah is sufficient as a protector. The Messiah does not condescend to be Allah's servant, nor do His favored angels. Those who disdain service to Him, and are filled with arrogance, Allah will gather them all together before Him.

61:6 *And remember when Jesus, son of Mary, said, "Children of Israel! I am Allah's messenger sent to confirm the Law which was already revealed to you and to bring good news of a messenger who will come after me whose name will be Ahmad." [Ahmad was one of Mohammed's names. This quote of Jesus is not found in any Christian scriptures.] Yet when he [Mohammed] came to them with clear signs, they said, "This is merely sorcery!" And who is more evil than the one who, when called to submit to Islam, makes up a lie about Allah? Allah does not guide the evil-doers! They wish to put out Allah's light with their mouths, but as much as the unbelievers hate it, Allah will perfect His light.*

61:9 *It is He who has sent forth His messenger with guidance and the true religion so that, though the idolaters hate it, He will make His religion victorious over all the others.*

5:112 *Remember when the disciples said, "Oh Jesus, Son of Mary, is your Lord able to send down a table to us spread with food from heaven?" He said, "Fear Allah if you are believers." They said, "We desire to eat from it, to satisfy hearts, to know that you have spoken the truth to us, and to be witnesses to the miracle." Jesus, Son of Mary, said, "Oh Allah, our Lord, send down a table spread with food from heaven that it will become a recurring festival from the first of us and to the last of us, and a sign from You, and do nourish us, for You are the best provider." Allah said, "I will send it down to you, but whoever among you disbelieves after that, I will surely inflict a punishment on him unlike any I have inflicted on any other creature."*

5:116 *And when Allah says, "Oh Jesus, Son of Mary, did you say to mankind, 'Take me and my mother as two gods, beside Allah?'" He will say, "Glory be unto You. It is not for me to say what I had no right to say. If I had said that, You would have known it. You know what is in my heart. I do not know what is in Your heart. You know all that is hidden. I only said what You commanded me to say, 'Worship Allah, my Lord and your Lord,' and I was a witness of their actions while I was among them. When You caused me to die, You watched them, and You are witness of all things. If You punish them, they are Your servants, and if You forgive them, You are mighty and wise."*

5:119 *Allah will say, "This day the truth will profit the truthful. They will have Gardens beneath which the rivers flow, and they will remain there forever." Allah is well-pleased with them and they with Him. This shall be the great bliss. Allah's is the sovereignty of the heavens and of the earth and of all that they contain. He is able to do all things.*

The Koran often uses the term People of the Book. At the time of Mohammed there were no books in Arabic. The written Arabic was used mostly for business. Since both Christianity and Judaism used religious texts this was distinctive. The term People of the Book can refer to either Jews, Christians, or both Jews and Christians. While in Medina Mohammed spoke of Allah's problems with the People of the Book.

> 4:53 *Should those who would fail to give even a penny to their fellow man have a share in the kingdom? Do they envy the people for what they have received from Allah's bounty? We gave the Scriptures and wisdom to the children of Abraham, and a grand kingdom. Some of them believe in His Messenger while others turn away from him. The flames of Hell are sufficient punishment for them! Those who reject Our revelations We will cast into the Fire. As soon as their skins are burnt away, We will give them new skins so that they will truly experience the torment. Truly Allah is mighty and wise!*
>
> 4:57 *But as for those who believe and do good works, We will lead them into the Gardens, watered by flowing rivers, where they will live forever; there they will be married to pure spouses, and We will lead them into the cool shade.*
>
> 3:64 *Say: People of the Book [Christians and Jews]! Let us settle upon an agreement: We will worship no one except Allah, we will set up no one as His equal, and none of us will take one from among us as a lord besides Allah. If they reject your proposal say, "Bear witness then that we are Muslims."*
>
> 3:65 *People of the Book! Why do you argue about Abraham [whether Abraham was a Jew or Christian] when the Law and the Gospel were not sent down until after him? Do you not understand? Listen, you are the ones who have argued about things of which you have some knowledge [arguments about Moses and Jesus], so then why do you argue about things of which you have no knowledge? Allah has knowledge, but you do not.*

OTHER RELIGIONS

CHAPTER 10

*4:69 Those who obey Allah and His Messenger will live
with the messengers and the saints and the martyrs
and the righteous. What wonderful company!*

The Koran condemns all religions that were not Islam.

4:116 Allah will not forgive those who worship idols, but He will forgive those He pleases for all other sins. Those who worship gods other than Allah have strayed into grievous error. Rather than calling on Him, they call upon female gods, and they pray to nothing but Satan, the rebel. Allah has cursed Satan because he said, "I will tempt a number of your servants and lead them astray and will arouse vain desires in them and command them to slit the ears of the cattle [a religious ritual for sacrificial animals]. I will command them to spoil Allah's creation [tattoos, scarification, piercing, etc.]." Whoever chooses Satan as a protector rather than Allah is ruined and beyond forgiveness.

4:120 Satan makes promises and stirs up vain desires within them, but he makes promises only to trick them. These will make their home in Hell, and they will not be able to escape it.

4:122 But those who believe and do good works, We will lead them into the Gardens beneath which rivers flow, where they will live forever. This is Allah's promise, and whose words hold more truth than His? This will not be according to your desires, nor to the desires of the People of the Book [Jews and Christians]. Those who do evil will be paid back with evil and will find no one but Allah to protect or help them. As for the believers who do good works, whether man or woman, they will enter Paradise, and they will not be treated unjustly in the least.

4:125 And whose religion is better than those who submit themselves to Allah, do good, and follow the faith of Abraham, the righteous? For Allah Himself took Abraham as a friend. All that is in the heavens and earth belongs to Allah; Allah surrounds all things.

The unbelievers, the Christians, Jews and pagans will burn forever in the fire of Hell.

98:1 The unbelievers among the People of the Book [Jews and Christians] and the idolaters did not turn away from their unbelief until the proof came to them in a messenger from Allah reading holy pages containing true scriptures. The People of the Book did not become divided until after the clear proof had come to them.

98:5 *And they were commanded nothing more than to serve Allah, worshiping none other than Him, being pure in their faith, being steadfast in their prayers, and paying the zakat [the poor tax]. For this is the true religion.*

98:6 *The unbelievers among the People of the Book and the idolaters will burn for eternity in the Fire of Hell. Of all the created beings, they are the most despicable. As for those who believe and do good works, they are the most noble of all created beings.*

98:8 *Their reward is with their Lord, in the Gardens of Paradise, beneath which are flowing rivers. They will live forever. Allah takes pleasure in them, and they take pleasure in Him. In this way those who fear Allah will be rewarded.*

22:1 *People, fear your Lord, for the earthquake of the Hour of will truly be a dreadful thing.*

22:2 *On that day, every nursing mother will abandon her infant, every woman who is pregnant will abort her burden, and you will see people staggering around as if they are drunk, even though they are not. Allah's wrath will be powerful upon them.*

22:3 *Among the people there are those who [Abu Jahl], in ignorance, argue about Allah and follow every rebellious devil. It is decreed that whoever takes him as a friend will be led astray, and they will be led to the torment of the Fire.*

22:5 *You people, if you are in doubt about the resurrection, remember how We created you from the dust, then from sperm, then from clots of blood, and then from pieces of flesh, both shaped and shapeless so that We may prove Our power to you. We cause you to remain in the womb for an appointed period; then We bring you forth as infants so that you may grow to maturity. There are some of you who die young, and others who live to be so old that they forget all they ever knew. And you have seen the earth parched and lifeless, but as soon as We send down rain, life begins to stir and swell, bringing forth every kind of luxuriant herb.*

22:7 *And undoubtedly the hour will come when Allah will raise all of those who are in the grave to life. And among the people there are some who argue about Allah without knowledge, guidance, or the illuminating scriptures. They turn away in contempt and lead others away from Allah's path. They will be disgraced in this world, and on the resurrection day they will be made to taste the torment of the Fire. And We will say to them, "This is what your misdeeds have earned you, for Allah is not unfair to His servants."*

22:11 *And there are some who say they serve Allah, yet they stand on the periphery of faith. If they are blessed with good fortune, they are satisfied with it, but when trials come upon them, they turn away in infidelity giving up this world and the world to come. That is a clear loss. They call upon gods that can neither harm them nor help them. This is a grievous sin. They call upon him who would rather harm them than help them. Truly evil is both the master and the friend.*

22:14 *But Allah will lead those who believe and do good works into Gardens watered by flowing rivers. Allah completes all that He plans.*

22:15 *If anyone thinks that Allah will not make His Messenger victorious in this world and the world to come, let them tie a rope to the ceiling of his house and hang himself with it. Then let him see if that course of action remedies his anger. We have sent down the Koran containing clear signs. Allah guides whom He pleases.*

Throughout history Allah has punished all cultures and civilizations who did not do what their prophets said.

64:1 *All that is in the heavens and in the earth give praise to Allah. The entire kingdom and all glory are His. He has power over all things.*

64:2 *It was He who created you, and although some of you are unbelievers and others believers, He sees everything you do. He created the heavens and the earth to reveal the truth. He created you and gave you your beautiful shape. All will return to Him.*

64:4 *He knows everything that is in the heavens and earth. He knows all that you hide and all that you make known. Allah knows all your deepest secrets.*

64:5 *Have you not heard of what happened to the unbelievers who came before you? They experienced the evil consequences of their actions, and a terrible punishment still awaits them. This is because when messengers came to them with clear signs they said, "Will simple humans be our guides?" So they rejected the message and turned away. Allah does not need them. Allah is self-sufficient and worthy of praise.*

64:7 *The unbelievers think that they will not be raised to life on the Day of Judgment. Say: Yes, you will be raised by my Lord, and you will be informed of everything you have ever done! That is easy for Allah. Therefore, believe in Allah and His messenger and in the light which we have sent down to you. Allah knows all your actions.*

64:9 *That day when He will gather you all together for a Day of Assembly, that will be a day of cheating. The believers will cheat the unbelievers out of their place in Paradise. Those who believe in Allah and do what is right, He will take away all their sins and lead them into the Gardens watered by flowing rivers, where they will live forever. This is the ultimate reward. But the unbelievers, those who reject Our revelations, will be prisoners of the Fire, where they will live forever. A torturous end!*

The Koran gives proof of Allah:

2:258 *Have you not remembered the one [Nimrod] who argued with Abraham about his Lord because Allah had given him power? Abraham said, "My Lord is the one who gives life and causes death." The other said, "I too have the power of life and death." "Allah causes the sun to rise in the east," Abraham said, "You make it rise in the west, then." The unbeliever was bewildered. Allah does not guide those who do evil.*

2:259 *Or remember the man [Esdras doubted that Jerusalem could be restored after its destruction by Nebuchadnezzar] who passed by a ruined and abandoned city and said, "How will Allah ever bring life to this city now that it is dead?" So then Allah caused him to die, and one hundred years later raised him back to life. "How long have you waited?" Allah asked him. He said, "A day, or part of a day." Allah said, "No, you have been gone a hundred years, but look at your food and drink which show no signs of having aged, and look at your donkey. And so We may use you as an example for mankind, see how We fix your bones and cover them with flesh." And when he [Esdras] realized what had happened to him he said, "I now know that Allah has the power to do all things."*

3:189 *All that is in the heavens and the earth belongs to Allah. Allah holds power over everything. In the creation of the heavens and the earth and in the changing of day to night, there are clear signs for those who are wise. Those who remember Allah when they stand, sit, and lie down, and reflect upon the creation of the heavens and earth say, "Lord! You have not made this creation in vain. All glory to You! Keep us from the torture of the Fire. My Lord! Surely those whom you cast into the Fire will be eternally shamed. The evil-doers will have no one to help them."*

3:193 *Lord! We have heard the voice of the one calling us to the true faith saying, "Believe in your Lord," and we have obeyed him. Lord! Forgive us of our sins and cleanse us of our evil deeds and cause us to die with the righteous. Lord! Give us that which Your messengers promised us, and keep us from shame on the Day of Resurrection. Truly, You never break your promise."*

Allah gave encouragement to Mohammed in his labors.

33:1 *Messenger! Fear Allah and do not listen to the unbelievers and hypocrites. Truly Allah is all-knowing and wise. Follow that which is revealed to you from your Lord, for Allah knows all that you do, and trust in Allah. Allah is sufficient as your protector.*

Allah changes His revelations when needed.

2:106 *Whatever of Our revelations We repeal or cause to be forgotten, We will replace with something superior or comparable. [There are as many as 225 verses of the Koran that are canceled by later verses. This is called abrogation.] Do you not know that Allah has power over all things? Do you not know that Allah reigns sovereign over the heavens and earth and besides Him you have no protector or helper?*

The Koran teaches more about the world of the jinns and magic.

2:102 They followed what the evil ones read against the kingdom of Solomon. It was not Solomon who was an unbeliever, but the evil ones teaching people sorcery and that which was revealed in Babylon to the angels Harut and Marut [The angels Harut and Marut were sent down from heaven to be tempted. They sinned and will be punished on Judgment Day. Until then they teach magic]. But neither of them instructed the people without first saying, "Truly we are only sent to tempt you; therefore, do not become disbelievers." And from the two angels they learned how to create animosity between husbands and wives, although they cannot cause harm unless it is Allah's will, and they learned what would harm them and what did not benefit them. And surely they know that those who bought into the sorcery would have no part in the life to come! And the price for which they sold their souls was vile; if they had only known! If they had kept their faith and guarded against evil, their reward from Allah would certainly have been better, if they had only realized!

PREACHING

Mohammed began to preach the religion of Islam to the Medinans just as he had the Meccans.

8:21 The vilest creatures in Allah's sight are the ones who are deaf, dumb, and without sense. If Allah had recognized any potential in them, He would have given them the ability to hear. Even if He makes them hear, they would still turn their backs and deny the faith. Believers! Answer the call of Allah and His messenger which gives you life. Know that Allah comes between a person and his own heart and that you all will be gathered to Him. Protect yourselves from sinning because it will not only be the unbelievers who will face temptation. Allah is severe in His punishment.

3:101 Believers! Fear Allah as He deserves to be feared! When death finds you, die as true Muslims.
3:103 Hold firmly to Allah's rope [the Koran] and do not be divided among you. And remember Allah's goodness to you, how when you were enemies He joined your hearts together in love so that through His grace you became like brothers. And when you were on the brink of the pit of Fire, He saved you. It is in this way that Allah makes His signs clear to you so you will find the right path. Let there be a group formed from among you who

calls for goodness, commands justice, and forbids what is wrong. These are the ones who will be victorious.

57:16 *Has not the time come for those who believe to submit to Allah's warning and to the truth He has sent down? This is so they will not be like those who came before and to whom the Scriptures were given, whose lives were prolonged but their hearts hardened, and many of them were evil-doers. Know that Allah gives life to the earth after it is dead. Now We have made Our signs clear to you so that you will understand.*

57:18 *Those who give to charity, whether they are men or women, and those who loan generously to Allah, will be paid back double what they have given. They will receive a noble reward.*

57:19 *Those who believe in Allah and His messenger are truthful ones who will testify [against the unbelievers] before the presence of their Lord. They will receive their reward and their light, but those who deny Allah will be the prisoners of Hell.*

57:20 *Know that the life of this world is only a game and an amusement, a show and vain boasting among you! The quest for more wealth and more children can be compared to the plants which spring up after the rain. Their growth makes the man rejoice, but soon they will whither and turn yellow becoming dry and crumbling away. In the world to come, either a terrible punishment or forgiveness and reward awaits you. The life of this world is only a fleeting joy.*

57:21 *Therefore, urge one another on in seeking forgiveness from your Lord and in earning admittance into a Paradise as vast as the heavens and earth prepared for those who believe in Allah and His messengers. That is the grace of Allah, and He gives it to whom He pleases. Allah's grace is boundless.*

57:22 *Every disaster that happens to the earth, or to yourselves, was preordained before We caused it to occur. Truly that is easy for Allah so that you will not grieve over good things that have passed you by or be overly joyous at the good you have received. Allah does not love the boastful, the arrogant, nor those who are selfish with their wealth and urge others to be the same. And those who turn away from Allah's path should know that Allah is self-sufficient, praiseworthy.*

57:25 *We have sent Our messengers with clear signs, and We have caused the Scriptures and the balance of justice to come down through them. We have sent down iron with its strength for war as well as its many other uses for mankind so that Allah would know those who would help Him and His messengers, although unseen. Allah is powerful and mighty.*

60:2 *If they have the upper hand of you, they will prove your enemies. They will stretch out their hands and tongues to hurt you and will desire that you reject the truth. Neither your kindred nor your children will be of profit to you on the Last Day. He will sever the connections between you. Allah sees your actions.*

60:4 *There is a good example in Abraham of those who followed him when they said to their people, "We are clear of you and of what you worship besides Allah. We renounce you, and between us a hatred and hostility has sprung up forever until you believe in Allah alone." Do not imitate the language of Abraham to his father, "I will pray for your forgiveness, but I will obtain nothing for you from Allah." Oh, our Lord, in You we trust, to You we repent, and to You we will return at last.*

60:5 *Oh, our Lord, do not make us a trial for those who disbelieve, but forgive us, Lord, for you are the mighty and wise. There is in them a good example for all who hope in Allah and in the Last Day. If any turn away, Allah is truly rich and praiseworthy. Allah will, perhaps, establish good will between yourselves and those whom you take to be your enemies. Allah is powerful, gracious, and merciful.*

5:55 *Your protectors are Allah and His Messenger and those who believe, who observe regular prayer and regular charity, and who bow in worship. And whoever takes Allah, His Messenger, and those who believe for friends, they truly are the people of Allah and must be triumphant. Oh, you who believe, do not take those who have received the Scriptures [Jews and Christians] before you, who have scoffed and jested at your religion, or who are unbelievers for your friends. Fear Allah if you are true believers. When you call to prayer, they make it a mockery and a joke. This is because they are a people who do not understand.*

The Koran extols the virtues and qualities of Allah.

2:255 *Allah! There is no god but Him, the living-one, the everlasting. He is not overtaken by slumber or sleep. All things in heaven and earth belong to Him. Who can intervene with Him except as He permits it? He knows what was before mankind and what is after them. They can only understand what He chooses for them to understand. His throne encompasses the heavens and the earth, and the preservation of them both does not tire Him. He is the most high, the great.*

64:11 *Nothing unfortunate occurs unless Allah wills it. Whoever believes in Allah, He will guide his heart. Allah knows all things. So obey Allah and His messenger. But if you turn your backs to them, Our messenger is not to blame, for his duty is only to deliver Our warning clearly. Allah! There is no god but Him! Let the faithful put their trust in Allah.*

62:1 *All that is in the heavens and earth sings the praises of Allah, the supreme Lord, the holy, the mighty, and the wise.*

62:2 *He sent to the people of Mecca a messenger from among their own to reveal His revelations to them, to make them pure, and to teach the*

Scriptures and wisdom, although before now they were clearly in error as well as the others among them who have not yet accepted the faith. He is the mighty and the wise! That is the grace of Allah; He gives it to whom He pleases. His grace is boundless.

3:1 *ELIF. LAM. MIM. There is no god except Him, the living, the eternal. He has sent down to you the Scriptures with the truth, which confirm the scriptures which came before it. And He has already sent down the Law of Moses and the Gospel of Jesus to guide mankind and to show them the difference between good and evil.*
3:4 *Those who reject Allah's revelations will receive severe punishment. Allah is mighty, Lord of revenge. Nothing in the earth or in heaven is hidden to Him. It is He who forms you in your mothers' wombs according to His pleasure. There is no god except Him, the mighty, the wise!*

JIHAD, WAR AGAINST ALL

CHAPTER 11

*4:42 On that day, the unbelievers and those who disobeyed
the Messenger will wish they could sink into the earth
for they cannot hide a single thing from Allah.*

In Mecca, Mohammed had divided the community into Islam and
those of the native Arabic religions. In Mecca he adopted all the classical
Jewish stories to prove his prophesy and spoke well of the Jews. But there
were almost no Jews living in Mecca, and therefore, no one to differ with
him.

In Medina half of the population were Jews, who let Mohammed know
that they disagreed with him. So in Medina, Mohammed argued with Jews
as well as the non-Muslim Arabs. Even though there were very few in the
town who were Christian, Mohammed argued against them as well. All
non-Muslims were verbally attacked in Medina.

I415 It was thirteen years after he started preaching and one to two years
after going to Medina that Mohammed prepared for war as commanded
by Allah. He would fight his enemies, those who were not Muslims.

JIHAD—THE FIRST KILLING

I416-423 Mohammed sent forth his fighters on seven armed raids to find
the trade caravans headed to Mecca.

I423-4 Mohammed sent Abdullah out with eight men. A caravan of the
Quraysh passed by the Muslims as they overlooked the road from a rise.
The caravan was loaded with leather and raisins. When the Quraysh saw
them they were scared because they had slept not too far from here, but
one of the Muslims had a shaved head. Now a shaved head was a mark
of pilgrim so the Quraysh felt better. They were safe. They were also in a
sacred month when weapons were not carried.

I425 The Muslims took council. They were in a dilemma. If they attacked the caravan now, they would be killing in a sacred month. Luckily,
the sacred month ended today and tomorrow there would be no taboo
about killing. But there was another problem. By tonight they would be in
the sacred area of Mecca. In the sanctified area, there could never be any

killing. They hesitated and talked about what to do. They decided to go ahead and kill as many as possible today and take their goods.

1425 Islam drew first blood against the Quraysh of Mecca. They attacked the unarmed men. Amr was killed by an arrow. He was the first man to be killed in jihad. One man escaped and they captured two prisoners. They took their camels with their goods and headed back to Mohammed in Medina. On the way they talked about how Mohammed would get one fifth of the stolen goods, spoils.

1425 When they got back, Mohammed said that he did not order them to attack in the sacred month. So he held the caravan and the two prisoners in suspense and refused to do anything with the goods or prisoners. The prisoners said, "Mohammed has violated the sacred month, shed blood therein, stolen goods and taken prisoners." But the Koran said:

> 2:216 *You are commanded to fight although you dislike it. You may hate something that is good for you, and love something that is bad for you. Allah knows and you do not. When they ask you about fighting in the holy month, say: Fighting at this time is a serious offense, but it is worse in Allah's eyes to deny others the path to Him, to disbelieve in Him, and to drive His worshipers out of the Sacred Mosque. Idolatry is a greater sin than murder. They will not stop fighting you until you turn away from your religion. But any of you who renounce your faith and die an unbeliever, will have your works count for nothing in this world and the world to come. These people will be prisoners of the Fire, where they will live forever.*

1426 To resist the doctrine of Islam and to try and persuade Muslims to drop their faith is worse than killing. Before Islam, the rule of justice in Arabia was a killing for a killing, but now to resist Islam was worse than murder. Those who argue against Islam and resist Islam can be killed as a sacred act. The spoils were distributed and a ransom set for the prisoners. The men who had killed and stolen were now concerned as to whether they would get their take of the spoils. So once again the Koran spoke:

> 2:218 *Those that have embraced the Faith, and those that have fled their land and fought for the cause of Allah, may hope for Allah's mercy. Allah is forgiving and merciful.*

1426 As Muslims who had been exiled and fought they were blessed by Allah. They received their spoils and Mohammed took his one fifth of the spoils of war.

> *You (Quraysh) count war in the holy month a grave matter*
> *But graver is your opposition to Mohammed and your unbelief.*
> *Though you defame us for killing Amr*

Our lances drank Amr's blood
We lit the flame of war. —Abu Bakr, the first caliph

FIGHTING IN ALLAH'S CAUSE—BADR

I428 Mohammed heard that Abu Sufyan was coming with a large caravan of thirty to forty Quraysh from Syria. Mohammed called the Muslims together and said, "Go out and attack it, perhaps Allah will give us the prey."

I428 As the caravan approached Medina, Abu Sufyan became worried and questioned every rider on the road about Mohammed. Then he heard intelligence that indeed Mohammed was going to attack. He sent out a fast rider to Mecca for aid.

I433 Mohammed and his men headed out of Medina for what was to prove to be one of the most important battles in all of history, a battle that would change the world forever.

I435 Mohammed was cheered. He said, "I see the enemy dead on the ground." They headed towards Badr where they camped near there for the night. He sent several scouts to the well at Badr and the scouts found two slaves with water camels. They felt sure they were from the Quraysh caravan and brought back them back to Mohammed. Two of Mohammed's men questioned them as Mohammed was nearby praying. The men replied that they were from the Quraysh. Mohammed's men began to beat them and torture the slaves as Mohammed prayed.

I436 Mohammed told his men that the slaves told them the truth until they started to beat and torture them. Then the slaves had lied but it had been the lie that they wanted to hear. Mohammed asked the men how many of the Quraysh there were and who were the leaders of the Quraysh. When they told him he was delighted and told his warriors that Mecca had sent their best men to be slaughtered.

I439-440 Both armies had an idea of the location of the other. Mohammed went ahead to chose a place to camp and set up for battle on the morrow.

I440-444 The Quraysh marched forth at daybreak. The battle started.

I445 Some arrows flew and one Muslim was killed. Mohammed addressed his army. "By Allah, every man who is slain this day by fighting with courage and advancing, not retreating, will enter Paradise." One of his men had been eating dates said, "You mean that there is nothing between me and Paradise except being killed by the Quraysh?" He flung the dates to the side, picked up his sword and set out to fight. He got his wish and was killed later.

1445 One of Mohammed's men asked what makes Allah laugh? Mohammed answered, "When he plunges into the midst of the enemy without armor." The man removed his coat of mail, picked up his sword and made ready to attack.

1445 Now the two armies started to close ranks and move forward. Mohammed had said that his warriors were not to start until he gave the order. Now he took a handful of pebbles and threw them at the Quraysh and said, "Curse those faces." The Muslims advanced. The battle had begun.

1451 As the battle wound down, Mohammed issued orders for the fighters to be on the look out for Abu Jahl, the enemy of Allah, among the slain. He was found still fighting in a thicket. A Muslim made for him and cut off his lower leg. Another Muslim passed by him as Abu Jahl lay dying and put his foot on his neck. The Muslim said, "Has Allah put you to shame, enemy of Allah?" Abu Jahl gasped, "How has He shamed me? Am I any more remarkable than any other you have killed?" The Muslim cut off his head.

1452 He took the head back to Mohammed and said, "Here is the head of the enemy of Allah" and threw it at Mohammed's feet. The Prophet said, "Praise be to Allah."

1455 As the bodies were dragged to a well, one of the Muslims saw the body of his father thrown in. He said, "My father was a virtuous, wise, kind, and cultured man. I had hoped he would become a Muslim. He died an unbeliever." His abode is hellfire forever. [Before Islam killing of kin and tribal brothers had been forbidden since the dawn of time. After Islam brother would kill brother and sons would kill their fathers. Fighting in Allah's cause—jihad.]

1454 The bodies of the Quraysh were thrown into a well. The Apostle of Allah leaned over the well and shouted at the bodies, "Oh people of the well, have you found what Allah promised to be true?" The Muslims were puzzled by his question. Mohammed explained that the dead could hear him.

1456 Now it was time to take the property from the dead who could no longer claim what had been theirs. It was now the spoils of jihad and the profit of Islam. Mohammed divided it equally among all who were there. He took one fifth for himself.

> 8:1 When they ask you about the spoils of war say: The spoils belong to Allah and His messenger. [This sura was written after the Battle of Badr.] Therefore, fear Allah and settle your arguments. Obey Allah and His messenger if you are truly believers.

I459 Off they set for Medina with the spoils of war and the prisoners to be ransomed. Except for one prisoner, who had spoken against Mohammed. He was brought in front of the Prophet to be killed and before the sword struck, he asked, "Who will care for my family?"

M230 The Prophet replied, "Hell!" After he fell dead, Mohammed said, "Unbeliever in Allah and his Prophet and his Book! I give thanks to Allah who has killed you and made my eyes satisfied."

I476 After the battle of Badr there came about an entire sura of the Koran. The eighth chapter is called War Treasure or Booty and also the Spoils of War. The idea of the battle of Badr was Mohammed's. Many of the Muslims had no desire to go to war. The armed Muslims wanted to attack the caravan, not the army.

I477 The Muslims were not alone. No, Allah sent a thousand angels to help kill those who worshiped in the ancient ways and rituals. To resist Mohammed was a death sentence from Allah. When a Muslim meets a non-Muslim in war, they should never turn their backs, except as a tactical maneuver. A Muslim fighting in Allah's cause must face the enemy. To not do so brings on the wrath of Allah and the judgment of Hell.

> 8:2 *The true believers are the ones whose hearts tremble with fear at the mention of Allah and whose faith grows stronger when His revelations are revealed to them and in Him they put their trust. True believers are dedicated to their prayers and give generously from that which We have given them. These are truly the believers. They will be raised up and receive forgiveness from their Lord, and they will receive generous provisions.*
>
> 8:5 *Remember how your Lord commanded you to leave your homes to fight for the truth, but some of the believers were opposed to it? They disputed the truth after you had revealed it, as if they were being led to certain death before their eyes.*
>
> 8:7 *And when Allah promised that you would defeat one of the two groups of enemies, you wished to attack the group that was defenseless. [Mohammed had started out to attack a large, unarmed Meccan caravan. But a thousand-man army from Mecca arrived to protect the caravan.] But Allah wished to justify the truth of His words and to cut the unbelievers down so that the truth would triumph and the lies would be shown false, much to the opposition of the guilty.*
>
> 8:9 *Remember when you begged your Lord for help and He said, "I will send the ranks of a thousand angels to your aid?" Allah gave this as a message of good news to bring them hope, for victory only comes from Allah. Allah is mighty and wise.*

8:11 *Remember when sleep overcame you, a sign of His reassurance? He sent down rain from the heavens to make you clean and to rid you of the grime of Satan, to strengthen your hearts and steady your feet. [The rain before the battle muddied the ground and hindered the Meccan cavalry.]*

8:12 *Then your Lord spoke to His angels and said, "I will be with you. Give strength to the believers. I will send terror into the unbelievers' hearts, cut off their heads and even the tips of their fingers!" This was because they opposed Allah and His messenger. Ones who oppose Allah and His messenger will be severely punished by Allah. We said, "This is for you! Taste it and know that the unbelievers will receive the torment of the Fire."*

8:15 *Believers! When you meet the unbelievers marching into battle, do not turn your back to them to retreat. Anyone who turns his back on them, unless it is for a tactical advantage or to join another company, will incur Allah's wrath and Hell will be his home, truly a tortuous end. It was not you, but Allah, that killed them. It was not you whose blows destroyed them, but Allah destroyed them so that He might give the believers a gift from Himself. Allah is all-hearing and all-knowing. Therefore, Allah will certainly thwart the plans of the unbelievers.*

8:19 *Meccans! If you sought a judgment, it has now come to you. If you cease in your persecution of the believers, it will be better for you, but if you continue in your war against the faithful, so will We continue to help them. Your vast forces will be no match for Us for Allah stands with the faithful.*

1478 When Mohammed speaks, a Muslim has only one choice. Listen and obey.

8:20 *Believers! Be obedient to Allah and His messenger, and do not turn your backs now that you know the truth. Do not be like the ones who say, "We hear," but do not obey.*

1480 If those who practice the old religions will submit to Islam then all will be forgiven. Only submission to Islam will save the unbeliever.

8:38 *Tell the unbelievers that if they change their ways, then they would be forgiven for their past. If, however, they continue to sin, let them remember the fate of those who came before them. Fight against them until they stop persecuting you, and Allah's religion reigns sovereign over all others. If they cease, Allah knows all they do, but if they turn their backs, know that Allah is your protector—an excellent helper.*

1481 After war and victory come, there are the spoils of war. One fifth is to go to the Apostle, Allah's prophet.

8:41 *Know that a fifth of all your spoils of war [the traditional cut for the leader was a fourth] belong to Allah, to His messenger, to the messenger's family, the orphans, and needy travelers. Sincerely believe in Allah and in what was sent down to you through His messenger on the day of victory when the two armies met. Allah is powerful over all things.*

The Koran shows how Allah helped the Muslims destroy the unbelievers.

8:42 *Remember when you were camped on the near side of the valley and the unbelievers were on the far side with the caravan below you? If you had made an agreement to meet in battle [against the caravan], you surely would have failed, but you went into battle [against the unbelievers army], nevertheless, so that Allah could accomplish his goal that those who were destined to die would die and so those who were meant to live would live. Allah hears and knows all.*

8:43 *Allah showed your enemies to you in a dream as an army few in number. If He had shown you a large army, you certainly would have been frightened and you would have had arguments among yourselves. But Allah spared you this for He knows your deepest secrets. And when you met them in battle, He made them appear to you as fewer in number than in reality so that Allah might carry out what had to be done. All things return to Allah.*

1482 In war (jihad) remember Allah all the time and you will prevail. Obey Mohammed, don't argue with him or each other. Don't quit, don't lose morale. Allah will see that you prevail. And when the unbelievers are slain, their troubles have just begun. Allah will use his angels to torture them forever.

8:45 *Believers! When you confront their army stand fast and pray to Allah without ceasing so that you will be victorious. Obey Allah and His messenger, and do not argue with one another for fear that you will lose courage and strength. Be patient for Allah is with the patient. Do not be like the Meccans who left home bragging and full of vainglory. They prevent others from following Allah's path, but Allah knows all that they do.*

8:48 *Satan made their sinful acts seem acceptable to them, and he said, "No one will defeat you this day, and I will be there to help you." When the two armies came within sight of one another, however, he quickly fled saying, "I am finished with you for I can see things which you cannot [the angels were helping to kill the unbelievers]. I fear Allah for Allah's punishment is severe."*

8:49 *The hypocrites [Muslims who were weak in their faith] and those with diseased hearts said, "Their religion has misled the Muslims." But those who have faith in Allah will discover that Allah is mighty and wise. If only you could witness the angels carrying off the unbelievers' souls! They slash their faces and backs saying, "Taste the torment of the Fire!"*

I483-4 Mohammed is to encourage war and lead the believers to war. With Allah 20 Muslims can kill and vanquish 200 of the non-Muslims. And 100 Muslims can destroy 1000 of the non-Muslims. The unbelievers are ignorant and easily defeated by jihad. Take no prisoners until Islam has made all submit. Forget the ransom and the money, submission of the non-believers is all that matters.

> 8:65 *Messenger! Call the faithful to fight. If there are among you twenty who will stand fast, they will overcome two hundred; and if there are a hundred of you, they will overcome a thousand unbelievers for they lack understanding. Allah has now lessened your burden because He knows that there is weakness in you. If there are among you a hundred men who will stand fast, they will overcome two hundred; and if there are a thousand among you, they will, by the permission of Allah, overcome two thousand. Allah is with the steadfast.*
>
> 8:67 *A prophet should not take prisoners of war until he has fought and slaughtered in the land. You desire the bounty of the world, but Allah desires the bounty for you of the world to come. Allah is mighty and wise. If there had not been a prior command from Allah, you would have been punished severely for what you had taken. But now enjoy the spoils you have taken, which are lawful and good, but fear Allah. Allah is forgiving and merciful.*

THE RAID ON THE TRIBE OF B. SULAYM

I540-543,T1365 Seven days after Mohammed returned from Badr, there were four more armed raids, but no contact with the enemy, the unbelievers.

I484 Mohammed was now a political force unlike any ever seen in history. The fusion of religion and politics with a universal mandate created a historic force that is permanent. There will be no peace until all the world is Islam. The spoils of war will provide the wealth of Islam. The awe of Mohammed is the fear of Allah.

> B1, 7, 331[1] *The Prophet said, "I have been given five things which were not given to anyone else before me.*
> *1. Allah made me victorious by awe, by His frightening my enemies for a distance of one month's journey.*
> *2. The earth has been made for me and for my followers a place for praying and to perform my rituals, therefore anyone of my followers can pray wherever the time of a prayer is due.*

1. The reference is to Bukhari's Hadith

3. The spoils of war has been made Halal (lawful) for me yet it was not lawful for anyone else before me.

4. I have been given the right of intercession on the Day of Resurrection.

5. Every Prophet used to be sent to his nation but only I have been sent to all mankind.

Mohammed left Mecca as a preacher and prophet. He entered Medina with about 150 Muslim converts. After a year in Medina there were about 250-300 Muslims and most of them were very poor. After the battle of Badr, a new Islam emerged. Mohammed rode out of Medina as a politician and general. Islam became an armed political force with a religious motivation, jihad.

JIHAD AND THE KORAN

CHAPTER 12

4:115 *Anyone who opposes the Messenger after having
received Our guidance and follows a path other than
that of the true believer will be left to their own devices.
We will lead them into Hell, an evil home.*

The Koran uses the term "fighting in Allah's cause" for jihad.

2:190 *And fight for Allah's cause [jihad] against those who fight you, but do
not be the first to attack. Allah does not love the aggressors.*

2:191 *Kill them wherever you find them, and drive them out of whatever
place from which they have driven you out, for persecution [the Meccans
made Mohammed leave] is worse than murder. But do not fight them inside the Holy Mosque unless they attack you there; if they do, then kill
them. That is the reward for the unbelievers, but if they give up their ways,
Allah is forgiving and merciful.*

2:193 *Fight them until you are no longer persecuted and the religion of Allah reigns absolute, but if they give up, then only fight the evil-doers. The
defilement of a sacred month and sacred things are subject to the laws of
retaliation. If anyone attacks you, attack him in the same way. Fear Allah
and know that He is with those who believe.*

2:195 *Spend your wealth generously for Allah's cause [jihad] and do not
use your own hands to contribute to your destruction. Do good, for surely
Allah loves those that do good.*

2:244 *Fight for Allah's cause [jihad] and remember that He hears and knows
everything.*

2:245 *Who will lend Allah a generous loan, which He will pay back multiple
times? Allah gives generously and takes away, and you will return to Him.*

2:246 *Have you not considered what the leaders of the Children of Israel
said to one of their messengers when Moses died? They said, "Appoint a
king for us, and we will fight for the cause of Allah." He said, "What if
you decline to fight when ordered to do so?" They said, "Why would we
not fight for Allah when we and our children have been driven out of our
homes?" But in the end, when they were ordered to fight all but a few refused. Allah knows the evil-doers.*

2:261 *Those who give their wealth for Allah's cause are like the grain of
corn that grows seven ears with each ear having one hundred kernels.*

Allah will multiply the wealth of those He pleases. Allah is caring and all-knowing. Those who give their wealth for Allah's cause [jihad] and do not follow their gifts with guilt-inducing comments or insults will be rewarded by their Lord. They will have nothing about which to fear or grieve.

8:59 *Do not let the unbelievers think that they will escape Us. They have no power to escape. Gather against them all of your armed forces and cavalry so that you may strike terror into the hearts of the enemies of Allah and your enemy, and others besides them whom you do not know but whom Allah knows. All that you give for Allah's cause [jihad] will be repaid. You will be treated with fairness.*

8:70 *Messenger! Tell the captives who are under your control, "If Allah finds good in your hearts [if the prisoners convert to Islam], He will give you something better than that which has been taken away from you, and He will show you forgiveness. Truly, Allah is forgiving and merciful." If, however, they plot to betray you, know that they have already betrayed Allah. He has therefore given you power over them. Allah is all-knowing and wise.*
8:72 *Truly, those who believe and have left their homes and have given of their wealth and lives for Allah's cause, and those who have taken them in and helped them, will be as close as family to each other. But those who believed but did not leave their homes, you are not beholden to them until they also go into exile. But if they seek your help on account of the faith, it is your duty to help them except those against whom you have a treaty. Allah knows all that you do.*
8:73 *The unbelievers give comfort and protection to each other, therefore, if you do not do the same for one another, there will be oppression in the land and widespread corruption.*
8:74 *Those who have believed and have left their homes and fought for Allah's cause [jihad], and those who have taken them in and given them help, they are the true believers. They will receive mercy and generous provisions. Those who have believed and left their homes to fight with you since then, they are also a part of your family. According to Allah those who are related to you by blood are the closest to you. Allah knows all things.*

47:1 *Those who deny Allah and prevent others from following Allah's path, He will make their plans fail. Those who believe and do good works, however, and believe in what Mohammed has revealed, as it is the truth sent down from their Lord, He will cleanse them of their sins and improve their circumstances.*
47:3 *This is because the unbelievers follow lies while the believers follow the truth sent down from their Lord. It is in this manner that Allah sets forth the rules of conduct for mankind.*

47:4 *When you encounter the unbelievers on the battlefield, cut off their heads until you have thoroughly defeated them and then take the prisoners and tie them up firmly. Afterward, either allow them to go free or let them pay you their ransom until the war is over. This you are commanded. If it had been Allah's will he would have taken out His vengeance upon them, but He has commanded this so that He may test you by using these others. As for those who are killed for Allah's cause [jihad], He will not let their sacrifice be in vain. He will lead them into Paradise, of which He has told them.*

47:7 *Believers! If you help Allah's cause [jihad], Allah will help you and make you stand firm. But as for those who deny Allah, they will be destroyed. He will make their plans fail because they have rejected His revelations. He will thwart their tactics.*

47:34 *Believers! Obey Allah and the messenger, and do not let your effort be in vain. Those who do not believe and who prevent others from following Allah's path and then die as unbelievers will not receive Allah's forgiveness. Therefore, do not be weak and offer the unbelievers peace when you have the upper hand, for Allah is with you and will not begrudge you the reward of your deeds.*

47:34 *Those who do not believe and who prevent others from following Allah's path and then die as unbelievers will not receive Allah's forgiveness. Therefore, do not be weak and offer the unbelievers peace when you have the upper hand for Allah is with you and will not begrudge you the reward of your deeds.*

47:36 *Truly this present life is only for play and amusement, but if you believe and fear Him, He will give you your reward and will not ask you to give up your worldly wealth. But if He were to ask you for all of it and strongly urge you, you would become greedy, and this would reveal your hatred.*

47:38 *You are called upon to give to Allah's cause [jihad], but some of you are greedy. Whoever of you acts miserly does so only at the expense of his own soul. Truly, Allah has no use for you, but you have need for Him. If you turn your backs on Him, He will simply replace you with others who will not act like you!*

61:1 *All that is in the heavens and earth gives praise to Allah for He is mighty and wise.*

61:2 *Believers! Why do you say you do things that you never actually do? [At the battle of Uhud, some who had pledged courage fled and failed to fight.] It is most hateful in Allah's sight when you say one thing and yet do another.*

61:4 *Truly Allah loves those who fight for His cause and stand together in battle array like a solid wall.*

61:5 Remember when Moses said to his people, "My People, why do you try to persecute me when you know that Allah has sent me to you?" So when they went astray, Allah allowed their hearts to wander for Allah will not guide evil-doers.

57:10 And for what reason should you not give to Allah's cause [jihad], when the heavens and earth are Allah's inheritance alone? Those of you who gave to the cause before the victory and fought will receive a greater reward than those who gave and fought after it. But Allah has promised a good reward to all of you. Allah knows all that you do. Who will loan generously to Allah? He will pay him back double what he is owed, and he will receive a noble reward.

4:91 You will also find others who seek to gain your confidence as well as that of their own people. Every time they are thrown back into temptation, they fall into it deeply. If they do not keep away from you or offer you peace or withdraw their hostilities, then seize them and kill them wherever they are. We give you complete authority over them.

4:94 Believers! When you travel abroad to fight for Allah's cause [jihad], be discerning, and do not say to everyone who greets you, "You are not a believer," only seeking the fleeting joys of this world [by killing the unbeliever and taking their property]. With Allah are abundant joys. You too were like them before Allah granted His grace to you. Therefore, be perceptive; Allah knows all that you do.

4:95 Believers who stay at home in safety, other than those who are disabled, are not equal to those who fight with their wealth and their lives for Allah's cause [jihad]. Allah has ranked those who fight earnestly with their wealth and lives above those who stay at home. Allah has promised good things to all, but those who fight for Him will receive a far greater reward than those who have not. They will be conferred ranks especially from Him, along with forgiveness and mercy, for Allah is forgiving and merciful.

22:39 Those who have been attacked are given permission to fight because they have been persecuted, and surely Allah is able to make them victorious. There are some who have been driven out of their homes unjustly just because they said, "Allah is our Lord." If Allah had not repelled some men by using others [war], the monasteries, churches, synagogues, and mosques, in which Allah's name is praised, would have been destroyed. But surely Allah will help those who help Him in His cause. Allah is strong and mighty. Allah will surely help those who, once we establish them as leaders in the land, pray regularly and pay the poor tax and command what is right and forbid what is wrong. And the final outcome of all things is in Allah's hands.

22:58 *Those who fled their homes for Allah's cause [jihad] and were killed or died as a result, surely Allah will provide for them generously, for Allah is the best provider. Allah will certainly lead them in with a pleasing welcome. Allah is all-knowing and gracious. So it will be. Whoever retaliates with the same force with which he was wronged and continues to be oppressed, Allah will help him. Allah is merciful and forgiving.*

22:78 *Fight valiantly for Allah's cause [jihad] as it benefits you to do for Him. He has chosen you, and has not made hardships for you in the religion; it is the religion of your father Abraham. It was Allah who called you Muslims, both in previous scriptures and now, so that the Messenger may be a witness for you and that you may be his witness against mankind. Therefore, pray regularly, pay the poor tax, and hold firmly to Allah, for He is your protector. He is the best protector and the best helper.*

9:19 *Do you compare him who gives drink to the pilgrims and who visits the Sacred Temple to him who believes in Allah and the Last Day and strives hard in Allah's cause [jihad]? They are not equal in the sight of Allah, and He does not guide the unrighteous.*
9:20 *They who have believed, have fled their homes, and have striven with all their might with their property and their souls in the cause of Allah [jihad] will have the highest rank with Him. These are the ones who are triumphant. Their Lord sends them tidings of mercy from Himself and of His good pleasure and Gardens in which lasting pleasure will be theirs. They will abide there forever. Allah's presence is the greatest reward of all.*

9:120 *The people of Medina and the Arabs of the desert around them had no cause to abandon Allah's Messenger or to prefer their own lives to his because anything they did or suffered was seen as a deed of righteousness. Whether they suffer thirst, fatigue, or hunger in the name of Allah, or take any steps that anger the unbelievers, or receive any damage from the enemy, it is all written down for them as a good work. Allah does not allow the reward of the righteous [those who die in jihad] to perish.*
9:121 *They could not spend anything in Allah's cause [jihad], small or great, nor cross any valley but it is written down in their credit. Allah may reward them with better than they have wrought.*

JIHAD, THE JEWS' EXILE

CHAPTER 13

*61:11 Believe in Allah and His messenger and fight valiantly
for Allah's cause [jihad] with both your wealth and your
lives. It would be better for you, if you only knew!*

THE AFFAIR OF THE JEWS OF QAYNUQA

1545 There were three tribes of Jews in Medina. The Beni Qaynuqa
were gold smiths and lived in a stronghold in their quarters. It is said by
Mohammed that they broke the treaty that had been signed when Mohammed came to Medina. How they did this is unclear.

1545 Mohammed assembled the Jews in their market and said: "Oh Jews,
be careful that Allah does not bring vengeance upon you like what happened to the Quraysh. Become Muslims. You know that I am the prophet
that was sent you. You will find that in your scriptures."

1545 They replied: "Oh Mohammed you seem to think that we are your
people. Don't fool yourself. You may have killed and beaten a few mer-
chants of the Quraysh, but we are men of war and real men."

1545 The response of the Koran:

> 3:12 *Say to the unbelievers, "Soon you will be defeated and thrown into
> Hell, a wretched home!" Truly, there has been a sign for you in the two
> armies which met in battle [at the battle of Badr, 300 Muslim defeated
> 1000 Meccans]. One army fought for Allah's cause, and the other army was
> a group of unbelievers, and the unbelievers saw with their own eyes that
> their enemy was twice its actual size. Allah gives help to whom He pleases.
> Certainly there is a lesson to be learned in this for those who recognize it.*

1546 Some time later Mohammed besieged the Jews in the their quarters. None of the other two Jewish tribes came to their support. Finally the
Jews surrendered and expected to be slaughtered after their capture.

1546 But an Arab ally bound to them by a client relationship approached
Mohammed and said, "Oh Mohammed deal kindly with my clients."
Mohammed ignored him. The ally repeated the request and again Mohammed ignored him. The ally grabbed Mohammed by the robe and
enraged Mohammed who said, "Let me go!" The ally said, "No, you must

deal kindly with my clients. They have protected me and now you would kill them all? I fear these changes." The response by the Koran:

> 5:51 *Oh, believers, do not take the Jews or Christians as friends. They are but one another's friends. If anyone of you take them for his friends, he surely is one of them. Allah will not guide the evildoers.*
> 5:52 *You will see those who have a diseased heart race towards them and say, "We fear in case a change of fortune befalls us." Perhaps Allah will bring about some victory or event of His own order. Then they will repent of the thoughts they secretly held in their hearts.*
> 5:53 *Then the faithful will say, "Are these the men who swore their most solemn oath by Allah that they were surely with you?" Their deeds will be in vain, and they will come to ruin. Oh, you who believe, if any of you desert His religion, Allah will then raise up a people whom He will love and who will be loved by Him. They will be humble towards the faithful and haughty towards the unbelievers. They will strive hard for Allah's cause [jihad], and not fear the blame of any blamer. This is the grace of Allah. He gives to whom He pleases. Allah is all-embracing and all-knowing.*

Mohammed exiled the Jews and took all of their wealth and goods.

THE RAID TO AL QARADA

1547 Mohammed's victory at Badr and ongoing jihad caused the Quraysh to go a different route to Syria. They hired a new guide to take them over the new route. Mohammed had intelligence about their route and sent a party to raid them. They were carrying a great deal of silver when the caravan stopped at a watering hole. The Muslims surprised them and the Quraysh managed to escape but Mohammed's men were able to steal all the caravan's goods, including the silver. The stolen goods were delivered to Mohammed in Medina.

THE ASSASSINATION OF AL ASHRAF, THE JEW

1548 When Al Ashraf, a Jew of Medina, heard that two of his friends had been killed at Badr, he said that the grave was a better place than the earth with Mohammed. So the "enemy of Allah" composed some poems bewailing the loss of his friends and attacking Islam.

1551 When Mohammed heard of Al Ashraf's criticism of his politics, he said, "Who will rid me of Al Ashraf?" A Muslim said, "I will kill him for you." Days later Mohammed found out that his assassin was not doing anything, including eating or drinking. Mohammed summoned him and asked what was going on. The man replied that he had taken on a task that was too difficult for him to do. Mohammed said that it was a duty which he should try to do. The assassin said, "Oh Apostle of Allah, I will have to tell a lie." The Prophet said, "Say what you like, you are free in the matter."

1552 By the use of lies three Muslims were able to kill Al Ashraf. When they returned to Mohammed, he was praying. They told him that they had killed the enemy of Allah. Their attack terrorized all the Jews. There was no Jew in Medina who was not afraid.

KILL ANY JEW THAT FALLS INTO YOUR POWER

1554 The Apostle of Allah said, "Kill any Jew who falls into your power." Hearing this Muhayyisa fell upon a Jewish merchant who was a business associate and killed him. His brother was not a Muslim and asked him how he could kill a man who had been his friend and partner in many business deals. The Muslim said that if Mohammed had asked him to kill his brother he would have done it immediately. His brother said, "You mean that if Mohammed said to cut off my head you would do it?" "Yes," was the reply. The older brother then said, "By Allah, any religion which brings you to this is marvelous." And he decided then and there to become a Muslim.

JIHAD, A SETBACK

CHAPTER 14

4:14 But those who disobey Allah and His Messenger
and go beyond His limits, will be led into the Fire to
live forever, and it will be a humiliating torment!

THE BATTLE OF UHUD

1555 Back at Mecca those who had lost at the battle of Badr told others, "Men of Quraysh, Mohammed has killed your best men. Give us money so that we may take revenge." Money was raised, men were hired. An army was put together.

1558 So the Meccans camped near Medina, ready for war. Ready for revenge. The Muslims now needed a strategy. Many, including Mohammed, wanted to sit and let the Meccans attack Medina. The town itself could be used in a defensive way—walls and rooftops would give any defender a strong advantage. But blood ran hot with the Muslim warriors. They were not afraid to meet the Meccans on the field of combat, man to man. After Badr, they were invincible. Allah had said as much. They said, "Mohammed lead us to our enemies, don't let them think that we are weak and cowards." The arguments went on until Mohammed went in his house and came out in his armor.

1559 But now, seeing him in his armor, the hot bloods repented and said that they should never try to persuade Mohammed to do anything. They had been wrong. Mohammed said, "When a prophet puts on his armor, he should not take it off until there has been war." So he marched out with a 1000 men to meet the Meccans.

1560 When they saw the Meccans, Mohammed said, "Let there be no fighting until I give the word." What they saw made the Muslims' blood boil. The Meccans had put their camels and horses into the crops of the Muslims. Mohammed placed 50 archers to protect his rear and flank. They must not move but hold that ground. Mohammed put on a second coat of mail.

1562 The morrow came and the battle was to begin. Now the Meccans had brought their women for the sole purpose to urge on the men. Men do not want to be cowards in front of women. The women began to beat their tambourines and chant poetry:

If you advance we will hug you
And place soft rugs beneath you
If you retreat we will leave you
Leave and no more love you.

I570 The Muslims fought without fear and the battle went against the Meccans who were cut off from their camp that had the spoils of war. The Muslim archers left their positions to get to the spoils. The battle might go to Islam, but the treasure would be theirs. This left the flank and rear open and the Meccan cavalry took advantage and charged the rear where Mohammed was. The battle suddenly went against the Muslims.

I571 The Muslims were put to flight and many were slain. Even Mohammed got hit in the face by a rock, broke a tooth and split his lip. He was incensed. The Meccans were all around and the Muslims had to protect him with their bodies.

I574 At one point the Meccans thought that they had killed the man who had brought them so much pain. But one Muslim recognized the prophet under his helmet and spread the news of his living. Mohammed fled the field. He was a heavy man, and wore two suits of armor. He almost could not climb the rocks and hill without help.

I583 The day went to the Meccans, the Quraysh. The Meccans did not press their advantage. They came to extract tribal justice and they killed about as many the Muslims had killed at Badr. They did not want to dominate Islam. Abu Sufyan, the Meccan leader, agreed through an emissary that they would meet in combat next year.

We have paid you back for Badr
And a war that follows a war is violent
I could not bear the loss of my friends
Nor my brother and his uncle and my first born.
I have slaked my vengeance and fulfilled my vow.
The slave who killed Hamza has cooled the burning in my breast
I shall thank the slave now free
Until my bones rot in the grave. —Hind

I586 The dead Muslims were buried in the battlefield. Mohammed said, "I testify that none who are wounded in jihad but what he will be raised by Allah with his bleeding wounds smelling like the finest perfume." When Mohammed heard the women weeping for their dead, but he wanted wailing for his uncle Hamza as well. So the women wailed for Hamza and Mohammed felt better.

1587 When Mohammed entered his house he handed his sword to his daughter and told her, "Wash the blood from this for by Allah it has served me well today." The next day he ordered all the fighters who had been at Uhud to marshal themselves and be ready to head out to pursue the enemy. This move was pure strategy to impress the enemy that he was still strong and not weakened by his losses. They went about eight miles from Medina and camped for three days before returning to Medina.

1589 Mohammed was the supreme master of the psychology of war. He sent an agent, who pretended to be a friend of the Meccans, to Abu Sufyan, the Meccan leader. Abu Sufyan was thinking about going back and finishing off the Muslims. But Mohammed's agent told Abu Sufyan that Mohammed was coming very soon with an army, the like of which had never been seen. They were in a state of total fury and would sweep into Hell all that were in front of them. Abu Sufyan, the merchant, left for Mecca and security. They had settled their score.

THE KORAN AND THE BATTLE OF UHUD

Since Allah had sent angels to the previous battle of Badr and the outnumbered Muslims triumphed, how could they fail at Uhud?

1593 Two of the clans of Muslims had doubts about the battle. But Allah was their friend and they did not doubt Islam and went on into the battle because of their belief in Allah and Mohammed.

> 3:121 *Remember when you [Mohammed] left your home early in the morning to lead the believers to their battle stations [battle of Uhud]? Allah heard and knew all. When two of your brigades showed cowardice, Allah protected them both. Let the faithful put their trust in Allah. Allah made you victorious at Badr when you were the weaker army. Therefore, fear Allah and be grateful to Him. Then you said to the believers, "Is it not enough for you that your Lord helped you by sending down three thousand angels?" Yes! And if you stand firm and fear Allah and you are suddenly attacked by your enemies, Allah will send down five thousand angels to wreak havoc upon them.*
>
> 3:126 *Allah intended this to be good news for you so your hearts will know peace. Victory comes from Allah alone, He is mighty and wise so that He might destroy a portion of the unbelievers, humiliate them, and keep them from their purpose. It is none of your concern whether He forgives them or punishes them for, truly, they are evil-doers. All that is in the heaven and earth belongs to Allah. He will forgive whom He pleases and punish whom He pleases. Allah is forgiving and merciful.*

1595 The reason for the loss was that the archers did not hold their ground, When they saw that the Meccans were cut off from their camp, they ran to get the spoils of war. Greed caused them to disobey Mohammed. So they should always obey Mohammed, he speaks for the Lord of all. Those who did not follow orders should ask for forgiveness. If they will see that it was their fault and be remorseful they can still get their reward of heaven.

> 3:131 *Obey Allah and His messenger so that you may receive mercy. Urge each other on to earn forgiveness from your Lord, and the Paradise as wide as heaven and earth is prepared for the righteous. Those who give freely, whether they are prosperous or poor; who control their anger; who are forgiving (for Allah loves those who do good); who, when they have sinned or wronged themselves, go to Allah and implore His forgiveness for their sins (for who except Allah can forgive you of your sins?) and do not knowingly continue in their sinning; these will be rewarded with their Lord's forgiveness and with the Garden watered by flowing rivers where they will live forever. The reward is great for those who serve Him!*
>
> 3:137 *There have been many religions that have come and gone before you. Travel the world and see what became of those who rejected the faith. The Koran is a clear statement for mankind: a guide and a warning to those who fear Allah. Therefore, do not lose heart or despair; if you are a true believer, you will be victorious.*

1597 The reason that Allah let the Meccans win was to test the Muslims. Now they will know their true selves. Are they fair weather friends of Mohammed or can they see their faults? If they obey Mohammed, then they can become true Muslims. A true Muslim never loses his morale, never falls into despair.

1596 If you have been wounded or suffered losses in the battle, don't forget that the non-Muslims have also suffered. Over the long view, fortunes go up and down. You must take the long view and believe in Mohammed and know that all will turn out well in the end. But those who died have the best reward. They are martyrs for Islam. Those who do wrong are the hypocrites, the pretenders.

> 3:140 *If you have been wounded [Muslims lost the battle of Uhud], be certain that the same has already befallen your enemies. We bring misfortune to mankind in turns so that Allah can discern who are the true believers, and so that We may select martyrs from among you. Allah does not love those who do evil. It is also Allah's purpose to test the believers and to destroy the unbelievers.*

1596 The Muslims must realize that Allah will purify them through tests such as the one they have just had. Those of true faith will not be discouraged. The hypocrites will be exposed and deprived of all blessing. Do you think you will get to heaven before Allah has tested you? Allah must know who is really a believer. A Muslim warrior must be given a trial. Losing at Uhud is merely a trial. After the big victory at Badr, those who were not there wanted to be part of the winning army. They were anxious to be able to show off as warriors, but when the actual killing started, many were not as good as they thought they would be.

> 3:142 *Did you think that you would be permitted into Paradise before Allah tested you to see who would fight for His cause [jihad] and endure until the end? You used to wish for death before you saw it, but now that you have seen it with your own eyes, you turn and run from it. Mohammed is only a messenger, and many messengers have come before him. If he died or was killed, would you turn your backs on the faith? But those who do in fact turn their backs will not hurt Allah in the least. And Allah will surely reward those who serve Him with gratitude.*
>
> 3:145 *No soul will ever die unless it is Allah's will. The length of each life is predetermined according to the Scriptures. Those who wish to receive their reward in this world will receive it, and those who wish to receive their reward in the world to come will also receive it. And We will undoubtedly reward those who serve Us with gratitude.*

1597 The Muslims should not think that they are the first to experience failure. In history many have failed in jihad, but they never lost heart or weakened. The lesson of Uhud is to be firm and not get depressed over a small failure.

> 3:146 *Many of the messengers have fought for Allah's cause [jihad] alongside large armies. They were never frightened by what they encountered on Allah's path, nor did they weaken or cringe with fear. Allah loves those who stand firm. Their only cry was this, "Lord! Forgive us of our sins and the things we have done that were against our duty; help us stand firm and make us victorious over the unbelievers." Therefore, Allah gave them their reward in this world, as well as an excellent reward in the world to come. Allah loves those who do good.*

1599 Do not think that the jihad is over. Soon Islam will bring terror to the unbelievers. After death, they will burn in Hell. The evil that will bring about their destruction is that they do not practice the religion of Islam.

> 3:149 *Believers! If you follow the unbelievers, they will cause you to reject the faith and lead you to eternal damnation. But Allah is your protector and the best of helpers. We will strike terror into the hearts of the*

unbelievers because they worship others besides Allah, which He gave them no permission to do. Their home will be the Fire, a terrible resting place for the evil-doers.

I599 Your slaughter of the unbelievers went well and you were about to wipe the unbelievers off the face of the earth, thanks to Allah. But then you disobeyed Mohammed. Allah did not destroy you because he is merciful. But your greed is of this world and you wanted the spoils of war of this world. But you must desire what comes after death, not the wealth of this world. You must learn this lesson with the grace of Allah.

> 3:152 *Allah fulfilled His covenant with you [Mohammed] when He allowed you to destroy your enemies [at the battle of Badr]. And then later, when you [the Muslims at Uhud] lost your courage, arguments broke out among you [the Muslims disobeyed orders and broke ranks to run and get the exposed spoils of the Meccans] and you sinned after you had come so close to what you wanted [spoils of war]. Some of you wish for the desires of this world and some of you for the world to come. Therefore, He caused you to be defeated so that you might be tested. Now He has forgiven you for Allah shows grace to the believers.*
>
> 3:153 *Remember when you [at Uhud the Muslims broke and fled] ran up the hill in cowardice and paid no attention to anyone and the messenger was behind you calling you back to the battle? Allah rewarded you with trouble for the trouble you caused Him so that you would not grieve for the spoils you lost or for what happened to you. Allah knows all that you do.*

I601 After the battle some were at ease, but others were in a state of anxiety because they did not trust Allah. The hypocrites divorced themselves from the decision and blamed others for failure. If they had their way then everyone would have been safe. But when Allah decrees your time has come, nothing can stay the hand of death. Death must come and it is better to die in jihad.

> 3:154 *Then, after the trouble Allah sent down upon you, He sent down calmness to wash over some of you. Some were overtaken by sleep, and others lay awake, stirred by their own passions, ignorantly thinking unjust thoughts about Allah. And they ask, "What do we gain by this affair?" Say: Truly the affair is entirely in Allah's hands. They hide in their hearts that which they do not want to tell you. They speak out saying, "If we had any say in this affair then none of us would have been killed here." Say: If you had stayed at home, those of you who were destined to be killed would have died regardless. This has taken place so that Allah might test your faith and see what is in your hearts. Allah knows the deepest secrets of every heart. Those of you who fled in cowardice on the day the two armies met in battle*

must have been tricked by Satan because of some evil you have done. But now Allah has forgiven you for Allah is forgiving and gracious.

Those who die in jihad will be rewarded by Allah.

3:156 *Believers! Do not follow the unbelievers' example when they say about their brothers who have been killed in a foreign country or in battle, "If only they had stayed at home they would not have died or have been killed!" Allah will make them regret what they have said. Allah is the giver of both life and death; Allah knows all that you do.*
3:157 *The forgiveness and mercy they, who die or are killed for Allah's cause, will receive from Allah will be far better than anything they could have gained. If you die or are killed, then surely you will all be gathered before Allah.*

1602 But Mohammed must be gentle with the Muslims. So he will overlook their faults and will forgive them. He will still consult with them, but the final decision must lie with Allah and Mohammed.

3:158 *It was because of Allah's mercy that you spoke so gently to them. For if you had dealt with them severely or been hard-hearted, they would have turned away from you. Therefore, forgive them and ask Allah to forgive them and counsel them in the affair of war; and when you have resolved the matters, put your trust in Allah. Allah loves those who trust Him. If Allah is helping you, no one can defeat you. But if He leaves you, who will be there to help you when He is gone? Therefore, let the faithful put their trust in Allah.*

1603 The Muslim's loss was a test that was brought on by their decisions. The hypocrites were told to fight in jihad or at least defend the city. Their excuses are those of an unbeliever.

3:165 *And when disaster [battle of Uhud] befell you, although it brought destruction twice as great to the unbelievers, you said, "Why is this happening to us?" Say to them, "You have brought this upon yourselves for Allah controls all things. The destruction which befell you the day the two armies met in battle was Allah's will so He would recognize who were the true believers and who were the hypocrites." And when they were told, "Come and fight for Allah's cause [jihad] and drive your enemies back," they replied, "If we knew how to fight, then we would have followed you."*
3:168 *Some of them were closer to unbelief than faith that day. What they said with their mouths was not what was in their hearts, but Allah knew what they were hiding in their hearts. It was these who said, while sitting at home, of their brothers, "If only they had listened to us, then they would not have been killed." Say: Try to avert your death if what you say is true!*

3:169 *Never believe that those who have been killed for Allah's cause [jihad] are dead. No, they are alive with their Lord and receive rich provisions. They rejoice in the bounty Allah gives them and are joyful for those left behind who have yet to join them that they will have nothing fear or regret. They are filled with joy for Allah's grace and blessings. Allah will not fail to reward the faithful.*

3:172 *As for those who answered the call of Allah and His messenger after they were defeated [battle of Uhud], those of them who do good works and fear Allah will be richly rewarded. They are the ones who when it was said to them, "Your enemies are gathering vast armies against you, so fear them," it only increased their faith and they said, "Allah's help is enough for us. He is the most excellent protector." It was in this manner that they earned Allah's grace and blessings, and no harm came to them. And they worked to please Allah for Allah is full of boundless grace.*

I606 The success that the unbelievers are experiencing is temporary. They will grow in their evil and they will be punished. Allah will not leave the believers in this state. But this trial will separate the weak from the strong. Those who have wealth should spend it on Allah's cause.

3:175 *It is only Satan who causes you to fear his followers [the leaders of the Meccans]. Do not fear them; fear Me if you are truly believers. Do not be distressed for those who turn away from the faith for Allah is not hurt by them. Allah will refuse them any part of the world to come. Severe torment awaits them. Those who trade their faith for unbelief will do no harm to Allah, and they will receive a painful punishment.*

3:178 *Do not let the unbelievers think that we lengthen their days for their own good. We give them time only hoping that they will commit more serious sins. They will receive a shameful punishment.*

3:179 *It is not Allah's will that the believers should remain in their present condition but only until He divides the bad from the good [reveals the hypocrites]. Neither is it Allah's will to reveal the secrets of the unknown, but Allah chooses those of His messengers whom pleases to know them. Therefore, believe in Allah and His messengers, and if you have faith and fear Allah, then you will receive a great reward.*

3:180 *Never let those who selfishly store up the wealth Allah has given them think that they are doing good. No! It will be bad for them. The wealth they have amassed will be a weight upon their shoulders on the Day of Resurrection. The heavens and the earth are Allah's inheritance, and Allah knows all that you do.*

ASSASSINATION AS JIHAD

M276 After Uhud, several tribes allied themselves under the leadership of Sufyan Ibn Khalid. Mohammed dispatched an assassin to kill him, for without his leadership the coalition would fall apart. So the assassin, Abdullah, joined his forces and waited until he was alone with him. He killed Sufyan and cut off his head and went back to Medina.

M276 Abdullah then went straight to Mohammed. Mohammed welcomed him and asked him how it went. Abdullah presented Mohammed with the head of his enemy. Mohammed was gratified and presented him with his walking stick. He said, "This is a token between you and me on the day of resurrection. Very few will have such to lean on in that day." Abdullah attached it to his sword scabbard.

JIHAD, THE JEWS SUBMIT

CHAPTER 15

58:20 *Those who oppose Allah and His Messenger will be laid low. Allah has declared, "Surely I will be victorious, along with My messengers." Truly Allah is strong and mighty.*

CLEANSING

1652 It had been four years since Mohammed came to Medina. Mohammed went to one of the two remaining Jewish tribes to ask for blood money for the two men his fighter had killed. At first they said yes, but as they talked about it they decided that this would be a good time to kill Mohammed. Here he was in their quarter of Medina sitting on a wall near a roof. Why not send a man up and drop a rock on this man who had been such a sorrow to them? Mohammed got word of the plot and left.

1653 This was as good a reason as any to deal with the Jews. The same Jews who insisted that he was not the prophet. He raised his army and went off to put their fortresses under siege. These Jews were farmers and they grew the finest dates in all of Arabia. So Mohammed cut and burned their date palms as they watched. They called out, "You have prohibited wanton destruction and blamed those who do that. Now you do what you forbid."

1653 Now the other Jewish tribe had assured them that they would come to their defense. But no Jew would stand with another Jew against Islam. With no help from their brothers, the besieged Jews cut a deal with the apostle of Allah. Spare their lives and let them go with what they could carry on their camels, except for their armor.

1654 When there was fighting in jihad, the fighter got four-fifths. But since there had been no fighting there was no reason to give four-fifths to the jihadists. All of the spoils went to Mohammed, not just one fifth.

1654 There were some new problems created—the burning of the date palms and all the money going to Mohammed. The Koran had the answers. It was Allah who wreaked his vengeance upon the Jews and gave Mohammed power over them. It was even Allah who caused the Jews to tear down their own houses.

59:2 It was He who caused the People of the Book [the Jews] to leave their homes and go into the first exile. They did not think they would leave, and they thought that their fortresses could protect them from Allah. But Allah's wrath reached them from where they did not expect it and cast terror into their hearts, so that they destroyed their homes with their own hands, as well as by the hands of the believers. Take warning from this example, you who have the eyes to see it!

1654 And the Jews were very fortunate that Allah let them go with a few worldly possessions. They got out alive, Allah did not slay them, but they will burn in Hell since they resisted Mohammed. Resist Islam and Allah will punish you. As far as the wanton destruction of the palm trees, that cannot be laid to Mohammed, it was the Jew's fault. They should have done what Allah wanted and then the Jews would not have suffered Allah's vengeance.

59:3 And if Allah had not decreed their exile, surely He would have punished them in this world. And in the world to come they will receive the punishment of the Fire because they had disobeyed Allah and His Messenger. Whoever disobeys Allah, knows that Allah is truly severe in His punishment.

59:5 Allah gave you permission to cut down some palm trees and leave others intact so as to shame the wicked [the Jews]. After Allah gave the spoils to His Messenger, you made no move with horses or camels to capture them [the Jews], but Allah gives His messengers power over what He chooses. Allah is all-powerful.

1654 As for all the spoils of war going to Mohammed, there was no actual fighting, hence no need to give spoils to fighters. Mohammed can do as he wishes.

59:7 The spoils of war taken from the people in the cities and given by Allah to His Messenger belong to Allah, to His Messenger and to his family, to the orphans, to the poor, and to the wayfaring traveler so that it will not stay among those of you who are wealthy. Take what the Messenger has offered you, and refuse what he has forbidden you. And fear Allah, for Allah is severe in His punishment.

59:8 A part of the spoils of war also belong to the poor refugees: the Immigrants driven from their homes and possessions who seek Allah's grace and help Allah and His Messenger. These are the sincere believers.

THE BATTLE OF THE TRENCH

1669 Some of the Jews who had been exiled from Medina decided that they needed to destroy Mohammed and to do that they needed allies. Since allies were to be found in Mecca, they went there and parlayed with the leaders of the Quraysh. But since this was a war of religion, the Quraysh wanted proof of religious supremacy to Mohammed. So the leaders said to the Jews, "You are People of the Book and you know our disagreement. Who has the better religion, us or Mohammed?" The leaders of the Jews replied that the Quraysh had the better religion.

I669 Now the Koran could not pass up such an insult to Mohammed. So the Koran says:

> 4:49 *Have you not seen those who praise themselves for their purity? But Allah purifies whom He pleases, and they will not be treated unjustly in the slightest degree. See how they make up lies about Allah! That in itself is a terrible sin. Have you not seen those [Jews allied with the Meccans] to whom part of the Scriptures were given? They believe in idols and sorcery, and they say of the unbelievers, "These are guided on a better path than the believers." It is on these whom Allah has laid His curse. Those who are cursed by Allah will have no one to help them.*
>
> 4:53 *Should those who would fail to give even a penny to their fellow man have a share in the kingdom? Do they envy the people for what they have received from Allah's bounty? We gave the Scriptures and wisdom to the children of Abraham, and a grand kingdom. Some of them believe in His Messenger while others turn away from him. The flames of Hell are suffi- cient punishment for them! Those who reject Our revelations We will cast into the Fire. As soon as their skins are burnt away, We will give them new skins so that they will truly experience the torment. Truly Allah is mighty and wise!*

I669-670 So the Meccans entered into an alliance with the Jews. Another Arab tribe joined the alliance as well.

As Mohammed had many spies in Mecca, so it took no time until he knew of the coming fight and he set out to prepare for it. There was a Persian who suggested to Mohammed that he build a trench as a barrier against the Meccans and their allies. For eight days the Arabs worked at building a trench, or ditch, around the weak points of Medina. To help with morale Mohammed personally pitched in and did his turn at manual labor.

I671 There was a fair amount of slacking and leaving work. The labor problems even worked their way into the Koran:

> 24:62 *Only those who believe in Allah and His Messenger are the true be- lievers, and when they are gathered together, do not leave until they have sought his permission. Those who ask your permission are the ones who truly believe in Allah and His Messenger. And when they ask your permission to*

leave for personal reasons, give permission to whom you please, and ask Allah for His indulgence on their behalf, for Allah is indulgent, merciful.

24:63 *Do not address the Messenger in the same way you address one another. Allah knows which of you leave quietly from the assemblies, hiding behind others. And let those who disobey his commands beware, for fear that some terrible punishment will come upon them.*

24:64 *Surely all that is in the heavens and earth belongs to Allah. He knows your intentions well. And one day all will be assembled before Him, and He will inform them of what they have done, for Allah knows all things.*

1673 But the work was done just in time. The Quraysh and the other allies camped near the trench. Mohammed and his army camped on their side of the trench and sent the women and children to the forts.

1674 One of the exiled Jews approached the last tribe of Jews in Medina to be allies with the attacking Meccans. At first the Jews would not even talk to him. After all, if Mohammed won, they would be left with the consequences of dealing with a man who had driven the other two tribes of Jews from Medina. But in the end the Jews agreed to lend aid if the battle started to go against Mohammed.

1677-683 Mohammed was able to use his agents to sow discord among those allied against him. The trench defense frustrated the Meccans. The weather was bad and the allies were distrustful of each other. In terms of actual combat only a handful of men were killed over the twenty-day siege. The Meccans broke camp and went back home. It was a victory for Mohammed.

33:9 *Believers! Remember Allah's grace when your enemies attacked you [the Battle of the Ditch], and We set a mighty wind against them [the Meccans and their allies, the confederates, put Medina under siege], and warriors they could not see, but Allah sees clearly all that you do. [The confederates' poor planning, poor leadership, and bad weather caused them to fail]*

33:10 *When they attacked you from above and from below, your eyes went wild, your hearts leapt up into your throats, and you doubted Allah's strength. There the believers were tried, and they were severely shaken. The hypocrites and the diseased of heart said, "Allah and His Messenger promised us only to deceive us." A group of them said, "People of Medina! It is not safe for you here. Therefore, go back to your city." Then another group said, "Our homes have been left defenseless," although they were not, and they really only wanted to run away.*

33:14 *If the enemy had infiltrated the entire city, the disaffected would have been incited to rebel, and they surely would have done so, but they would have maintained control for only a short while. Before they had pledged to*

Allah that they would never turn their backs and flee. A pledge to Allah must be answered for. Say: Fleeing will not help you. If you are running away from death or slaughter, even if you do escape, you will only be left to enjoy this world for a short time. Say: Who will keep you from Allah if it is His will to punish you or to show you mercy? Only Allah is your guardian and a helper.

JIHAD, THE JEWS AGAIN

CHAPTER 16

*58:5 Those who oppose Allah and His Messenger will
be laid low, just as those who came before them.*

THE SOLUTION FOR THE JEWS

1684 That same day the angel Gabriel came to Mohammed at noon.
He asked if Mohammed were through fighting. Gabriel and the angels
were going to attack the last Jewish tribe in Medina. Gabriel said, "Allah
commands you to go to the Jews. I am headed there now to shake their
stronghold."

1684 So Mohammed called upon his troops and they headed to the forts
of the Jews. Now the Jews of Medina lived in forts that were on the outskirts of Medina. Mohammed rode up to the forts and called out, "You
brothers of apes, has Allah disgraced you and brought His vengeance
upon you?"

1685-689 Mohammed put the Jews under siege for twenty-five days. Finally, the Jews offered to submit their fate to a Muslim, Saed, with whom
they had been an ally in the past. His judgment was simple. Kill all the
men. Take their property and take the women and children as captives.
Mohammed said, "You have given the judgment of Allah."

1690 The captives were taken into Medina. They dug trenches in
the market place of Medina. It was a long day, but 800 Jews met
their death that day. Mohammed and his twelve year old wife sat and
watched the entire day and into the night. The Apostle of Allah had
every male Jew killed.

1693 Mohammed took the property, wives and children of the Jews, and
divided it up amongst the Muslims. Mohammed took his one fifth of the
slaves and sent a Muslim with the female Jewish slaves to a nearby city
where the women were sold for pleasure. Mohammed invested the money
from the sale of the female slaves for horses and weapons.

1693 There was one last piece of spoils for Mohammed. The most beautiful Jewess was his slave for pleasure.

1696-7 In the battle of the Trench it was Allah who had won the day.
Allah is what gives the Muslim his strength and will. No matter what the

unbelievers do Allah will triumph. Allah totally approves of the killing of the Jews, enslaving the women and children. It was good to give the Jew's property to the Muslim warriors. After all, Allah wanted it done and helped to do it.

> 33:25 *And Allah drove back the unbelievers in their wrath, and they gained nothing by it. Allah aided the believers in the war, for Allah is strong and mighty. He brought down some of the People of the Book [the Jews] out of their fortresses to aid the confederates and to strike terror into their hearts. Some you killed, and others you took captive. He made you heirs of their land, their homes, and their possessions, and even gave you another land on which you had never before set foot. Allah has power over everything. [800 male Jews were executed, their property taken, and women and children enslaved.]*

THE KILLING OF THE JEW, SALLAM

I714-6 A Jew named Sallam helped to plan and organize the confederation of the tribes that attacked Mohammed in the Battle of the Trench. Mohammed sent five Muslim men to assassinate Sallam. When the men had done their work, they returned to Mohammed and fell to arguing as to who actually killed Sallam. Mohammed demanded to see their swords. He examined them one by one and then pointed to the sword that had been the killing weapon. It had food on it still from the thrust to the stomach.

The Koran's last words about the Jews:

> 5:12 *Allah did, of old, make a covenant with the children of Israel, and We appointed twelve leaders among them, and Allah said, "I will be with you if you observe regular prayer, practice regular charity, believe in My messengers and help them, and offer Allah goodly gifts. I will surely wipe away your sins, and I will bring you into Gardens beneath which the rivers flow. Whoever of you does not believe this has gone astray from the even path."*
> 5:13 *Because they [the Jews] broke their covenant, We have cursed them and have hardened their hearts. They changed the words of Scripture [Islam claims that the Jews removed the references to Mohammed's coming from their Scripture.] from their places and have forgotten part of what they were taught. You will always discover them in deceits, except for a few of them, but forgive them and overlook their misdeeds. Allah loves those who act generously.*
>
> 5:41 *Oh, Messenger, do not let those who hurry to disbelief grieve you. Whether it is those who say the words, "We believe," while their hearts do not believe, or, it is the Jews, who will listen to any lie but do not come to you. They change words from their contexts and say, "If you are given this,*

take it, if you are not given this, then beware of it." For whomever Allah would mislead, you will be no help for him against Allah. Those whose hearts Allah does not desire to cleanse will suffer disgrace in this world and a grievous punishment in the next.

5:42 They [the Jews] are fond of listening to lies or devouring anything forbidden. If they do come to you [Mohammed], judge between them, or refuse to interfere. If you withdraw from them, they cannot harm you in any way, but if you judge, then judge between them with equity. Allah loves those who deal equitably. Why would they make you their judge since they possess their own law, the Torah, which holds the commands of Allah, yet they have not obeyed it? These are not believers.

5:44 We have sent down the Torah, which was a guidance and light. The messengers who professed Islam used the Torah to judge the Jews, the rabbis, and the doctors because they were required to be the keepers and the witnesses of the Book. Therefore, Oh Jews, do not fear men but fear Me, and do not sell my signs for a miserable price. Whoever will not judge by what Allah revealed are the unbelievers.

5:45 We ordained in the Book, "Life for life, and eye for eye, and nose for nose, and ear for ear, and tooth for tooth, and for wounds retaliation." Whoever will give up retaliation, it is an act of atonement for his sins. Whoever does not use the laws of Allah to judge is unjust.

MORE OF THE KORAN AND JIHAD

CHAPTER 17

4:59 Believers! Obey Allah and obey His Messenger and those among you with authority. If you have a disagreement about anything, refer it to Allah and His Messenger if you believe in Allah and the Last Day. This is the best and fairest way to settle a dispute.

4:60 Have you not noticed those who act like they believe in that which has been revealed to you and that which was revealed before you? They wish to seek the judgment of Satan, although they have been commanded to deny him, and Satan wishes to lead them astray into grievous sin. And when it is said to them, "Come and be judged by what Allah has revealed and by His Messenger," you see them turn their heads in disgust. But how would they act if some disaster came upon them because of what they have done with their own hands? They would come to you, swearing by Allah, "We wish nothing but goodwill and reconciliation." But Allah knows the secrets of their hearts. Therefore, turn away from them and warn them, speaking words that will pierce their souls.

4:64 We have sent messengers only so that people will obey them by Allah's permission. If the people hurt themselves by their own error, and they came to you to ask Allah's forgiveness, and you asked Allah's forgiveness on their behalf, they would certainly have found Allah forgiving and merciful. But no, I swear by your Lord, they will not believe until they make you judge in all their disputes. Then they will have no doubt in the fairness of your judgment and will entirely submit to you.

4:66 If We had commanded them, "Lay down your lives," or "Abandon your homes," only a few of them would have obeyed. But if they had done as they were commanded, it would have been better for them and it would have strengthened their faith. We would have given them of Ourselves a great reward and guided them to the right path.

4:69 Those who obey Allah and His Messenger will live with the messengers and the saints and the martyrs and the righteous. What wonderful company! This is the bounty of Allah, and Allah's infinite knowledge is sufficient. Believers! Be cautious, and either march forward in groups or advance all together. There are some among you who are sure to hang back, and if a disaster came upon you, would say, "Allah has dealt with us graciously because we were not in the battle." If, however, you were met with victory, they, as if there were no friendship between you, would

161

say, "If only I had been with them! Surely I would have been greatly successful!"

4:74 Let those who would sell the life of this world for the world to come fight for Allah's cause [jihad]. Whoever fights for Allah's cause, whether he is killed or is victorious, We will grant him a great reward. How could you not fight for Allah's cause? For the weak men, women, and children who plead, "Lord! Rescue us from this city of oppressors [Mecca]. Send us a protector from Your presence; send a defender from Your presence."

4:76 The believers fight for Allah's cause [jihad] and the unbelievers fight for Satan. Therefore, fight against the friends of Satan. Truly Satan's strategy is weak.

4:77 Look at those who were told, "Lay down your arms of war for a time, attend to your prayers, and pay the poor tax." When they were told to resume fighting, some of them feared their fellow man more than they should have feared Allah, and said, "Lord! Why have you commanded us to fight? Why could you not have given us a longer respite?" Say: The joys of this world are fleeting. The world to come will be better for those of you who fear Allah, and you will never be treated unfairly in the least. Wherever you are, death will find you, even if you lock yourselves in high towers! If something good happens to them they say, "This is from Allah," but if something evil happens to them they say, "It was the Messenger's fault." Say: Everything is from Allah! But what is wrong with these people that they fail to understand what is told to them?

4:79 Whatever good comes to you is from Allah, but whatever evil happens to you is from yourself. We have sent you to mankind as a Messenger, and Allah is sufficient as your witness. Those who obey the Messenger obey Allah. As for those who turn away from you, We have not sent you to watch over them.

4:81 They promise obedience to you, but when they leave you, they gather together at night and plan to do other than what you say. Allah writes down all they say. Therefore, leave them alone and put your trust in Allah. Allah is sufficient as your protector. Will they not study the Koran? Were it not from Allah, they surely would have found many contradictions in it. And when they hear any news, whether it is good or bad, they announce it to everyone. On the other hand, if they had told the Messenger or those in authority, the wise among them would have learned it from them. If it were not for Allah's grace and mercy, all but a few of you would have followed Satan!

4:84 Therefore, fight for Allah's cause [jihad]. Do not lay the burden on anyone but yourself, and stir up the faithful. It may be that Allah will restrain the unbelievers' fury. Allah is mightier and stronger in His punishment.

4:85 *Those who mediate between people for a good cause will gain from it, but those who mediate for an evil cause will bear the consequences. Allah has power over all things.*

66:6 *Oh, believers, save yourselves and your families from the Fire whose fuel is men and stones [ritual objects made from stone], over which are set fierce and mighty angels. They do not resist Allah's commands, but do precisely what they are commanded. Oh, unbelievers, do not make excuses for yourselves this day. You are only being rewarded for your deeds.*
66:8 *Oh, believers, turn to Allah in true penitence. Maybe your Lord will cancel your evil deeds and will bring you into the Gardens beneath which the rivers flow on the day when Allah will not humiliate the Messenger or those who have shared his faith. Their light will run before them and on their right hands. They will say, "Lord perfect our light, and pardon us. You have power over all things."*
66:9 *Oh, Messenger, make war on the unbelievers and hypocrites, and be hard on them. Hell will be their home, and wretched is the passage to it.*
66:10 *Allah sets forth as an example to unbelievers the wife of Noah and the wife of Lot. They were under two of Our righteous servants yet they both deceived them, so their husbands did not help them at all against Allah. It was said to them, "Enter into the Fire with those who enter."*
66:11 *Allah also holds forth to those who believe the example of the wife of Pharaoh. She said, "Lord, build me a house with you in Paradise and deliver me from Pharaoh and his doings and deliver me from the wicked."*
66:12 *Mary, the daughter of Imran who guarded her chastity and into whose womb We breathed of Our spirit, accepted the words of her Lord and of His revelations. She was one of the obedient.*

THE RAID ON THE MUSTALIQ TRIBE

1725 When Mohammed heard that the Arab tribe, the Mustaliq, were opposed to him and were gathering against him, he set out with his army to attack them. He contacted them at a watering hole and combat started. Islam was victorious and the Mustaliq and their women, children, and goods were taken as spoils of war and distributed to the fighters.

1729 The captives of the tribe of Mustaliq were parceled out as spoils. There was a ransom price set upon their heads. If the ransom were not paid then the people were treated as spoils and slaves. Now one of them was a beautiful woman with a high price on her. She came to Mohammed and asked him to see if the price could be reduced. Mohammed had a better idea. He would pay the ransom for the beautiful woman and she would become his wife. Now in spite of the fact that she was already married, there was no problem. It was a deal. Mohammed paid the ransom and the beautiful woman became wife number seven.

1729 This marriage had a side effect. The captives were now related to Mohammed's wife. They were all released without ransom.

THE DEATH OF A POETESS

1996 There was a poetess who wrote a poem against Islam. Mohammed said, "Who will rid me of Marwan's daughter?" One of his followers heard him and on that very night he went to the woman's home and killed her.

M239 The assassin was able to do the work in the dark as the woman slept. Her other children lay in the room, but her babe lay on her breast. The stealthy assassin removed the child and drove the knife into her with such force that he pined her to the bed.

1996 In the morning he went to Mohammed and told him. Mohammed said, "You have helped Allah and his Apostle." When asked about the consequences, Mohammed said, "Two goats won't butt their heads together over this."

M239 Mohammed turned to the people in the mosque, he said, "If you wish to see a man who has assisted Allah and his Prophet, look here." Omar cried, "What, the blind Omeir!" "No," said Mohammed, "call him Omeir the Seeing."

1996 The poetess had five sons and the assassin went to them and said, "I killed Bint Marwan, Oh sons. Withstand me if you can; don't keep me waiting." Islam became powerful that day and many became Muslims when they saw the power of Islam.

MOHAMMED'S FAMILY LIFE

CHAPTER 18

48:13 We have prepared a blazing Fire for these unbelievers
who do not believe in Allah and His Messenger.

Mohammed had many wives. The Koran goes into detail about his romances.

THE LIE

When Mohammed went on his missions to attack those who resisted Islam, he took one of his wives with him. Which one got to go was determined by lots. Mohammed took Aisha with him on this trip to fight in Allah's cause in attacking the Mustaliq tribe.

1731 Now there was a problem in taking one of Mohammed's wives on an expedition and that was privacy. By now the veil had been prescribed for his wives. So the wife was not supposed to be seen or heard. To accomplish this a light cloth-covered howdah was used. Basically this was a box with a seat that could be mounted on a camel's saddle. On the way back on the expedition Aisha had gone out in the morning to relieve herself. When she got back she discovered that she had lost a necklace and went back to find it. The tent had been struck and the men in charge loaded the howdah on the camel and off they went without Aisha.

1732 When Aisha got back the entire group had moved on. She returned on a camel lead by a young Muslim who had lagged behind the main body and brought her back to Medina.

1732 Tongues began to wag, imaginations worked overtime and gossip spread. Aisha fell ill and was bedridden for three weeks.

1734-5 Tempers flared and men offered to kill the gossips. Something had to be done. In the end the innocence or guilt of Aisha was determined by revelation in the Koran which to this day is the sharia (Islamic law) about adultery.

> *24:1 A sura [chapter] which We have sent down and ordained, and in which We give you clear signs so that you will take warning. The man and woman who commit adultery should each be beaten with a hundred lashes, and do not let your pity for them prevent you from obeying Allah. If you believe in Allah and the Last Day, then allow some of the believers to*

witness their punishment. An adulterer can only marry an adulteress or an unbeliever, and a adulteress cannot marry anyone other than an adulterer or an unbeliever. Such marriages are forbidden for believers.

24:4 *Those who make accusations against honorable women and are unable to produce four witnesses should be given eighty lashes. Thereafter, do not accept their testimony, for they are terrible sinners, except those who repent afterwards and live righteously. Allah is truly forgiving and merciful.*

24:6 *If a husband accuses his wife of adultery but he has no witnesses other than himself, his evidence can be accepted if he swears by Allah four times that he is telling the truth and then calls down Allah's curse upon him if he is lying. If, however, the wife swears by Allah four times that she is innocent and calls Allah's curse down upon herself if she is lying, then she should not be punished.*

24:10 *If it were not for Allah's grace and mercy towards you and that Allah is wise, this would not have been revealed to you.*

24:11 *Truly there is a group among you who spread that lie [During an armed raid, Aisha—Mohammed's favorite wife since their marriage when she was age six—accidentally spent a day alone with a young jihadist. Gossip about what might have happened consumed the Muslims], but do not think of it as a bad thing for you [Aisha was cleared of doubt of sexual infidelity by a revelation in the Koran] for it has proved to be advantageous for you. Every one of them will receive the punishment they have earned. Those who spread the gossip will receive a torturous punishment.*

24:12 *Why did the believing men and women, when they heard this, not think better of their own people and say, "This is an obvious lie"? Why did they not bring four witnesses? And because they could not find any witnesses, they are surely liars in Allah's sight.*

24:14 *If it were not for Allah's goodness towards you and His mercy in this world and the world to come, you would have been severely punished for the lie you spread. You [the Muslims] gossiped about things you knew nothing about. You may have thought it to be only a light matter, but it was a most serious one in Allah's sight. And why, when you heard it, did you not say, "It is not right for us to talk about this. Oh, Allah! This is a serious sin." Allah warns you never to repeat this if you are true believers. Allah makes His signs clear to you, for Allah is all-knowing, wise. Those who take pleasure in spreading foul rumors about the faithful will be severely punished in this world and the world to come. And Allah knows, while you do not.*

24:20 *If it were not for Allah's grace and mercy towards you, you would have been punished long ago, but know that Allah is kind and merciful.*

24:21 *Believers, do not follow in Satan's footsteps for those who do so will be commanded to commit shameful and evil acts. If it were not for Allah's grace, not one of you would be pure. And Allah purifies those He pleases, and Allah is all-hearing.*

24:22 *And do not allow those among you who are wealthy and have many possessions to swear that they will not give to their family, the poor, and those who have fled their homes for Allah's cause [jihad]. Instead, let them be forgiving and indulgent. Do you not want Allah to show you forgiveness? Allah is forgiving and merciful.*

24:23 *Truly, those who carelessly slander believing women will be cursed in this world and the world to come. Their own tongues, hands, and feet will one day testify against them concerning their own actions. On that day Allah will give them what they have earned, and they will know that Allah is the clear truth.*

Since there were not four witnesses, then there was no adultery and the gossips got eighty lashes.

1736 But the scandal did not end here. One of those who got flogged for gossip was a poet and propagandist for the Muslim cause. The young warrior who led Aisha's camel was in a poem written by the poet and was offended. So he took his sword and cut the poet badly. The poet and his friends managed to bind the young warrior and take him to Mohammed. Mohammed wanted this to all go away. He gave the wounded poet a nice home and a Christian slave girl of pleasure as compensation for the sword blow.

Islam was no longer poor, indeed, the money from jihad poured in. But Mohammed was a simple man and had no attraction to money. Hence, his household was poor and the wives complained.

33:28 *Messenger! Say to your wives, "If you desire a life of this world and all its glittering adornment, then come. [All of the money from the spoils of war was spent on support of the Muslims and jihad. Mohammed's wives complained about the lack of household money.] I will provide for you and release you with honor. If, however, you seek Allah and His Messenger and the world to come, then know that Allah has prepared a great reward for those of you who do good works.*

33:30 *Wives of the Messenger! If any of you are proven guilty of public indecency, then you will be doubly punished; that is easy for Allah. But those of you who obey Allah and His Messenger and do good works will be doubly rewarded. We have prepared honorable provisions for you.*

33:32 *Wives of the Messenger! You are not like any other women. If you fear Allah, then do not be too lax in your speech for fear that lecherous-hearted men will lust after you. Stay in your homes and do not go out in public dressed in your fine clothes as they did in the time of ignorance [all non-Islamic history, civilization and customs are of the time of ignorance], but pray regularly, pay the poor tax and obey Allah and His Messenger. It is Allah's desire to remove all that is unclean from you, People of His House, and to make you pure. And remember what is said to you in your homes of Allah's revelations and wisdom, for surely Allah knows all mysteries and is aware of all.*

33:35 *Allah has prepared forgiveness and a great reward for the men and women who submit to Him and believe, who are devout, truthful, patient, humble, generous, and pure; who fast, are modest, and always remember Allah.*

33:50 *Messenger! We allow you your wives whose dowries you have paid, and the slave-girls Allah has granted you as spoils of war, and the daughters of your paternal and maternal uncles and aunts who fled with you to Medina, and any believing woman who gives herself to the Messenger, if the Messenger wishes to marry her. This is a privilege for you only, not for any other believer. We know what We have commanded the believers concerning wives and slave-girls. We give you this privilege so you will be free from blame. Allah is forgiving and merciful!*

33:51 *You may turn away any of them that you please, and take to your bed whomever you please, and you will not be blamed for desiring one you had previously set aside for a time. Therefore, it will be easier for you to comfort them and prevent their grief and to be content with what you give each of them. Allah knows what is in your hearts, and Allah is all-knowing and gracious.*

33:52 *It will be unlawful for you to marry more wives after this or to exchange them for other wives, even though you are attracted by their beauty, except slave-girls you own. [Mohammed had nine wives and several slave-girls.] And Allah watches over all things.*

MARY, THE COPTIC SLAVE OF PLEASURE

M425 Mohammed was given two Coptic (Egyptian Christian) slaves. One he gave to another Muslim but he kept Mary, fair of skin with curly hair. He did not move her into the harem, but set up an apartment in another part of Medina. Mary gave something in sex that none of his wives could—a child and it was a male child, Ibrahim. Mohammed doted on him.

M426 The harem was jealous. This non-Arab slave had given Mohammed his best gift. One of his wives, Hafsa, was away and Mohammed took Mary to Hafsa's apartment in the harem. Hafsa returned and there was a scene. The harem was incensed. A slave in one of their beds was an outrage and a scandal. The wives banded together and it was a house of anger and coldness.

M427 Mohammed withdrew and swore he would not see his wives for a month and lived with Mary. Omar and Abu Bakr were appalled as Mohammed, their son-in-law had abandoned their daughters for a slave. But at last Mohammed relented and said that Gabriel had spoken well of Hafsa and he wanted the whole affair to be over.

The Koran:

> 66:1 *Why, Oh, Messenger, do you forbid yourself that which Allah has made lawful to you? Do you seek to please your wives? [Mohammed was fond of a Coptic (Egyptian Christian) slave named Mary. Hafsa found Mohammed in her room with Mary, a violation of Hafsa's domain. He told a jealous Hafsa that he would stop relations with Mary and then did not. But Hafsa was supposed to be quiet about this matter.] Allah is lenient and merciful. Allah has allowed you release from your oaths, and Allah is your master. He is knowing and wise.*
>
> 66:3 *When the Messenger confided a fact to one of his wives, and when she divulged it, [Hafsa had told Aisha (Mohammed's favorite wife) about Mary and the harem became embroiled in jealousy.] Allah informed Mohammed of this, and he told her [Hafsa] part of it and withheld part. When Mohammed told her of it, she said, "Who told you this?" He said, "He who is knowing and wise told me."*
>
> 66:4 *"If you both [Hafsa and Aisha] turn in repentance to Allah, your hearts are already inclined to this, but if you conspire against the Messenger, then know that Allah is his protector, and Gabriel, and every just man among the faithful, and the angels are his helpers besides. Perhaps, if he [Mohammed] divorced you all, Allah would give him better wives than you—Muslims, believers, submissive, devout, penitent, obedient, observant of fasting, widows, and virgins."*

M429 Ibrahim became a favorite of Mohammed. But when the child was fifteen months old, he fell sick. Mary and her slave sister attended the child during his illness. Mohammed was there at his death and wept mightily. Mohammed was to suffer the Arabic shame of having no living male children to succeed him.

MARRIAGE TO HIS DAUGHTER-IN-LAW

M290 Mohammed had an adopted son, Zaid, and went by his house. Zaid was not there and Mohammed went on in the house. He wound up seeing his daughter-in-law, Zeinab, in a thin dress, and her charms were evident. Mohammed was smitten and said, "Gracious Lord! Good Heavens! How thou dost turn the hearts of men!"

M290 Well, Zeinab, had turned the head of the future king of Arabia and she told her husband what Mohammed said. The step-son went to

Mohammed and said that he would divorce Zeinab so he could have her. Mohammed said no. But Zaid went ahead and divorced her anyway. In Arabia a union between a man and his daughter-in-law was incest and forbidden. But while Mohammed was with Aisha, he had a revelation and said, "Who will go and congratulate Zeinab and tell her that Allah has blessed our marriage?" The maid went right off to tell her of the good news. So Mohammed added another wife.

> 33:4 *Allah has not given any man two hearts for one body, nor has He made your wives whom you divorce to be like your mothers, nor has He made your adopted sons like your real sons. [Previous to this verse, an Arab's adopted children were treated as blood children. This verse relates to verse 37 of this sura.] These are only words you speak with your mouths, but Allah speaks the truth and guides to the right path. Name your adopted sons after their real fathers; this is more just in Allah's sight. But if you do not know their fathers' names, call them your brothers in the faith and your friends. There will be no blame on you if you sin unintentionally, but that which you intend in your heart will be held against you. Allah is forgiving and merciful.*

> 33:36 *And it is not the place of a believer, either man or woman, to have a choice in his or her affairs when Allah and His Messenger have decided on a matter. Those who disobey Allah and His Messenger are clearly on the wrong path. And remember when you said to your adopted son [Zaid], the one who had received Allah's favor [converted to Islam], "Keep your wife to yourself and fear Allah," and you hid in your heart what Allah was to reveal, and you feared men [what people would say if he married his daughter-in-law], when it would have been right that you should fear Allah. And when Zaid divorced his wife, We gave her to you as your wife, so it would not be a sin for believers to marry the wives of their adopted sons, after they have divorced them. And Allah's will must be carried out.*
> 33:38 *The Messenger will not be blamed for anything that Allah has given him permission to do. This was Allah's way with the messengers who came before you, and Allah's commands are absolute. The messengers fulfilled Allah's mission and feared Him, and feared no one but Allah. Allah takes sufficient account. Mohammed is not the father of any man among you. He is Allah's Messenger and the last of the messengers. Allah knows all things.*

Since Zaid was adopted, he was not really a son, so there was no incest. M292 It was about this time that the veil was imposed. The wives became mothers of the faithful and could not marry after Mohammed died.

33:55 *There is no blame on the Messenger's wives if they speak unveiled with their fathers, sons, brothers, nephews on either their brother's or sister's side, their women, or their slave-girls. Women! Fear Allah, for Allah witnesses all things.*

JIHAD, THE FIRST DHIMMIS

CHAPTER 19

4:80 *Those who obey the Messenger, obey Allah. As for those who turn away from you, We have not sent you to watch over them.*

KHAYBAR

1756 After the treaty of Al Hudaybiya, Mohammed stayed in Medina for about two months before he collected his army and marched to the forts of Khaybar, a community of wealthy Jewish farmers who lived in a village of separate forts about 100 miles from Medina.

1758 Mohammed seized the forts one at a time. Among the captives was a beautiful Jewess named Safiya. Mohammed took her for his sexual pleasure. One of his men had first chosen her for his own slave of pleasure, but Mohammed traded him two of her cousins for Safiya. Mohammed always got first choice of the spoils of war and the women.

1759 On the occasion of Khaybar, Mohammed put forth new orders about sex with captive women. If the woman was pregnant, she was not to be used for sex until after the birth of the child. Nor were any women to be used for sex who were unclean with regards to the Muslim laws about menstruation.

1764 Mohammed knew that there was a large treasure hidden somewhere in Khaybar, so he brought forth the Jew who he thought knew the most about it and questioned him. The Jew denied any knowledge. Mohammed told one of his men, "Torture the Jew until you extract what he has." So the Jew was staked on the ground, and a small fire built on his chest to get him to talk. When the man was nearly dead and still would not talk, Mohammed had him released and taken to one of his men who had a brother killed in the fight. This Muslim got the pleasure of cutting off the tortured Jew's head.

1764 At Khaybar Mohammed instituted the first dhimmis. After the best of the goods were taken from the Jews Mohammed left them to work the land. Since his men knew nothing about farming, and the Jews were skilled at it, they worked the land and gave Mohammed half of their profits.

1774 There were a total of 1,800 people who divided up the wealth taken from the beaten Jews of Khaybar. A cavalry man got three shares, a foot soldier got one share. Mohammed appointed eighteen chiefs to divide the loot. Mohammed received his one-fifth before it was distributed.

FADAK

1777 The Jews of Fadak panicked when they saw what Mohammed did at Khaybar. They would be next, so they surrendered to Mohammed without a fight. Since there was no battle Mohammed got 100% of their goods and they worked the land and gave half to Mohammed each year. They became dhimmis like those of Khaybar.

MOHAMMED'S FINAL JIHAD

CHAPTER 20

3:53 "Our Lord! We believe in what Thou hast
revealed, and we follow the Apostle; then write
us down among those who bear witness."

THE PILGRIMAGE

1789 After returning from Khaybar, Mohammed sent out many raiding parties and expeditions. Seven years after Mohammed moved to Medina and one year after the treaty of Hudaybiya, Mohammed led the Muslims to the Kabah in Mecca. While there he kissed one of the stones of the Kabah and trotted around the Kabah. When he got to the corner with the Black Stone, he walked up and kissed it. He did this for three circuits of the Kabah.

1789 As Mohammed entered Mecca, the man leading his camel said this poetry:

> *Get out of his way, Kafirs, make way*
> *I know Allah's truth in accepting it*
> *We will fight you about its interpretation*
> *As we have fought you about its revelation*
> *We will cut off your head and remove friend from friend.*

1790 After his three day stay in Mecca, the Quraysh asked him to leave as per the treaty. Mohammed asked to stay and have a wedding feast and he would invite the Quraysh. The Quraysh said no, please leave. He left.

THE RAID ON MUTA

1791-3 Mohammed sent an army of 3000 to Muta soon after his return from Mecca. Now Muta was north of Medina, near Syria. When they arrived the Muslims found a large army of the Byzantines. They argued about what to do. One of them said, "Men, you are complaining of what you came here to do. Die as martyrs. Islam does not fight with numbers or strength but with Islam. Come! We have only two prospects. Victory or martyrdom, both are fine. Let us go forward!"

1796 The Muslims were cut to ribbons. The Byzantines were professionals and superior in numbers.

1798 The Muslims who remained behind in Medina scorned the returning fighters. They threw dirt at them and said, "You are runaways. You fled from the way of Allah. You fled from jihad." Poetry was written to the effect that the men kept their distance from the Byzantine army and were afraid of death. They loved life too much and feared death.

MECCA CONQUERED

1803 At the treaty of Hudaybiya, it was agreed that the Meccans and Mohammed could make alliances between themselves and other tribes. There were two different Arab tribes, one allied with the Meccans and the other allied with Mohammed. As tribes are prone to do, there was a murder and subsequently retaliation by the other tribe. Then it was escalated by the Quraysh of Mecca when they helped out their ally. A chief came to Mohammed to tell of his losses and how it was time for Mohammed to take the cause of his ally and punish the Quraysh of Mecca.

1811 As a result of the fighting between a tribe allied with the Meccans and a tribe allied with Mohammed, he marched on Mecca with 10,000 men to punish them.

1813 The Muslims camped at a small town near Mecca. The Meccans needed to know whether Mohammed was going to enter Mecca. Many lives would be saved if the people would come out and seek protection, so they would not be killed.

1813-4 The chief of the Meccans, Abu Sufyan, came to the Muslim camp to negotiate. Abu Sufyan, the chief Meccan, spent the night in the Muslim army camp and went to Mohammed the next morning. Mohammed spoke, "Isn't it time for you to recognize that there is no god but Allah?" Abu answered, "I thought that there had been another god with Allah, he would have helped me." Mohammed replied, "Woe to you, Abu Sufyan, is it not time to recognize that I am Allah's apostle?" Abu Sufyan said, "As to that I have some doubt." He was told, "Submit and testify that there is no god but Allah and that Mohammed is his apostle before you lose your head!" So he submitted.

Abu Sufyan went ahead and announced to Mecca that Mohammed's army was coming. They were not to resist but to go into their houses, his house or the Kabah and that they would be safe.

1819 Mohammed had told his commanders only to kill those who resisted. Otherwise they were to bother no one except for those who had spoken against Mohammed. The list of those to be killed:

- One of Mohammed's secretaries, who had said that when he was recording Mohammed's Koranic revelations sometimes Mohammed let the secretary insert better speech. This caused him to lose faith and he became an apostate.
- Two singing girls who had sung satires against Mohammed.
- A Muslim tax collector who had become an apostate (left Islam).
- A man who had insulted Mohammed.

1821 Mohammed went to the Kabah and rode around it seven times. Each time he went past the Black Stone, he touched it with his stick. Then he called for the key to the Kabah and entered. There was a wooden dove carved that he picked up and broke and threw out the door. There were 360 ritual objects representing the gods of the various Arab faiths. Mohammed had them all destroyed by burning.

Mohammed announced the end of all feuds, all revenge killings, payment of blood money. Veneration of the ancestors was over.

KHALID'S DESTRUCTION OF THE NATIVE SHRINE

1840 Mohammed sent Khalid to an ancient temple near Mecca that was used by several tribes for worship. When Khalid got there, he destroyed it completely.

THE BATTLE OF HUNAIN

1840 When Mohammed took Mecca, the surrounding Arab tribes saw that if he was not opposed he would be King of Arabia. The Hawazin Arabs decided to oppose him under the leadership of Malik.

1842 Mohammed sent a spy to gather intelligence about the Arabs. When he received the information, he set about for jihad. He first borrowed armor and lances from a wealthy Meccan and then marched out with 12,000 men.

1845 When the army descended into the broad area, they found the enemy prepared and hiding, waiting to attack. The Muslim troops broke and ran. Mohammed stood in his stirrups and called out, "Where are you going? Come to me, the Apostle of Allah." Most of the men continued to retreat except his battle hardened core troops who regrouped around him. About a core of 100 lead the charge to turn the tide. They were steadfast. Mohammed looked at the carnage and said, "Now the oven is hot!"

1847 One of the Muslim women was near Mohammed and said about those who were retreating, "Kill those who flee just as you kill those who are attacking us."

> 9:25 *Allah has helped you in many battlefields, and on the day of Hunain, when your great numbers elated you [there were 12,000 Muslims and 4000 unbelievers], but availed you nothing [the Muslims panicked and fled], and the earth, for all its breadth, constrained you, you turned your backs in flight.*
>
> 9:26 *Then Allah sent down His tranquility on His Messenger and on the faithful, and He sent down invisible forces and He punished the unbelievers. This is the reward for those without faith. After this, Allah will turn to whom He pleases, for Allah is oft-forgiving and merciful.*

THE RAID ON TABUK

1894 Mohammed decided to raid the Byzantines. Normally he never let his men actually know where he was headed. He would announce a destination, but after they were on the way, he would announce the actual place. But this raid was far away in very hot weather, so greater preparations would need to be made. The men began to prepare, but with no enthusiasm due to the heat, it was time for harvest to begin and they remembered the last combat with the Byzantines—they lost badly.

1894 When Mohammed asked one of his best men if he wanted to go, the man replied, "Would you allow me to stay? You know how much I love women and when I see the Byzantine women, I don't know if I will be able to control myself." So Mohammed told him to stay. But the Koran had a comment:

> 9:45 *The only ones who will ask leave of you are those who do not believe in Allah and the Last Day, whose hearts are full of doubts, and who waver in their doubts. If they had intended to go to war, they would have prepared for war. But Allah was opposed to their marching forth and held them back. It was said, "Sit at home with those who sit." If they had taken the field with you, they would not have added to your strength but would have hurried about among you, stirring up dissension. Some of you would have listened to them. Allah knows the evildoers. They had plotted dissension before and made plots against you again until the truth arrived. Then the decree of Allah prevailed, much to their disgust.*
>
> 9:49 *Some of them say to you, "Allow me to remain at home, and do not expose me to temptation." Have they not already fallen into temptation? Hell will surround the unbelievers. If a success befalls you [Mohammed], it annoys them. If a misfortune befalls you, they say, "We took our precautions," and they turn their backs and are glad.*

1895 There was much grumbling about the heat.

> 9:81 *Those who were left behind were delighted at sitting behind Allah's Messenger. They hated to strive and fight with their riches and their lives for Allah's cause [jihad] and said, "Do not go out in the heat." Say: The Fire of Hell is a fiercer heat." If they would only understand. Let them laugh a little for they will weep much in payment for their deeds.*
>
> 9:83 *If Allah brings you back from the fight and they ask your permission to march out with you the next time, say, "You will never come out with me or fight an enemy with me. You were well pleased to sit at home at the first crisis, so sit at home with those who lag behind."*

1896 So Mohammed set off, but there were many Muslims who were slow to leave or they came with misgivings. After the first camp some of the Muslims left and returned to Medina. These were called hypocrites.

> 9:51 *Say: Nothing will happen to us except what Allah has destined for us. He is our protector. Let the faithful put their trust in Allah. Say: Can you expect for us anything other than one of the two best things—martyrdom, or victory? Allah will inflict a punishment Himself or at our hands. So wait, and we will wait with you.*
>
> 9:53 *Say: Pay your offerings willingly or unwillingly. It cannot be accepted from you because you are a wicked people. The only reasons their contributions are not accepted are because they reject Allah and His Messenger. They do not keep prayer but with sluggishness, and they do not make offerings willingly.*
>
> 9:55 *Do not let their riches or their children amaze you. Allah's plan is to punish them by means of these in this present life and for their souls to depart while they are unbelievers. They swear by Allah that they are believers when they are unbelievers, but they are people who are afraid of you [Mohammed]. If they could find a place of refuge, or caves, or a hiding place, they surely would have turned towards it running in haste.*

1902 When they got to Tabuk, the people there paid the poll tax, jizya. By paying the poll tax, a per person tax, they would not be attacked, killed or robbed by the Muslims. Those who paid the jizya were under the protection of Islam.

The Battle of Tabuk was hard for Mohammed. The Muslims did not come out to be jihadists as they had before. But the Koran makes clear that jihad is an obligation.

> 9:85 *Do not let their riches or their children astonish you. Through these Allah is inclined to punish them in this world and to let their souls depart while they are still unbelievers. When a sura [chapter] was sent down saying, "Believe in Allah and strive and go to war with His Messenger," those*

of them who are possessed of riches demanded exemption saying, "Leave us behind that we may be with those who sit at home." They are well contented to be with those who stay behind for their hearts are sealed. They do not understand.

9:88 The Messenger and those who share his faith strive hard for their faith with their with purses and lives. All good things await them. These are the ones who will prosper. Allah has made ready for them Gardens beneath which the rivers flow, where they will remain forever. This is the supreme felicity.

9:90 Some Arabs of the desert came with excuses to avoid fighting. They who had rejected Allah and His Messenger sat at home. A painful doom will fall on those who do not believe. It will be no crime in the weak, in the sick, or in those who find no resources to contribute to Allah's cause [jihad] to stay at home provided they are sincere with Allah and His Messenger. There is no cause of blame against those who act virtuously. Allah is gracious and merciful. Nor is their blame against those who, when they came to you asking to be provided with mounts, were told, "I do not find mounts for you." They turned their backs, their eyes shedding tears of grief, because they found no means to contribute.

9:93 The cause for blame is only against those who ask for exemption though they are rich. They are pleased to be with those who stay behind, and Allah has set a seal upon their hearts so they do not know. They will present their excuses to you when you return to them. Say: Do not present excuses. We cannot believe you. Allah has informed us about you. Allah and His Messenger will behold your doings. You will return to the knower of the seen and the unseen. He will tell you the truth of what you have done.

ETERNAL JIHAD

T448 After all the victories, some Muslims said that the days of fighting were over and even began to sell their arms. But Mohammed forbid this, saying, "There shall not cease from the midst of my people a party engaged in fighting for the truth, until the Antichrist appears." Jihad was recognized as the normal state of affairs. Indeed, the Koran prepares the way for this:

9:122 The faithful should not all go out together to fight. If a part of every troop remained behind, they could instruct themselves in their religion and warn their people when they return to them that they should guard against evil.

9:123 Believers, fight the unbelievers who are near you, and let them find you to be tough and hard. Know that Allah is with those who guard against evil.

ABU BAKR LEADS THE PILGRIMAGE

1919-20 Abu Bakr led the pilgrimage from Medina to Mecca. While they were in Mecca major changes were made to the treaty of Hudaybiya, which are recorded in the Koran. The treaty is only good for four more months, then jihad will be declared if the non-Muslims don't submit to Islam.

> 9:1 *A declaration of immunity from Allah and His Messenger to the unbelievers with whom you have made a treaty: Travel freely in the land for four months, but know that you cannot escape Allah and that those who do not believe will be put to shame by Allah.*
>
> 9:3 *Allah and His Messenger proclaimed to the people on the day of the greater pilgrimage: "Allah and His Messenger are free from any obligations with the unbelievers. If you repent to Allah, it will be better for you, but if you turn away, then know that you cannot escape Allah. Announce a painful punishment to those who do not believe. But this does not concern those unbelievers with whom you have an agreement and who have not failed you, nor aided anyone against you. So fulfill your agreement with them to the end of its term, for Allah loves those who fear Him.*
>
> 9:5 *When the sacred months [by ancient Arab custom there were four months during which there was to be no violence] are passed, kill the unbelievers wherever you find them. Take them as captives, besiege them, and lie in wait for them with every kind of ambush. If they submit to Islam, observe prayer, and pay the poor tax, then let them go their way. Allah is gracious and merciful. If anyone of the unbelievers seeks asylum with you, grant it that he may hear the word of Allah; then take him to a place of safety. This is because they are an ignorant people.*

1922 After this time, those who practice the old native religions of Arabia will no longer be able to come to Mecca for pilgrimage.

> 9:17 *It is not for the unbelievers to visit or maintain the mosques of Allah while they witness against their own souls to disbelief. Their work bears no fruit; they will abide in the Fire forever. Only he who believes in Allah and the Last Day should visit the temples of Allah, observe regular prayer, and practice regular charity, and fear only Allah. These will be among the rightly guided.*

1924 The non-Muslims are unclean and must not approach the Kabah. The money that will be lost from their pilgrimages will be taken care of by Allah. Jihad will bring in the lost money.

> 9:28 *Oh, believers, only the unbelievers are unclean. Do not let them come near the Sacred Temple after this year of theirs. If you fear poverty from the loss of their business [breaking commercial ties with the Meccans], Allah*

will enrich you from His abundance if He pleases. Allah is knowing and wise.

1924 The Koran then turns to the issue of the raid on the Byzantines at Tabuk. Muslims must answer the call to jihad. It is an obligation. If the Byzantine raid had been short and had made for easy war spoils, the Muslims would have joined readily. But instead they made excuses. A Muslim's duty is not to avoid fighting with their person and money.

> 9:38 *Oh, believers, what possessed you that when it was said, "March forth in Allah's cause [jihad]," you cling heavily to the earth? Do you prefer the life of this world to the next? Little is the comfort of this life compared to the one that is to come. Unless you march forth, He will punish you with a grievous penalty, and He will put another in your place. You will not harm Him at all, for Allah has power over everything.*
>
> 9:40 *If you do not assist your Messenger, it is no matter for Allah assisted him when the unbelievers drove him out, he [Mohammed] being only one of two men. When the two [Mohammed and Abu Bakr] were in the cave, the Messenger said to his companion, "Do not be distressed, for Allah is with us." Allah sent His tranquility upon him, and strengthened him with hosts you did not see. He humbled the word of those who disbelieved and exalted the word of Allah, for Allah is mighty and wise. March forth both the lightly and heavily armed, and strive hard in Allah's cause [jihad] with your substance and your persons. This is better for you if you knew it.*
>
> 9:42 *Had there been a near advantage and a short journey [Mohammed marched to Tabuk against the Greeks. It was a long, hot campaign]; they would certainly have followed you, but the journey was too long for them. Yet they will swear by Allah saying, "If we only could have, we would surely have gone forth with you." They would destroy their own souls. Allah knows that they are surely lying.*
>
> 9:43 *Allah forgive you, Mohammed. Why did you give them permission to stay behind before you knew those who told the truth from those who lied? Those who believe in Allah and in the Last Day do not ask for exemption from fighting with their wealth and their lives. Allah knows those who fear Him.*

1926 Those who try to avoid jihad are hypocrites. The Prophet should struggle against them. They are bound for Hell.

> 9:73 *Oh, Prophet, strive hard against the unbelievers and the hypocrites, and be firm with them. Hell will be their dwelling place: A wretched journey.*

1927 In the past Mohammed had prayed at funerals and gone to the graves for some of the hypocrites. But now a Muslim should not pray for a non-Muslim or stand at their grave.

> 9:84 *Never pray over nor stand over the grave of anyone of them who dies because they did not believe in Allah and His Messenger and died in their wickedness.*

Those who believe in Allah and the Apostle and enter jihad with their wealth and selves will prosper and enter Paradise. This is a promise from Allah.

> 9:111 *Allah has bought from the believers their lives and their wealth, and in return, theirs is the Garden of Paradise. They will fight on the path of Allah so they slay and are slain. It is a promise binding on Him in truth through the Law, in the Gospel, and in the Koran, and who is more faithful to His promise than Allah? Rejoice, therefore, in the pledge that you have made, for this will be the great bliss.*

1933 When Mohammed had taken Mecca and Tabuk, deputations began to come from the Arabs. The Arabs were waiting to see what would happen between the Quraysh and Mohammed. When Mohammed was victorious, the Arabs came in groups and joined with him.

> 110:1 *When the help of Allah and the victory arrive, and you see men entering the religion of Allah in ranks, then celebrate the praises of your Lord and pray for His forgiveness, for He is always ready to show mercy.*

1956 The kings of Himyar wrote to Mohammed that they had submitted to Islam. Mohammed wrote them back, "… I received your message and am informed of your Islam and your killing Kafirs. Allah has guided you. … send the one fifth of the spoils of war and tax the believers… Christians and Jews who do not convert must pay the poll tax…"

1965 Mohammed sent out tax collectors to every part of Islam to collect the tax.

THE SHARIA

CHAPTER 21

4:170 People! The Messenger has come to you with truth
from your Lord. If you believe, it will be better for you.

The Sharia is the law of Islam that is based upon the Koran, the Hadith and the Sira. It is the political aim of Islam to replace all legal codes and constitutions (which are man-made) with the Sharia, which comes from Allah.

MARRIAGE/DIVORCE/SEX

4:34 Allah has made men superior to women because men spend their wealth to support them. Therefore, virtuous women are obedient, and they are to guard their unseen parts as Allah has guarded them. As for women whom you fear will rebel, admonish them first, and then send them to a separate bed, and then beat them. But if they are disobedient after that, then do nothing further; surely Allah is exalted and great!
4:35 If you fear a breach between a man and wife, then send a judge from his family, and a judge from her family. If they both want to come to a reconciliation, Allah will bring them back together. Truly Allah is all-knowing and wise!

24:30 Tell the men who are believers that they should look away from that which tempts them and control their lustful desires. Therefore, they will be more pure. Allah is well aware of all they do. And tell the women who are believers that they should lower their eyes and guard their purity, and they should not display their beauty and adornments except that which is normally shown. They should cover their breasts with their veils and only show their adornments to their husband, father-in-law, sons, step-sons, brothers, nephews, or their female servants, eunuch slaves, and children who are innocent and do not notice a woman's nakedness. And do not let them stamp their feet so as to reveal their hidden adornments [ankle bracelets]. Believers, all of you turn to Allah and repent so that it will go well for you.
24:32 And marry those among you who are single, or an honorable male or female servant. And if they are poor, then Allah will give them riches from His own bounty. Allah is bountiful and all-knowing. And for those who cannot afford to marry, let them stay pure until Allah fulfills their needs

from His bounty. In regard to your slaves who wish to buy their freedom, grant it if you see there is good in them, and give them a part of the wealth that Allah has given you. Do not force your female slaves into prostitution just to gain the wealth of this world if they wish to remain pure. Yet if they are forced to do so, then truly Allah will be merciful.

2:221 *You will not marry pagan women unless they accept the faith. A slave girl who believes is better than an idolatress, although the idolatress may please you more. Do not give your daughters away in marriage to unbelievers until they believe, for a slave who is a believer is better than an idolater, though the idolater may please you more. These lure you to the Fire, but Allah calls you to Paradise and forgiveness by His will. He makes His signs clear to mankind so that they may remember.*
2:222 *They ask you about women's menstrual cycle. Say: It is a discomfort. Therefore, keep away from them during this time and do not come near them until they are clean again. But when they are clean, you may lie with them as Allah has commanded. Allah loves those who turn to Him and seek cleanliness.*
2:223 *Your women are your plowed fields: go into your fields when you like, but do some good deed beforehand and fear Allah. Keep in mind that you will meet Him. Give good news to the believers.*

4:15 *If any of your women are guilty of adultery or fornication, then bring in four of you as witnesses against them. If they admit their guilt, then shut them up in their houses until they die or until Allah makes some other way for them. If two of your men are guilty of an indecent act [homosexuality], punish both of them. If they ask for forgiveness and change their ways, then leave them alone, for Allah is forgiving and merciful!*
4:17 *Allah will forgive those who sin unknowingly and then turn away and repent soon thereafter; Allah will show them mercy, for Allah is knowing and wise! But as for those who do evil, and then when they are about to die say, "Now I truly turn to Allah!" or those who die as unbelievers, they will not be forgiven, and a painful punishment is prepared for them.*
4:19 *Believers! It is not allowed for you to inherit the wives of your deceased family members against their will, or to prevent the wives from re-marrying in order to take away part of the dowry you have given them unless they are guilty of flagrant indecency. Treat them kindly for if you hate them, it may be that you hate that in which Allah has placed abundant goodness.*
4:20 *If you want to exchange one wife for another, do not take anything away from the dowry you have given her. Would you take it by slandering her and doing her obvious wrong? How could you take it back when you have slept with one another and entered into a firm covenant?*

LEGAL

5:38 *As to the thieves, whether men or women, cut off their hands in payment for their deeds. This is a penalty by way of warning from Allah Himself. Allah is mighty and wise. But whoever repents after his wickedness, and makes amends, Allah will turn to him, for Allah is forgiving and merciful. Do you not know that the sovereignty of the heavens and of the earth is Allah's? He punishes whom He will and forgives whom He will. Allah has power over all things.*

2:178 *Believers! Retaliation is prescribed for you in the matter of murder: the free man for the free man, a slave for a slave, a female for a female. If the brother of the slain gives a measure of forgiveness, then grant him any sensible request, and compensate him with a generous payment [blood money]. This is a merciful indulgence from your Lord. He who sins after having been pardoned will suffer a terrible fate. And there is life for you in the law of retaliation, men of understanding, so that you will protect yourselves against evil.*
2:180 *It is ordered that when you are on the verge of death that you dispense your possessions equally to parents and near relatives. This is the duty of the Allah-fearing. One who hears the will and then changes it will be guilty, for Allah is all-hearing and all-knowing. But if anyone fears an error or partiality on the part of the testator and brings about an agreement among the parties, then he is not to blame. Allah is forgiving and merciful.*

4:92 *A believer should never kill a Muslim unless an accident occurs. Whoever kills a fellow Muslim by accident must free one of his believing slaves and pay blood-money to the victim's family unless they give it to charity. If the victim was a believer from a people at war with you, then freeing a believing slave is enough. But if the victim was from a people with whom you have an alliance, then his family should be paid blood-money and a believing slave must be set free. For those who cannot afford to do this, they must fast for two months straight. This is the penance commanded by Allah. Allah is all-knowing and wise!*
4:93 *For those who intentionally kill another Muslim, Hell will be their punishment, where they will live forever. The wrath of Allah will be upon them, He will curse them, and they will receive terrible torture.*

RELIGIOUS

2:172 *Believers, eat the good things We have given you, and give thanks to Allah if it is truly Him you worship. He has forbidden that you eat carrion [animals found dead], blood, and pork, also any other meat that has been sacrificed to any other besides Allah. But if one is forced by necessity and does not intend to sin, then he will be held blameless. Allah is forgiving and merciful.*

2:183 *Believers, fasting is commanded for you as it was for those before you so that you will learn to protect against evil. Fast a particular number of days, but if any of you are sick or on a journey you may fast the same number of days at a later time, Those who are unable to endure it may be redeemed by feeding a poor person. Whoever does good on his own will be rewarded; it is better for those of you who fast, if you only knew it.*

2:185 *During the month of Ramadan, the Koran was sent down as a guide for mankind with clear signs of guidance for distinguishing right and wrong. Therefore, whoever of you is present must fast that month, and whoever is sick or on a journey will later fast the same number of days. Allah desires your comfort, not your discomfort. He wishes you to fast the entire month so that you will glorify Him for His guidance.*

2:186 *When my servants question you about Me, then surely I am near. I will answer the prayer of each who requests when he calls to Me. Let them hear My call and trust in Me so that they will be guided to the right path.*

2:187 *It is now permitted for you to lie with your spouses on the nights of fasting; you are a consolation for one another. Allah knew what you did secretly between yourselves, but He has turned to you in forgiveness. Therefore, you may now lie with one another and fulfill what Allah has ordained. Eat and drink until you are about to distinguish a white thread from a black thread in the light of the approaching dawn; then fast again until nightfall and do not touch your spouse, but instead pray at the mosque. These are the limits set by Allah, so do not come near them. It is in this way that He makes his signs clear to mankind so that they practice self-discipline.*

2:188 *Do not take one another's property by unfair means or seek to bribe the judges to take another's wealth unjustly and knowingly.*

2:189 *When they ask you about the moon's phases say: They are signs for mankind to mark the seasons and the pilgrimage. It is not righteousness if you enter your houses from the back as the pagans do. [Pilgrims of the old Arabic religions entered their houses from the back after pilgrimage.] Righteousness is found in fearing Allah. Enter your houses through the proper doors and observe your duty to Allah so that you will find success.*

CUSTOM

49:9 *If two parties of the believers are at war, then make peace between them. If one of them wrongs the other, fight against that party that does wrong until they come back to the commands of Allah. If they come back, make peace between them with fairness and act impartially. Allah loves those who act with justice. Only the believers are brothers, so make peace between your brothers, and fear Allah so that you may obtain mercy.*

MOHAMMED'S LAST YEAR

CHAPTER 22

*24:51 But when Allah and His Messenger call
the true believers to judge between them, their
response is, "We have heard, and we obey."*

THE FAREWELL PILGRIMAGE

1968 Ten years after entering Medina Mohammed made what was to be
his last pilgrimage to Mecca. There he made his farewell address. He told
the Muslims that usury was abolished, Allah would judge them and their
works. All of the blood shed before Islam was to be left unavenged. The
lunar calendar was the sacred calendar and it was not to be adjusted with
respect to the solar calendar.

1969 The men have rights over their wives and the wives have rights
over the men. The wives must never commit adultery nor act in a sexual
manner towards others. If they do, put them in separate rooms and beat
them lightly. If they refrain from these things, they have the right to food
and clothing. Lay injunctions on women lightly for they are prisoners of
the men and have no control over their persons.

M473 Feed and clothe your slaves well.

1969 Every Muslim is a Muslim's brother. Only take from a brother what
he gives you.

1970 Mohammed led the Muslims through the rituals of the pilgrimage.

THE FINAL STATE OF CHRISTIANS AND JEWS

M453 When Mohammed first started preaching in Mecca, his religion
was Arabian. Then Allah became identified with Jehovah and Jewish elements were introduced. When Mohammed moved to Medina, he argued
with the Jews when they denied his status as a prophet in the Judaic line. He
then annihilated the Jews and makes no more connections between Islam
and the Jews. In his last statement, Jews and Christians became perpetual second class political citizens, dhimmis (pay the dhimmi tribute, jizya,
and are subdued). Only those Christians and Jews who submit to Islam are
protected. Islam defines Judaism and Christianity. The real Christians are
those who deny the Trinity and accept Mohammed as the final prophet.

The real Jews are those who accept Mohammed as the final prophet of their god, Jehovah. Both Christians and Jews must accept that the Koran is the true Scripture and that the Old Testament and New Testament are corrupt and in error. The contradictions between the Koran and the New and Old Testament are proof of the corruption of the nonbelievers.

All other Jews and Christians are false and unbelievers.

> 9:29 *Make war on those who have received the Scriptures [Jews and Christians] but do not believe in Allah or in the Last Day. They do not forbid what Allah and His Messenger have forbidden. The Christians and Jews do not follow the religion of truth until they submit and pay the poll tax [jizya], and they are humiliated.*
>
> 9:30 *The Jews say, "Ezra is the son of Allah," [this tradition is unknown in the Old Testament] and the Christians say, "The Messiah is a son of Allah." Such are the sayings in their mouths, but they resemble the saying of the unbelievers of old. Allah destroy them. How they are deluded from the truth.*
>
> 9:31 *They take their rabbis and their monks and the Messiah, son of Mary, for Lords besides Allah [Both Jews and Christians of that area used the term "rabbi" for their religious leaders. Islam only applied rabbi to Allah], though they were bidden to worship one Allah only. There is no god but Allah. He is far from having the partners they associate with Him.*
>
> 9:32 *They desire to put out Allah's light with their mouths, but Allah only desires to perfect His light, though the unbelievers detest it. He sent His Messenger with the guidance and a religion of the truth that He may make it victorious over every other religion, though the unbelievers will detest it.*
>
> 9:34 *Oh, Believers of truth, many of the rabbis and monks devour the substance of man and hinder them from the way of Allah. To those who store up gold and silver and do not spend it on Allah's cause [jihad], give tidings of grievous torment. On that day their treasures will be heated in Hellfire and their foreheads, their sides, and their backs will be branded with them, "This is the treasure you have buried for yourselves. Now, taste your riches."*

The Christians have hidden their prophesies that Mohammed would come to fulfill the work of Christ. To believe in the divinity of Christ is to refuse to submit to Islam. Those Christians are unbelievers and infidels. Like the Jews, only those Christians who submit to Islam and become dhimmis and are ruled by the sharia (Islamic law) are actual Christians. Islam defines all religions. No religion defines itself, except Islam.

> 5:14 *We made a covenant with those who say, "We are Christians," but they, too, have forgotten a part of what they were taught [Islam claims that the Christians suppressed the prophecies of Jesus that Mohammed would be the final prophet] so We have stirred up animosity and hatred among*

them that will last until Resurrection Day. In the end, Allah will tell them what they have done.

5:15 *Oh, people of the Scriptures, Our Messenger has come to you to clear up what you have hidden of those Scriptures and to pass over many things that are now unnecessary. Now you have a new light and a clear Book from Allah. He will use it to guide whoever seeks to follow His good pleasure to paths of peace. He will bring them out of the darkness to the light, and, by his decree, will guide them to the straight path.*

5:17 *Surely they are unbelievers who say, "Allah is the Messiah, son of Mary." Say: Who has any power against Allah if He chose to destroy the Messiah, son of Mary, his mother, and all who are on the earth together? Allah's is the sovereignty of the heavens and of the earth and of all that is between them. He creates what He will, and Allah has power over all things.*

5:72 *The unbelievers say, "Jesus is the Messiah, Son of Mary," for the Messiah said, "Oh, Children of Israel, worship Allah, my Lord and your Lord." Whoever will join other gods with Allah, He will forbid him in the Garden, and his abode will be the Fire. The wicked will have no helpers. They surely blaspheme who say, "Allah is the third of three [the Trinity]," for there is no god except one Allah, and if they do not refrain from what they say, a grievous penalty will fall on those who disbelieve. Will they not turn to Allah and ask His forgiveness? For Allah is forgiving and merciful.*

5:75 *The Messiah, Son of Mary, is but a messenger. Other messengers have passed away before him, and his mother was a saintly woman; they both ate food. See how Allah makes His signs clear to them; then see how they turn from the truth. Say: Will you worship, beside Allah, that which can neither hurt nor help you? Allah hears and knows all things.*

A SUMMARY OF MOHAMMED'S ARMED EVENTS

1973 In a nine year period Mohammed personally attended twenty-seven raids. There were thirty-eight other battles and expeditions. This is a total of sixty-five armed events, not including assassinations and executions, for an average of one armed event every seven weeks.

MOHAMMED'S DEATH

I1000 When Mohammed spoke to Aisha, his favorite wife, He complained of a headache. Mohammed said, "No, Aisha, Oh my head. Would it distress you if you were to die before me so that I might wrap you in your shroud and pray over you?" Aisha said, "I think that if you did that, that after you returned to the house you would simply spend the night with one of your other wives." But the pain became worse and he took his final illness in the house of Aisha.

I1006 Mohammed weakened and was in a great deal of pain. Later he died with his head in Aisha's lap. His final words were the perfect summation of Islam, political action based upon religion.

> B4, 52, 288 *Mohammed said, "There should be no other religions besides Islam in Arabia" and that the money should be continued to be paid to influence the foreign unbeliever ambassadors.*

T1831 Mohammed was buried beneath his bed. The bed was removed and a grave was dug where the bed had stood.

JIHAD, CONQUEST

CHAPTER 23

*8:13 This was because they opposed Allah and
His messenger. Ones who oppose Allah and His
messenger will be severely punished by Allah.*

After Mohammed's death, Abu Bakr was elected caliph (political and
religious leader) to rule over Islam. He went to war against the many Muslims who wished to leave Islam after Mohammed's death. Thousands of
these apostates were killed in the Riddah wars, the war against apostasy.
The rule of political Islam in Arabia was now permanent.

Umar became the next caliph and put Mohammed's final command
into effect by expelling every Christian and Jew in Arabia. To this day
there is no temple, church, synagogue, shrine or any house of worship except that of Islam in Arabia. Umar then launched the jihad and conquest
of every neighbor of Arabia. The Islamic Empire was born and political
Islam became a permanent part of world politics.

FIGURE 23.1: PRE-JIHAD 600 A.D.

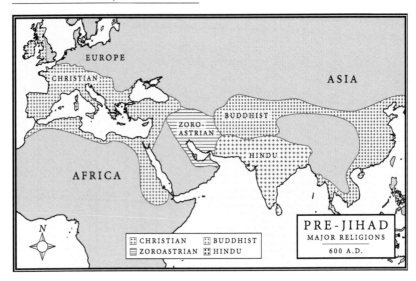

FIGURE 23.2: ISLAM AFTER MOHAMMED'S JIHAD 632 A.D.

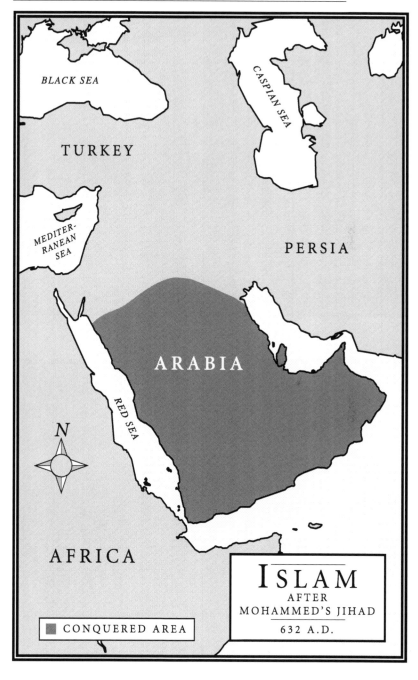

FIGURE 23.3: ISLAM AFTER UMAR'S JIHAD 661 A.D.

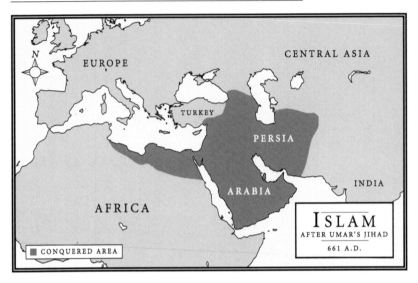

FIGURE 23.4: ISLAM IN PRESENT DAY

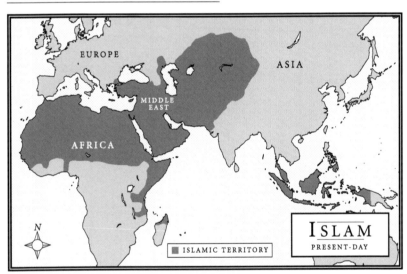

CONCLUSIONS

CHAPTER 24

THE KORAN AND PHILOSOPHY

The Koran lays out a complete philosophic system including politics and ethics. Its metaphysics claim that the only reality is Allah and humanity is to worship Him. Human life has been pre-determined by Allah. The highest form of living is to die for Allah in jihad. Death, Paradise, and Hell are the values of Islam. The proper relationship between Allah and humanity is master/slave (Muslims are the slaves of Allah) and fear (there are over 300 references to the fear of Allah, the Merciful).

The epistemology (what is knowledge and how knowledge is acquired) of the Koran and Islam is revelation. But since Mohammed is the final prophet, the door to further knowledge is closed.

LOGIC

The Koran advances a logical system. Truth is determined by revelation. No fact or argument may refute the Koran. Logical persuasion is based upon repetition and continued assertion. Another part of the persuasion is personal attacks against those who resist Islam. The Koran advances its argument through threats against specific people and groups. If persuasion fails, then force may be used to settle the logical or political argument.

Another aspect of Koranic logic is the use of name calling and personal insults to advance the truth. The Koran, with its poetical language and repeated threats and physical violence, bases its logic on emotions. Although its intellectual truth can be contradictory, the contradictions do not need to be resolved. Understanding apparent contradictions is a key to understanding Islamic logic. In unitary logic, a contradiction shows the theory or argument is false. But in the Koran, a contradiction does not prove an argument to be false. What appears to be logical contradictions are statements of duality that offer two true choices, depending upon the circumstances. This is a dualistic logic.

How do we know that the Koran is true? Because it contains the words of Allah. How do we know that these are the words of Allah? Mohammed said they were Allah's words. How do we know that Mohammed is Allah's messenger? Mohammed reported that Allah said that Mohammed is His messenger. The foundational assumption of Islam is based on circular reasoning.

DUALITY

The constant theme of Islam's perfect, eternal, and universal Koran is the division between those who believe Mohammed, and those who don't. This sacred division is dualism; Kafirs are not fully human and fall under a separate moral code. The dualistic separation is in politics, culture and religion. This duality is carried further by two different approaches to the Kafir in the Koran of Mecca and the Koran of Medina.

Some verses of the Koran contradict each other, but the text states a principle for resolving the contradictions. The later verse abrogates (nullifies) the earlier verse. However, since the entire Koran comes from Allah, then all verses are true, and no verse is actually false. The later, contradictory verse is merely stronger than the earlier, weaker verse. In practice, both sides of a contradiction can be true—logical duality.

ETHICS

The ethical system of the Koran is dualistic. How a person is treated depends upon his being a believer or a Kafir. There is one set of ethics for the believer and another set of ethics for the Kafir. Deceit, violence and force are acceptable against the Kafirs who resist the logic of the Koran. Believers are to be treated as brothers and sisters. There are 13 Koran verses which tell Muslims that they can be friendly with Kafirs, they are never their friends.[1]

POLITICS

The story of the Koran culminates in the dominance of political Islam. The Koran teaches that Islam is the perfect political system and is destined to rule the entire world. The governments and constitutions of the world must all submit to political Islam. If the political systems of the Kafirs do not submit, then force, jihad, may be used. All jihad is defensive, since refusing to submit to Islam is an offense against Allah. All Muslims must support the political action of jihad. This may take several forms—fighting, proselytizing or contributing money.

---

1   http://cspipublishing.com/statistical/pdf/Friends.pdf

The basis of the Islamic dualistic legal code, the Sharia, is found in the Koran. The Sharia treats Kafirs, including Jews and Christians, as inferior to believers. This legal inferiority is sacred, eternal and universal.

RELIGION

Some English translations of the Koran use the word God instead of Allah. In an English speaking culture the word God is synonymous with the God of the Hebrew Bible and the New Testament. However, the meaning of both Allah and Jehovah/Yahweh is based upon their textual attributes. Allah is defined by the Koran. Yahweh is defined by the Old Testament. On a textual basis Jews, Muslims, and Christians do not worship the same God. As an example, red and blue are both colors, but red is not blue. Likewise, Allah and Jehovah/Yahweh are both a God, but they are not the same God. Allah is not Jehovah/Yahweh[2]. Hence, Allah is the only acceptable term for the God of the Koran.

CATEGORIES AND THE KORANIC ARGUMENT

The key to understanding the Koran is Context, Chronology (the right time order of events), and Categories, CCC. Both the context and chronology come from Mohammed's life.

Some categories are obvious, such as retold tales from the Jews. But the less obvious category is *Koranic Argument*. The Koran is filled with violent threats against those who do not believe Mohammed and who did not believe the prophets of Allah in the past.

The stream of violence that runs throughout the Koran gives insight into its structure and how to select the topics and their divisions. The violence is not random, but turns out to have a structure. Take Hell, for instance. If you highlight the violent references to the Kafirs, you will find that there are five elements that accompany the violence:

1. A description of the threat or violence
2. Who is threatened
3. What they did to deserve the violence
4. How they are wrong
5. Words from Allah to support his messenger, Mohammed

---

2. Arab Christians also use the word Allah. The word allah is derived from *ilah*, deity or god, and *al*, meaning the. So Allah means The-God. But the meaning of the name Allah of Arab Christians is taken from the Christian scriptures. The meaning of the name Allah of Islam comes from the Koran. The Allah of Arab Christians is not the Allah of Islam. But for Arab Christians Allah is the same as Jehovah.

This structure is named the Koranic Argument. The argument goes like this: the Kafirs are wrong; Mohammed is right; and violence will come to those who deny him. The Koranic Argument is a *pericope*, a coherent unit of thought.

The violence of the Koran is not random, but develops around certain themes. If colored pens are used on printouts of the Koran to mark each of the above five elements with a different color, it will produce a colored "map" of the structure of the Koranic Argument that can be easily seen.

The Koranic Argument is a natural organizational element of thought in the Koran. A verse is typically only a sentence. People who use individual verses to prove anything about the Koran would never turn around and analyze Kant, Plato or Marx on the basis of a single sentence. No, you want to analyze thoughts, and a sentence is too small a unit for critical, systemic thought. The Koranic Argument allows easy textual analysis of thought, ideas and theme.

Example:

> 16:82 *However, if they [the Meccans] turn away, your only duty is to preach the clear message. They recognize the favors of Allah and then deny it. Most of them are ungrateful.*
>
> 16:84 *One day We will raise up a witness from every nation; then no excuses will be accepted from Kafirs, and they will not be allowed to make amends. When the wicked see the penalty waiting for them, it will not be made lighter for them nor will they be reprieved.*
>
> 16:86 *When those who ascribe partners to Allah see their false gods, they will say, "Lord, these are the equals to whom we used to pray rather than You." But their gods will reply, "You are liars!" They will openly submit to Allah that day, and all of their inventions will desert them. Because they have spoken against Allah, We will add punishment to their punishment for all those who rejected Allah and kept men from the way of Allah.*
>
> 16:89 *One day We will raise up from every people a witness who will testify against his own people. We will bring you [Mohammed] to testify against your people. We have revealed the Scripture to you as a way of explaining everything, and as a guide, a mercy, and good news for those who submit to Allah.*

- The threat of violence is: We will add punishment to their punishment
- Who is threatened: they (the Meccans)
- What they did: ascribed partners (polytheism) to Allah
- How they are wrong: being ungrateful
- Support for Mohammed: We will bring you [Mohammed] to testify against your people. We have revealed the Scripture to you as a way

of explaining everything, and as a guide, a mercy, and good news for those who submit to Allah.

As a measure of the importance of Koranic Argument, consider:

TABLE 24.1: IMPORTANCE OF THE KORANIC ARGUMENT

Mohammed's Teaching	Mecca In Private	Mecca In Public	Mecca Argument	Medina
Number of times Koranic Argument is used	40	65	70	36
Percentage of text devoted to the Koranic Argument category	70.5%	63.7%	67.2%	12.8%

The Meccan Koran[1] can be divided into three phases. At first Mohammed only told those who were close to him about his message in private teachings. Then he taught Islam publicly. The third phase in Mecca was during the intense resistance of the Meccans against Mohammed.

The reason there are so few Koranic Arguments in Medina was that in Medina, Mohammed threatened little and killed a lot. Threats were replaced by action.

This data mirrors the history of Mohammed's life. In the Meccan religious phase, the violence took the form of threats of punishment that were to occur after death in Hell. Or the mentioned violence was in ancient history, i.e. the Pharaoh being destroyed because he would not listen to Allah's prophet, Moses. In Mecca the Koranic violence referred to the far future or the distant past. However, in Medina, there is much less preaching about Hell, and much more physical violence against political enemies. The action of jihad replaces the rhetoric of the threat of punishment.

Approximately two-thirds of the Koran of Mecca is devoted to the Koranic Argument of "listen to Mohammed, the prophet of the only god, Allah, or you will suffer eternal torture in Hell." When Mohammed achieved political power, the religious threats became political reality. The Koranic Argument of religion in Mecca became the political practice in Medina.

The Koran of Mecca is an exact record of what took place in the intellectual and political sphere. Koranic persuasion is a recording of actual events of debate and persuasion. In many cases, there are actual quotes of Mohammed's opponents. The Koran contains an intimate and exact view of Arabian history.

---

1 Mohammed first preached the religion of Islam in Mecca for 13 years. He then went to Medina for the last 10 years of his life. The Koran written in Mecca differs greatly from the one in Medina.

The Meccan Koran is an historical and political document of Mohammed's campaign to convince the Arabs of the superiority of Islam. Even the repetition shows it to be history of the persuasion campaign. The Medinan Koran chronicles the exact history of the rise of Islamic political power. The Koran is both a religious text and a political/historical text. As a political/historical text, the Koran can be viewed as a biography of Mohammed.

STATISTICS AND THE KORAN

The Koran of Medina has much of its text devoted to the subject of jihad, but so does the rest of the Trilogy[1].

FIGURE 24.1: AMOUNT OF TRILOGY TEXT DEVOTED TO JIHAD

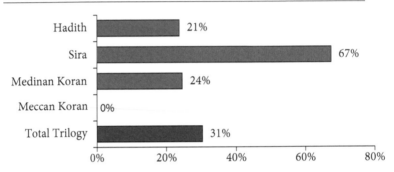

Note that the Koran of Mecca has no jihad, but the Koran of Medina has a very large amount, 24%. This is part of Islamic dualism. Islam is the religion of peace; Islam is the politics of total war.

There is a large amount of text devoted to the Kafir[2]. This is what makes Islam a political ideology, hence, political Islam.

FIGURE 24.2: AMOUNT OF TEXT DEVOTED TO KAFIR

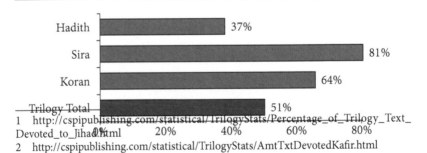

1   http://cspipublishing.com/statistical/TrilogyStats/Percentage_of_Trilogy_Text_Devoted_to_Jihad.html
2   http://cspipublishing.com/statistical/TrilogyStats/AmtTxtDevotedKafir.html

Religious Islam is defined as doctrine concerned with going to Paradise and avoiding Hell by following the Koran and the Sunna. The part of Islam that deals with the "outsider", the Kafir, is defined as political Islam. Since so much of the Trilogy is about the Kafir, the statistical conclusion is that Islam is a political system and a religious system.

Mohammed's success depended on politics, not religion. The Sira, Mohammed's biography, gives a highly detailed accounting of his rise to power. He preached the religion of Islam for 13 years in Mecca and garnered 150 followers. He was forced to move to Medina and became a politician and warrior. During the last 9 years of his life, he was involved in an event of violence every 6 weeks. When he died every Arab was a Muslim. Mohammed succeeded through politics, not religion.

An estimate can be made that there were 100,000 Muslims[3] when Mohammed died. Using this information allows a graph to be drawn:

FIGURE 24.3: GROWTH OF ISLAM

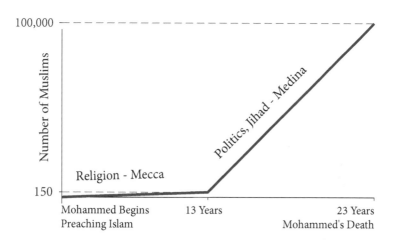

There are two distinct growth processes—religion and politics. By preaching the religion, Islam grew at a rate of about 12 new Muslims per year. Politics and jihad brought in roughly 10,000 new Muslims per year, an enormous increase. This is a process yield improvement of over 800. Politics was roughly a thousand times more effective than religion.

If Mohammed had continued with preaching religion, we can extrapolate that there would have been fewer than 300 Muslims when he died,

---

3   *The History of al-Tabari*, volume XI, SUNY, Albany, NY, page 9. Khalid, the Sword of Allah, went into battle in 633 AD, with 10,000 Muslim Arab troops at the Battle of Chains. A nation at full conflict can field an army of about 10% of its population. If 10% is 10,000, then the total population is 100,000. This is a very rough estimate.

instead of the 100,000 that resulted from his politics and jihad. This gives us an estimate of 300 conversions due to religion and over 99,000 conversions to due the political jihad process. We can calculate the relative contributions of religion and politics in growth. Islam's success was less than 1% religious and more than 99% political at the time of Mohammed's death, 632 AD.

This graph above is a very strong indicator of how effective politics was to establish Islam and how religion its was a failure.

The entire Trilogy text has a great deal of Jewish hatred material. However, in the Meccan Koran, there is very little[1]. From the graph on the next page, the favorable Jew content in the Koran is almost all in the early Meccan Koran. Actually, all of the Jew hatred in Mecca occurs in the thirteenth and last year. The first 12 years of the Koran written in Mecca contains no Jewish hatred. This is the Koranic dualism about Jews. The Jewish hatred material in the Koran illustrates how the Sira is necessary to understand the Koran.

FIGURE 24.4: ANTI-JEWISH TEX IN TRILOGY

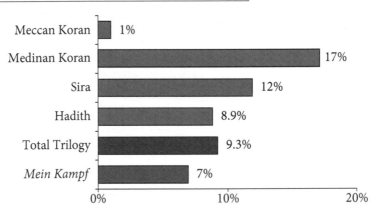

The Koran's treatment of women is of interest[2]. This chart was prepared by collecting all of the verses that include any mention of women. These are then sorted into neutral, low status, high status and equal status. The neutral verses are not included in the study.

---

1   http://cspipublishing.com/statistical/TrilogyStats/Amt_anti-Jew_Text.html
2   http://cspipublishing.com/statistical/TrilogyStats/Womans_Status_in_the_Koran.html

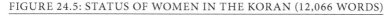

FIGURE 24.5: STATUS OF WOMEN IN THE KORAN (12,066 WORDS)

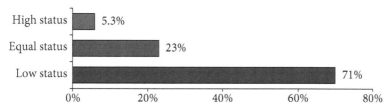

The high status verses are about women as mothers. The equal status refers to women and men being held responsible for their actions on judgment day. Low status means that men are dominant over the women.

THE METHODOLOGY OF THE ABRIDGED KORAN

The *Abridged Koran* is a reconstruction of the historical Koran of Mohammed's day. It was prepared by the CCC analytic method of:

Context—using Mohammed's life to give the circumstances and environment of the text.

Chronology—putting the verses in the original historical order[3].

Category—the method of grouping verses around the same subject. There can be discussion about which categories to use, but the Koranic Argument method of categorization produces the simplest text.

With the analytic tools of Context, Chronology and Category, the Koran becomes a clear and simple text. The CCC analytic method most closely duplicates the historical words spoken by Mohammed.

In scientific philosophy the term, Occam's Razor, refers to the idea that the simplest theory that will explain the facts is the best theory. Using the criteria of Occam's Razor shows that Context, Chronology and Category is the best method to show the meaning of the Koran. No other method produces clarity, hence, the CCC is the superior method of organization of the Koran.

The classical method of ordering the Koranic text is based upon the length of the chapters. It starts with the longest sura and ends with the shortest sura. This methodology was devised by the secretary Zaid under the caliph, Uthman, and there were arguments about it at the time. It is an arbitrary method of presenting the words spoken by Mohammed. It has failed to produce a text that can be easily understood. Mohammed did not produce or use the classical method of presenting the Koran.

---

3 The Noldeke-Schwally order was used. Other methods of ordering differ in minor ways.

The classical method was designed to produce a difficult text by obscuring meaning.

The Koran is highly repetitive, which adds to its difficulty. The *Abridged Koran* removes the duplicated verses and leaves the most representative verses. You miss no meaning.

THE FOUNDATIONALIST SCHOOL

The actions and words of Muslims have their foundation in the doctrine of Islam found in the Koran, the Sira and the Hadith—the Trilogy. This doctrine must be analyzed and understood on a rational basis and on its own merits. Know the foundational doctrine of Islam and apply it to every action by Muslims, but first know the doctrine.

The Foundationalist school is fact-based and scientific. It posits a cause and effect relationship between Islamic doctrine and the behavior and speech of Muslims. If an opinion or comment about Islam does not have a reference, or a possible reference, to the Trilogy, then the opinion has no merit.

The Foundationalist school sees Islamic history as being the fruit of its doctrine. Since both past and present Islam are based upon the same unchanging doctrine, it is possible to understand from the actions of Muslims today what the future will bring.

FOR MORE INFORMATION

www.politicalislam.com
www.cspii.org
Facebook: @BillWarnerAuthor
Twitter: @politicalislam
YouTube: Political Islam

BIBLIOGRAPHY

Watt, W. Montgomery and Bell, Richard. *Introduction to the Quran.* Edinburgh: Edinburgh University Press, 1970.

Robinson, Neal. *Discovering the Koran.* London: SCM Press, 1996.

Arberry, A. J. *The Koran Interpreted,* NY: Touchstone, 1996.

Pickthall, Mohammed M. *The Meaning of the Glorious Koran.* Kuwait: Dar Al-Islamiyya.

Warraq, Ibn. *What the Koran Really Says.* Amherst, NY: Prometheus Books, 2002.

Dawood, N. J. *The Koran,* London: Penguin Books, 1999.

Rodwell, J. M. *The Koran,* North Clarendon, VT: Tuttle Publishing, 1994.

Ali, Maulana Muhammad. *Holy Koran.* Columbus, Ohio: Ahmadiyyah Anjuman Ishaat Islam 1998.

Watt, W. Montgomery and M.V. McDonald. *The History of al-Tabari, vol. VI, Muhammad at Mecca.* New York: The State University of New York Press, 1987.

McDonald, M.V. and W. Montgomery Watt. *The History of al-Tabari, vol. VII, The Foundation of the Community.* New York: The State University of New York Press, 1987.

Michael Fishbone, *The History of al-Tabari VIII The Victory of Islam.* New York: The State University of New York Press, 1987.

Poonawala, Ismail K. *The History of al-Tabari, vol. IX, The Last Years of the Prophet.* New York: The State University of New York Press, 1987.

Muir, Sir William. *Life of Mohammed.* New York: AMS Press, 1975.

Guillaume, A. *The Life of Muhammad,* (Ishaq's—*Sirat Rasul Allah*). Karachi: Oxford University Press, 1967.

The Hadith of Abu Al-Bukhari, *Sahih Bukhari,* and the Hadith of Abu Muslim, *Sahih Muslim,* are best found on the web, e.g. http://www.usc.edu/org/cmje/religious-texts/hadith/

INDEX

A

.

Printed in Great Britain
by Amazon

43837868R00142